CFAs AND RISK ASSESSMENT
IN PRACTICE

AUSTRALIA
Law Book Co.
Sydney

CANADA and USA
Carswell
Toronto

HONG KONG
Sweet & Maxwell Asia

NEW ZEALAND
Brookers
Wellington

SINGAPORE and MALAYSIA
Sweet & Maxwell Asia
Singapore and Kuala Lumpur

CFAs AND RISK ASSESSMENT IN PRACTICE

by

Nigel Tomkins

and

Claire Edwards

LONDON
SWEET & MAXWELL
2002

Published in 2002 by Sweet & Maxwell Limited of
100 Avenue Road, Swiss Cottage,
London NW3 3PF

Typeset by YHT
Printed in Great Britain by Ashford Colour Press Ltd,
Gosport, Hampshire

No natural forests were destroyed to make this product;
only farmed timber was used and replanted

**A CIP catalogue record for this book is available from the British
Library**

ISBN 0421 786 205

This is a very rapidly developing area of law. To the best of the
authors' abilities, the text reflects the law as at November 25th 2002.
No responsibility for loss obtained to any person acting or refraining
from action as a result of any material in this publication can be
accepted by the authors or publishers.

Contents

Contents

Table of Cases

TABLE OF CASES

Table of Statutes

Table of Statutory Instruments

INTRODUCTION

The Essential Approach to Modern CFA Work

In the "good old days" lawyers did not have to fund litigation. Cases were mainly funded by the client, their trade union, a legal expenses insurer or perhaps best of all, the Legal Aid Board. Lawyers were often paid in advance, on account, or on an interim billing basis. Lawyers were of course barred from funding litigation themselves or supporting funding for their clients.

Today with legal aid abolished and trade unions embracing collective conditional fee options, more and more of a lawyer's work is funded by what the client knows as "no win no fee". In other words, it is funded by the lawyers themselves. Lawyers are no longer paid up front. Lawyers are now rarely paid interim fees. Lawyers are increasingly often only paid after the case is finally over. Most importantly, if a lawyer loses a case they are frequently paid nothing.

So now in many cases lawyers are only paid if they win. In theory to compensate for all the pain, suffering and anguish that this produces for lawyers, the government allows them a "success fee" in cases funded under conditional fee agreements (or at least some of them). There are many risks associated with running cases on a Conditional Fee Agreement (CFA) bases funding. It is not just a matter of the risk of failure, that risk is simply the most obvious of risks. There are a host of risks associated with running a CFA based business.

This book is designed to provide practitioners with the essential information necessary to operate a successful

1

Conditional Fee Agreement personal injury practice. The book is meant to be practical with the aim of ensuring not only a comprehensive understanding of the subject but also how to make certain that your understanding relates to everyday case handling, management and control of the risks being taken.

Conditional fees were only introduced for personal injury cases as recently as 1995. They were extended to all civil non-family cases in 1998. Under the Access to Justice Act 1999 a solicitor became able to recover, from a losing opponent, the success fee and any after the event legal expense insurance purchased either supporting a conditional fee agreement or covering both sides costs. This can be done subject to the requirements of the Civil Procedure Rules and the Practice Directions on Costs.

The Conditional Fee Agreement Regulations 2000 set out the requirements for a Conditional Fee Agreement to be enforceable. These Regulations apply to agreements entered into after April 2000. The Conditional Fee Agreements Regulations 1995 (SI 1995/1675) govern agreements which were entered into before this date. On November 30, 2000 the Collective Conditional Fee Agreement Regulations 2000 (SI 2000/2988) came into force enabling bulk purchasers of legal services (such as trade unions and commercial organisations) to enter into collective conditional fee agreements covering specific areas of their work.

In this book the essential law and principles of Conditional Fee Agreements are covered. Insurance principles for Conditional Fee Agreement work are examined. Risk assessment and risk control is the core of this work and our approach combines the practical first hand experience of those from the practitioner and insurer sides of the world of personal injury. We deal with cases within the jurisdiction of England and Wales and in relation to personal injuries sustained worldwide. This single volume is designed to be clear, concise and user friendly with guides and flow charts to aid understanding.

We begin by addressing the risk of selecting the wrong funding option. That in itself can lead to disaster. We then look at the risk of suffering a loss simply by failing to provide the correct information to the right people at the right time.

Next we address the risks linked to the recovery of a success fee and follow it by addressing the risk of failing to recover an after the event insurance premium.

Risk is big business for one industry in particular. That of course is the insurance industry. We look at applying insurance risk principles generally and specifically to conditional fee work. There are of course a number of risks associated with the after the event insurance aspects of conditional fee work, and we address those head on in Chapter 7 on working with after the event insurance.

It is only at this stage that we look directly at conditional fee risk assessment. We start by considering the need to have a strategy for identifying case risk factors. Then we address the act of carrying out a risk assessment itself. This is followed by perhaps the most important of all of the aspects of risk control and management. The best practice in all other areas can be ruined so easily where the risks are not managed and controlled adequately.

In Appendix 1 we have drawn together some of the essential materials practitioners need to have readily available. We have also included what we hope you will find to be a series of useful precedents. The first of those is the Law Society's *Conditional Fees—Funding Arrangements—Guide to Provisions*. Others are referred to in the main text throughout the book.

In Appendix 2 we have included a report on the decision of the House of Lords in *Callery v Gray* [2002] UKHL. This case has significance in many areas covered by this book. It impacts on issues including recoverability of an after the event insurance premium, reasonableness of premium amounts, the level of success fees or uplifts and how they should be assessed. Most of the references in the main text relate to the earlier decision of the Court of Appeal (EWCA Civ 1246) as it was upheld by the Lords and remains good law.

Lord Bingham, in his judgment, set out in the clearest terms the history and background leading to the current funding situation that we find ourselves in today.

"For nearly half a century, legal aid provided out of public funds was the main source of funding for those of modest means who sought to make or (less frequently) defend claims in the civil courts and who needed professional help to do so. By this means access to the courts was made available to many who would otherwise, for want of means, have been denied it. But as time passed the defects of the legal aid regime established under the Legal Aid and Advice Act 1949 and later statutes became more and more apparent. While the scheme served the poorest well, it left many with means above a low ceiling in an unsatisfactory position, too well off to qualify for legal aid but too badly off to contemplate incurring the costs of contested litigation. There was no access to the courts for them.

Moreover, the effective immunity against adverse costs orders enjoyed by legally-aided claimants was always recognised to place an unfair burden on a privately-funded defendant resisting a legally-aided claim, since he would be liable for both sides' costs if he lost and his own even if he won. Most seriously of all, the cost to the public purse of providing civil legal aid had risen sharply, without however showing an increase in the number of cases funded or evidence that legal aid was directed to cases which most clearly justified the expenditure of public money.

Recognition of these defects underpinned the Access to Justice Act 1999 which, building on the Courts and Legal Services Act 1990, introduced a new regime for funding litigation, and in particular personal injury litigation with which alone this opinion is concerned ... The 1999 Act and the accompanying regulations had (so far as relevant for present purposes) three aims.

One aim was to contain the rising cost of legal aid to public funds and enable existing expenditure to be refocused on causes with the greatest need to be funded at public expense, whether because of their intrinsic importance or because of the difficulty of funding them otherwise than out of public funds or for both those reasons.

A second aim was to improve access to the courts for members of the public with meritorious claims. It was appreciated that the risk of incurring substantial liabilities in costs is a powerful disincentive to all but the very rich from becoming involved in litigation, and it was therefore hoped that the new arrangements would enable claimants to protect themselves against liability for paying costs either to those acting for them or (if they chose) to those on the other side.

A third aim was to discourage weak claims and enable successful defendants to recover their costs in actions brought against them by indigent claimants. Pursuant to the first of these aims publicly-funded assistance was withdrawn from run-of-the-mill personal injury claimants. The main instruments upon which it was intended that claimants should rely to achieve the second and third of the aims are ... conditional fee agreements and insurance cover obtained after the event giving rise to the claim.

At the time when the 1999 Act was enacted and brought into effect, new Civil Procedure Rules were also in the course of being implemented. The objects underlying these rules were not new, but the rules gave a sharply increased emphasis to the need for expedition in the conduct of legal proceedings, to the need for simplicity and to the need to avoid unnecessary and disproportionate costs. To achieve these ends new and detailed procedures were devised to moderate the traditional adversarial approach to the making and defending of claims. There was inevitably a bedding-down period during which both judges and practitioners adjusted to the practical implications of the new procedural regime to which they were required to give effect.

If the objects underlying the new procedural regime were not new, those underlying the new funding regime were. Arrangements which had until relatively recently been professionally improper were to become the norm. It was however evident that the success of the new funding regime was threatened by two contingencies which, had they occurred, could have proved fatal. One was that lawyers, in particular solicitors, would decline to act on a conditional fee basis.

To counter that risk the maximum permissible uplift, on the first introduction of conditional fees in 1995, had been fixed, despite very strong opposition, at 100% and this high level of permissible uplift was retained. It was no doubt felt, rightly as events have proved, that if solicitors were permitted in some cases to earn, as the reward for success, double the fee otherwise receivable, they would be tempted into the market. The other contingency was that no accessible market would develop in after the event insurance. There was at the outset very little knowledge and experience of whether or how such a market would develop.

Even if these contingencies did not occur, the new funding regime was obviously open to abuse in a number of ways. One possible abuse was that lawyers would be willing to act for claimants on a conditional fee basis but would charge excessive fees for their basic costs, knowing that their own client would not have to pay them and that the burden would in all probability fall on the defendant or his liability insurers. With this expectation the claimant's lawyers would have no incentive to moderate their charges.

Another possible abuse was that lawyers would be willing to act for claimants on a conditional fee basis but would contract for a success uplift grossly disproportionate to any fair assessment of the risks of failure in the litigation, again knowing that the burden of paying this uplifted fee would never fall on their client but would be borne by the defendant or his insurers.

A third possible abuse was that claimants, although able to obtain after the event insurance, would be able to do so only at an unreasonably high price, the after the event insurers having no incentive to moderate a premium which would be paid by the defendant or his insurers and which might be grossly disproportionate to the risk which the insurer was underwriting. Under the new regime, a claimant who makes appropriate arrangements can litigate without any risk of ever having personally to pay costs either to those acting for him or to the other side and without any risk of ever having to pay an after the event insurance premium whatever the outcome: the practical result is to transfer the entire cost of funding this kind of litigation to the liability insurers of unsuccessful defendants (and defendants who settle the claims made against them) and thus, indirectly, to the wider public who pay premiums to insure themselves against liability to pay compensation for causing personal injury.

The front-line responsibility for making the new funding regime work fairly and effectively and in accordance with the objects both of the 1999 Act and the new Civil Procedure Rules lay with lawyers agreeing to act under conditional fee agreements and insurers offering after the event insurance cover. The role of watchdog would be exercised, in the first instance, by district judges and costs judges, on whose judgment and insight in assessing recoverable costs much would depend. If they were too restrictive in the level of success fees or after the event insurance premiums which they allowed, lawyers and clients might be deterred from acting or proceeding on this basis and the objects of the new regime would be defeated. If they were too generous and too uncritical, excessive fees and premiums might be allowed and an unfair and disproportionate burden placed on defendants and their liability insurers, thereby undermining one of the key objects of the Civil Procedure Rules.

The difficult task entrusted to district judges and costs judges called for a clear understanding of the object of both the 1999 Act and the Civil Procedure Rules, an understanding how the new funding regime was developing in practice and an alert willingness to make appropriate orders if and when signs of abuse appeared. However carefully and attentively district judges and costs judges applied themselves to their task, it was inevitable that occasions would arise when judges misdirected themselves and made erroneous orders, and given the number of orders made by different judges in different parts of the country disparities in practice would be likely to arise. The responsibility for curbing errors and giving guidance to district judges and costs judges on the exercise of their powers in this context, of correcting erroneous orders and of seeking to harmonise practice between various courts rests with circuit judges and then, importantly, with the Court of Appeal."

Some of the key worries about the new system were voiced by Lord Hope when he said in his judgment:

"I accept that the new regime is not beyond criticism. It is plain that it has transferred the burden of meeting the cost of access to justice in these cases from the taxpayer through the medium of the legal aid fund. Instead a different kind of taxation is involved. The burden of meeting the cost of access to justice now falls on liability insurers. It thus falls indirectly on their policy holders, who are likely to have to face increased premiums. Furthermore, unless the new regime is controlled very carefully, its effect may be to benefit ATE insurance providers unreasonably and to place a burden on liability insurers which is disproportionate. It may lead to a culture of incurring additional costs which lacks any incentive on claimants to keep costs down."

These are difficult times for personal injury lawyers particularly those acting for claimants. To make them even harder the defendants' insurers who loose or settle cases are still attacking success fees. Just for good measure, defendants who loose or settle cases are still attacking the premiums charged by the claimant's after the event insurers who backed the litigation in the first place. They are also regularly attacking the legitimacy of charging arrangements in their entirety by challenges attempting to establish defects in Conditional Fee Agreements or failure to comply with the complex rules and regulations.

All of this means that judges are now in the business of assessing the fees which lawyers recover in a way they never did before. Step by step we are seeing just what all of this means. The decision of the Court of Appeal on September 2, 2002 in *Halloran v Delaney* [2002] EWCA Civ 1258 (see Chapter 8) illustrates how there remains the continued potential for change and an ongoing lack of certainty. It also illustrates that success fees will not be recovered without proper risk assessments being carried out and made available to the court to back them up. Each court decision is another piece in the jigsaw. Our aim is to pull all of this together so far as is possible at the present time. There may yet be twists and turns and there are some pieces still to be put into place. However, this is where we are today. Our aim is to help practitioners stay in the black and to understand, manage and control the risks that they are now facing every day.

Claire Edwards & Nigel Tomkins

1

Picking the Right Funding Option

Conditional fees for personal injury cases were only intro-   **1.001**
duced in the UK in 1995. Conditional fees were extended to all
civil non-family cases in 1998. They are now seen as the main
means funding much civil litigation and, in particular, personal injury cases.

The big change from the earlier CFA position it that under
the Access to Justice Act 1999, a solicitor is able to recover
from a losing opponent the success fee and any legal expenses
insurance purchased either supporting a Conditional Fee
Agreement or covering both sides costs, subject to the Civil
Procedure Rules and Practice Directions on Costs.

The Conditional Fee Agreement Regulations 2000 set out
the requirements for a Conditional Fee Agreement to be
enforceable. These Regulations apply to agreements entered
into from April 1, 2000. The Conditional Fee Agreements
Regulations 1995 govern agreements that were entered into
before this date. These are not our concern. We are dealing
with the current position, not the past. On November 30, 2000
the Collective Conditional Fee Agreement Regulations 2000
came into force enabling bulk purchasers of legal services
(such as trade unions and commercial organisations) to enter
into collective Conditional Fee Agreements covering specific
areas of their work. That completed the picture as far as CFA
options were concerned. However none of this means that a
Conditional Fee Agreement is automatically going to be the

proper means of funding a piece of litigation. The first thing to do is pick the right funding option.

PICKING THE RIGHT FUNDING OPTION

1.002 Any failure to comply with the rules and regulations covering conditional fee work can result in serious costs consequences. Picking the wrong funding option is one of those potential failures. There are a series of steps which if taken should avoid this pitfall and ensure the opportunity exists to obtain full costs recovery.

FUNDING OPTION STEPS

1.003 When a potential new client comes to see you and tells you that they would like you to take their case on a "no win no fee" basis, before you agree, it is essential to be certain that it is the appropriate option. Before you can agree to accept instructions and to fund the cases by a Conditional Fee Agreement, there are a whole series of questions you need to address before you should offer the client case funding by that means. The starting point is your overriding duty to give your client the best advice.

Ignoring any other requirements, the basic principle must always be to give your client the best possible advice for them in relation to their potential action. This now includes advice on the most suitable funding option for their case. In practice, if you do this you will comply with all of the various rules and regulations. It is therefore essential to remember what those rules and regulations are, so that your client really is in fact given "the best advice".

Remember to start by applying the Solicitors' Practice Rules most relevant to Conditional Fee Agreement funding: rules 8, 15 & 18.

Rule 8

(1) A solicitor who is retained or employed to prosecute or   **1.004**
defend any action, suit or other contentions proceed-
ings shall not enter into any arrangement to receive a
contingency fee in respect of that proceeding, save one
permitted under statute or by common law.

Rule 15

Solicitors shall: **1.005**

(a) give information about costs and other matters

(b) operate a complaints handling procedure

In accordance with a Solicitors' Costs Information and Client
Care Code made from time to time by the Council of the Law
Society with the concurrence of the Master of Rolls.

Rule 18

Defines a contingency fee as one which is "any sum (whether   **1.006**
fixed, or calculated either as a percentage of the proceeds or
otherwise howsoever) payable only in the event of success in
the prosecution or defence of any action, suit or other contentious proceeding."

WHAT ELSE MATTERS?

The Costs Practice Direction

You need to consider the requirements of the Costs Practice   **1.007**
Direction supplementing Parts 43–48 of the Civil Procedure
Rules 1998 (CPR). All funding arrangements must comply
with the Indemnity Principle. This will mean that under normal circumstances if your client is successful in their claim
they will be able to recover their base costs from the other

party. In essence, notwithstanding the CPR changes in respect of costs, the basic principle remains that they will normally "follow the event." However, this does not mean that the paying party will be automatically responsible for any additional liabilities. Although the Civil Procedure (Amendment No.3) Rules 2000 and the Costs Practice Direction provide for payment of success fees and insurance premiums by losing parties, they will only be recoverable when they can be justified. We shall consider the requirements for justification later.

Section 11 of the Costs Practice Direction looks at the factors to be taken into account by the court in deciding the amount of costs recoverable under rule 44.5. Practice Direction section 11.4 allows a party who has entered into a "funding arrangement" to include an "additional liability."

What is a Funding Arrangement?

1.008 A funding arrangement can be one of three quite different things:

(1) A Conditional Fee Agreement with a success fee.

(2) An "after the event" insurance policy.

(3) An agreement with a membership organisation to meet costs.

Both a success fee and an insurance premium are regarded as costs even though common sense would tell you that "an insurance premium" is a disbursement.

What is an Additional Liability?

1.009 An "additional liability" is defined as:

"A success fee, an insurance premium, or an additional amount in respect of provision made by a membership organisation."

In essence, there are two matters to consider. The first is whether or not a Conditional Fee Agreement with a success fee is appropriate for the case and therefore whether a success

12

fee will be recoverable in the event of success. The second is whether the premium paid for the insurance product linked to the Conditional Fee Agreement will be fully recoverable.

ESTABLISHING AN ENTITLEMENT TO RECOVER A SUCCESS FEE

Consideration of level of success fee is secondary to estab- **1.010** lishing that there is an entitlement to recover a success fee at all. If the court concludes that the case should not have been run on a Conditional Fee Agreement with a success fee at all, then no success fee will be recoverable. The first risk that you run is therefore the risk that you have funded a case by this means when the court will conclude it was not appropriate. In the Costs Practice Direction section 11.8(1), the relevant factors to be taken into account by the court in deciding whether a percentage increase is reasonable includes consideration of what other methods of financing the costs were available to the receiving party.

WHAT METHODS OF FINANCING DO YOU NEED TO CONSIDER?

Private Funding

Some would say the best method of funding any litigation is **1.011** private funding, where the client backs their case with their own money and therefore takes all of the risk. However, the whole concept of "best advice" includes advising a client on the need to contain their financial exposure. It would not therefore, seem to be a bar to recovery of a success fee or after the event insurance premium if instruction were accepted on a Conditional Fee Agreement with success fee when in theory the client might have been sufficiently wealthy to put up the money to fund the case privately. If this was a bar conditional fee funding would not be available in commercial disputes between vast corporations and of course it is.

Giving best advice to the client on the implications of private funding when compared to the transfer of the risk of financial exposure to an after event insurer and shared with the CFA, must be a choice option available to any person regardless of private financial position. It should not be for defendants to establish that a man of apparent wealth should not derive the benefit of transfer of that financial exposure.

Therefore, the choice of CFA back with after the event insurance, where the only alternative was private funding, should be a bar to recovery of the additional liabilities.

Community Legal Service Funding

1.012 As the replacement for legal aid, there can be no doubt that if community legal service funding were available to your client, it would in many cases, clearly be the best option. However, this route is seriously limited as the Access to Justice Act 1999, in Sch. 2, para. 2(a) excludes from the community legal service remit all claims from "negligently caused injury, death or damage to property, apart from allegations relating to clinical negligence". According to para. 3.2.1 of the Decision Making Guidance in the Funding Code, this is because the great majority of cases of this type are suitable for funding by way of Conditional Fee Agreements.

Nevertheless, there will be circumstances where investigative support could be applied for when prospects of success are so unclear that investigation may be required before a Conditional Fee Agreement can be agreed if the case has a value exceeding £5,000. This is only an option when the likely cost of investigation would exceed £3,000 at prescribed rates or disbursements, including counsel's fees would exceed £1,000.

In reality, other than in clinical negligence cases, community legal service funding, as an alternative to Conditional Fee Agreement funding will normally only need to be considered where the personal injury aspect of the claim is linked to another matter. For example, a housing disrepair claim with an associated claim for asthma could be pursued with community legal service funding provided that the law firm is franchised, the client meets the means test requirements and the case passes the merits test.

Other Funders

An "other funder" can include a person or organisation pre- **1.013**
pared to financially back a case, such as a trade union, a trade association or an insurance company. Whoever they are, the funder needs to avoid the pitfalls of "maintenance and champerty".

Maintenance was described by Lord Denning M.R. in *Re Trepca Mines Limited (No.2)* [1963] Ch. 199 at 219 as;

> "improperly stirring up litigation and strife by giving aid to one party to bring or defend a claim without just cause or excuse".

Champerty was described by Scrutton L.J. in *Ellis v Torrington* [1920] 1 KB 399 at 412 as;

> "only a particular form of maintenance, namely where the person who maintains takes as a reward a share of the property recovered".

There is a good deal of case law on this subject which we do not need to consider in any detail here. The authorities make it plain that an agreement with the funder of litigation enabling him to share in the proceeds of the litigation remains unlawful on the ground that it is champertous. It is clear that the only relaxation to that law has been the statutory approval of Conditional Fee Agreements. There has never been any objection to an organisation such as a trades union or an insurance company funding litigation on behalf of its members or insured, basically because there has never been any question of them sharing in the proceeds. Accordingly, although it would be legitimate for any organisation to provide assistance to a litigant, whether financial or practical, it is clear that for important policy reasons that the law stops well short of sanctioning a true contingency agreement.

The effect of this is that where an other funder seeks to

recover a payment equivalent to an "after the event" insurance premium to compensate them for the risk that they are covering, they must ensure that the funding arrangement complies fully with the Collective Conditional Fee Agreement Regulations 2000. Since those regulations came into force in November 2000, Collective Conditional Fee Agreements have by regulation 8, which is an amendment to the original Regulations, been excluded from the Conditional Fee Agreements Regulations 2000.

Is the other funder option always going to be best advice? In the past, if a client was entitled to financial support from a source such as their trade union, it would have been very difficult to justify any alternative means of funding on best advice principles. However, that may not always be the case now and other options including a privately arranged Conditional Fee Agreement with commercial after the event insurance should not automatically be ruled out. As an option it may be at least as good and possibly sometimes actually better.

If a case is funded by way of Collective Conditional Fee Agreement there is no reason to suppose that this will be more attractive or more economic than the individual alternative. There may be no free choice of lawyer as usually a lawyer is appointed by the trade union. They may not be local to the client and it may be difficult to have face to face dealings with them. The cost to the defendant, if the claimant's case is successful, is not likely to be greater than if the case is run by a non-union lawyer. Provided that the risk assessment is properly carried out, the success fee sought should be more or less the same on a Conditional Fee Agreement or Collective Conditional Fee Agreement (CCFA). If on the Collective Conditional Fee Agreement a sum equivalent to an "after the event" premium is just that, equivalent, then whether it is a true insurance premium or not, should make no difference in terms of consideration by the court when it comes to the recoverability of costs.

In *Sarwar v Alam*, which we also consider below and in Chapter 5 dealing with recoverability of insurance premiums, the Court of Appeal said that in normal circumstances if a claimant making a relatively small claim in a road traffic case who had access to pre-existing before the event legal expenses cover which appeared to be satisfactory for a claim of that size should use it.

In addition it was not thought reasonable for trade unions to offer CCFA's with ATE or section 30 cover in such cases either. This may well turn out to be the view of the courts in non road traffic cases as well. The Court of Appeal accepted that it is not in the interests of motorists or the general public that motor liability insurers should have to pay unnecessary costs that raise premium costs. The same could be said about other insured people with other forms of before the event legal expenses insurance. The legal expenses insurance option needs to be looked at in all cases.

LEGAL EXPENSES INSURANCE

Whatever you do before entering into a Conditional Fee **1.014** Agreement backed by after the event insurance, it is essential to look at any appropriate before the event policies first. The duty imposed by the Court of Appeal in *Sarwar v Alam* is very clear. Their guidance is that in normal circumstances if a claimant making a relatively small (*i.e.* under £5,000) claim in a road traffic case has access to pre-existing before the event legal expenses cover which appears to be satisfactory for a claim of that size, then it should be used.

The arguments that it would be reasonable for claimants in such cases to sign CFAs and to take out after the event policies even if reasonable before the event cover was available were rejected. As we have already seen, this even applies when trade unions offer their members legal support using collective Conditional Fee Agreements with either an after the event policy or section 30 cover.

The court suggested that a solicitor should normally invite a client, using a standard form letter, to bring to the first interview any relevant motor and household insurance policy, as well as any stand-alone legal expenses insurance policy belonging to the client and/or their spouse or partner. They recognised that regard had always to be had to the amount at stake, and a solicitor was not obliged to embark upon what they called a "treasure hunt". However, clients who were passengers should be asked to obtain a copy of their driver's policy, where reasonably practicable. If the driver's consent to use by the passenger is required, the solicitor should ask the client to try to obtain it.

A draft letter designed to cover this aspect will be found in the precedents section in Appendix 1?Essential Materials and Useful Precedents.

So far as before the event legal expenses cover linked to credit cards is concerned, at present the Court of Appeal considered at the present time it is likely to be disproportionate to investigate. The question of practicability is necessarily fact-sensitive.

If there is in place a before the event legal expenses insurance policy it could well provide the best advice funding option. The question is must legal expenses insurance be used if there is a policy? The short answer is no. There are a series of matters to consider.

The Indemnity Limit Offered

1.015 Before the event insurance unless otherwise stated, generally within the maximum limit of indemnity, will include cover for both sides costs.

Will this limit be sufficient to pay both sides costs in a worst possible case scenario?

You need to remember that your opponent may be funded by Conditional Fee Agreement with a success fee of up to 100 per cent. The limit of the indemnity should be viewed with caution as in real terms it may be worth perhaps as little as one quarter of the indemnity figure provided by an after the event insurance policy. This is because an after the event insurance policy linked to a CFA only has to cover the winning party's costs, not both sides.

The indemnity under before the event legal expenses policies was considered by the Court of Appeal in *Murphy & Murphy v Young & Co.'s Brewery Plc & Sun Alliance* [1997] 1 W.L.R. 1591. The major question raised was what happens when an unsuccessful party has had its legal costs funded under legal expenses insurance, should the insurer be held liable to pay all of the successful party's costs? The Murphy's were insured by Sun Alliance under the American Express Legal Expenses Plan. The limit of cover in respect of any claim arising out of the same original cause was £25,000.

The relevant cover was expressed as follows:

Legal benefits

(a) Fees, expenses and other disbursements reasonably and properly incurred by the appointed representative (a solicitor, firm of solicitors or appropriately qualified person appointed to act for you) in connection with any claim or legal proceedings including any costs incurred by us.

(b) Costs and expenses of expert witnesses.

(c) Any costs payable by you following an award of costs by a court or tribunal in connection with a claim or proceedings.

There were conditions attached to the policy as there always are. Cover was subject to the conditions that the insurer's consent to pay legal benefits had firstly been obtained in writing. The consent was only to be given if the insured was able to satisfy the insurer that they had reasonable grounds for pursuing or defending the legal proceedings or it was reasonable for legal benefits to be provided in a particular case. The decision to grant consent was to take into account the opinion of the insured's appointed representative as well as that of the insurer's own advisers. There was power to require the obtaining of an opinion of counsel on the merits of the claim or legal proceedings. If consent was refused the insurer had to give reasons with a right where the insured disagreed to invoke an arbitration procedure.

The Murphy's exhausted their right to indemnity in respect of the action, because their own legal costs exceeded the limit of £25,000. Sun Alliance denied that they could be under any liability to meet Young's costs. Young's contended that it was just and reasonable that Sun Alliance should pay their costs and that the authorities demonstrated that it was appropriate for the court so to order on the facts of this case.

These were Young's points:

(1) Sun Alliance funded the Murphys' conduct of the litigation.

(2) Sun Alliance did so pursuant to a commercial agreement.

(3) Sun Alliance exercised a degree of control over the conduct of the litigation.

Young's argued that in these circumstances to seek to rely on the limit of liability in answer to Young's claim was objectionable and contrary to public policy. Sun Alliance for their part denied that they had exercised control over the litigation. They argued that legal expense insurance was in the public interest and that limits of cover were a usual and necessary feature of such insurance. Costs should only be ordered against a non-party in exceptional circumstances. There were no such circumstances in the case and it would be contrary to public policy to hold Sun Alliance liable to pay costs beyond the limit of their cover.

The critical question was whether the mere fact that Sun Alliance had funded the Murphys' legal expenses under a policy of insurance, up to the limit of the cover under that policy, made it reasonable and just that Sun Alliance should be ordered to pay Young's costs. In other words should a legal expense insurer be permitted to cap its liability, or should the provision of such cover render the insurer liable to pay the costs of a successful adverse party, regardless of any contractual limit of liability?

For Sun Alliance, Mr Stuart Isaacs Q.C. argued that legal expense insurance is in the public interest. He referred the court to the approval of such insurance in the final report of Lord Woolf M.R. on Access to Justice, *Overview*, section 1 para. 12, in support of that submission. He submitted that, if insurers are not permitted effectively to limit their liability, they will be less ready to provide such cover.

The submission that legal expense insurance is in the public interest was accepted. The Court of Appeal held that such insurance not only provides desirable protection to the insured party but it is of benefit to the adverse party in that it is likely to ensure that careful consideration is given to the merits of the litigation at an early stage. It also provides a potential source of funding of the adverse party's costs, should the insured party be unsuccessful. The latter proved illusory in the *Murphy* case because of the limit of cover and evidence before the court suggested that it is unusual for the limit of cover to be exceeded. The court held that an order that a non-party pay costs will only be justified when exceptional circumstances make such an order reasonable and just. This case did not fall into any of them.

They reached the conclusion that the existence of legal expenses insurance with a limit of cover that has been exhausted does not make it reasonable or just to order the insurer to pay the costs of the adverse successful party. Accordingly, if the indemnity is exhausted the client is still exposed to the risk of personally having to satisfy an adverse costs order. This case is quoted by before the event legal expenses insurers as justification for their refusal to allow an insured person to "top up" their indemnity by the payment of an additional premium when it appears that their indemnity may be about to be exhausted. To agree to extending cover in this way could potentially open them up to unlimited financial liability.

In effect, to use before the event insurance to back a case a party needs to be certain that the indemnity is enough to cover that worst case scenario. If there is doubt then an alternative means of funding needs to be found and after the event insurance linked to a Conditional Fee Agreement will be the usual route. The choice not to use before the event legal expenses insurance in these circumstances should not be a bar to recovery of a success fee or after the event insurance premium.

Choice of Legal Representative

Many before the event insurance policies take away from the **1.016** insured person the right to select their own legal representative. In *Maltez v Lewis* (1999) 96(21) L.S.G. 39, Mr Justice Neuberger was faced with an applicant seeking an order making use of the "level playing field" envisaged by CPR R.1.1(2)(a) and the requirement of proportionality under CPR R.1.1(2)(c). The applicant sought, but was refused, an injunction to restrain the respondent from instructing senior counsel. Neuberger J., held that the CPR did not qualify the established principle that a litigant was entitled to be represented by the counsel of his or her choice. The right to choose your own legal representative must be a basic human right. Lack of freedom to chose your own legal representative may in itself be a sufficient reason to reject the use of the before the event insurance policy.

There are two separate situations covered by the European Directive (87/344/EEC) on legal expenses insurance. Article 4 requires any contract of legal expenses insurance to expressly recognise that the insured person shall be free to choose their lawyer.

Article 4 states:

(1) Any contract of legal expenses insurance shall expressly recognise that:

    (a) where recourse is had to a lawyer or other person appropriately qualified according to national law in order to defend, represent or serve the interests of the insured person in any inquiry or proceedings, that insured person shall be free to choose such lawyer or other person;

    (b) the insured person shall be free to choose a lawyer or, if he so prefers and to the extent that national law so permits, any other appropriately qualified person, to serve his interests whenever a conflict of interests arises.

The intention of the directive could not be clearer. Freedom of choice of your legal representative is a core right.

There is only one exception which can be found in Article 5. Article 5 states:

(1) Each Member State may provide exemption from the application of Article 4(1) for legal expenses insurance if all the following conditions are fulfilled:

(a) the insurance is limited to cases arising from the use of road vehicles in the territory of the Member State concerned;

(b) the insurance is connected to a contract to provide assistance in the event of accident or breakdown involving a road vehicle;

This appears to mean that unless the accident arises from the use of a road vehicle and the cover arises from insurance linked to a road vehicle and the insurance is connected to a contract to provide assistance in the event of accident or breakdown of a road vehicle, it is a breach of the European Directive if the insurer refuses to allow their insured to select their own legal representative.

For this reason, with legal expenses policies linked to straightforward household insurance, credit cards and so on, the legal expenses insurer should never attempt to compel their insured to use a designated lawyer. With the one very limited exception there is no basis in the directive to restrict choice. For the exemption to take effect *both* (a) and (b) must apply, not just one or the other. In all other circumstances, on the basis of the directive, the insurer should allow their insured freedom of choice to appoint their preferred lawyer. The denial of that right is a breach of the requirements of the directive.

The United Kingdom government had a duty to ensure that the directive was properly implemented in United Kingdom law. The Insurance Companies (Legal Expenses Insurance) Regulations 1990 (SI 1990/1159) was the mechanism used to achieve this. Regulation 6 states:

(1) Where under a legal expenses insurance contract recourse is had to a lawyer (or other person having such qualifications as may be necessary) to defend, represent or serve the interests of the insured in any inquiry or

proceedings, the insured shall be free to choose that lawyer (or other person).

(2) The insured shall also be free to choose a lawyer (or other person having such qualifications as may be necessary) to serve his interests whenever a conflict of interests arises.

(3) The above rights shall be expressly recognised in the policy.

Regulation 7 follows on saying: regulation 6 does not apply where—

(a) the legal expenses cover is limited to risks arising from the use of a road vehicle in the United Kingdom and is connected with a contract to provide assistance in the event of accident or breakdown involving a road vehicle,

(b) neither the legal expenses insurer nor the assistance insurer carries on any class of liability insurance business, and

(c) there are arrangements for securing that, where the parties to a dispute are insured in respect of legal expenses by the same insurer, legal advice and representation are provided for each of them by completely independent lawyers.

The UK Government clearly appears to have fulfilled its duty to fully implement the directive in the wording of the regulations.

Notwithstanding the limited nature of the exemption in the European Directive and the regulations, some years ago the then insurance ombudsman made it clear that in his view an insured person was only entitled to exercise the right to chose their lawyer in the event that proceedings became necessary.

In one case, following a road traffic accident, the policy holders made claims on their legal expenses policies, nominating their own solicitors to act for them. The insurer had advised them that, under the terms of the policy, the insurers own claims handling department could deal with the case and that the insurer was entitled to reject the policy holder's nominee. Counsel had advised the insurer that para. 6(1) of the regulations, meant in effect that the freedom to chose a lawyer did not arise until it became mandatory, unless the insured was to represent himself as a litigant in person, for him to be represented by a solicitor in any proceedings or inquiry. From the time of the issue of proceedings but not before the insured would be free, as against his legal expenses insurer, to select his own solicitor.

The insurance ombudsman was concerned that freedom of choice should be limited in this way, since the majority of cases never reached the courts. The ombudsman expressed the view that the time at which a policy holder would need the services of his own chosen lawyer would be immediately after the dispute had arisen so that he could receive wholly impartial and independent advice as to whether he should institute of defend proceedings at all.

Nevertheless, in the absence of any authority that para. 6(1) of the regulations was wider that its wording suggested to him, he upheld the insurers position that the freedom to chose a lawyer did not arise until administrative or legal proceedings had actually started. Up until that point he held that the insurer could properly retain "in house" technical staff or nominate a lawyer from one of his panels.

The ombudsman added an important rider. He indicated that if the freedom to chose a lawyer is to be limited in this way, it is crucial that this is made clear to policy holders prior to proposal. In other words, any brochure or summary of cover should emphasise that the insurance only covers legal expenses after proceedings have started. The ombudsman said that he might well require the insurer to give freedom of choice at an earlier stage.

If the policy does not clearly indicate that there is a restriction on the choice of lawyer, any attempt at restriction should not be enforceable unless it has been clearly brought to the insured's attention by other means. If it is claimed that it was brought to the insured's attention by other means then how and when should be demonstrated by the insurer. When challenged on this point without a proper response the insured's chosen lawyer should always be allowed to act. Most legal expenses insurers readily accept this to be the case.

In the decision of the Court of Appeal in *Stephen Callery v Charles Gray* [2001] 1 W.L.R. 2112, the question of whether the term "proceedings" included "contemplated proceedings" was considered. The argument was based on interpretation of the terms of section 29 of the Access to Justice Act 1999 headed "Recovery of Insurance Premiums by way of Costs". The section states:

> "where in any proceedings a costs order is made in favour of any party who has taken out an insurance policy against the risk of incurring a liability in those proceedings, the costs payable to him may, subject in the case of court proceedings to rules of court, include costs in respect of the premium of the policy."

The conclusion of the Court of Appeal on the definition of costs in "costs only proceedings" under CPR Part 8, which post dated the Access to Justice Act 1999, can only sensibly mean "the costs which would have been recoverable in the proceedings had the proceedings been commenced". By section 29 of the Access to Justice Act 1999, such costs include the cost of an after the event insurance premium paid on a policy taken our in contemplation of commencement of substantive proceedings.

It is arguable whether or not this decision is of wider application in particular the definition of proceedings for the purpose of instruction of solicitors in before the event insurance funded cases. It is in any event very difficult to see how the relevant words from the directive "where recourse is had to a lawyer ... in order to defend, represent or serve the interests of the insured person in any inquiry or proceedings, that insured person shall be free to choose such lawyer or other person" can be said to be limited to post proceedings. Nevertheless that is where we were until very recently.

The real difficulty was caused by an insured person being unable to recognise at what point in time it would be appropriate to conclude that court proceedings should be issued and to seek to transfer the case to his or her own chosen lawyers. In the event of a denial of liability there would be a clear cut-off point. In other circumstances, the cut-off point might not be so easy to ascertain. One remedy was for an insured person, unable to instruct a lawyer of their choice, to seek and obtain written confirmation from the legal expenses insurer that if liability was not admitted or settlement was not achieved within a reasonable period, the insurer would automatically agree to transfer the handling of the case to the insured's chosen lawyer. This would allow litigation to be commenced and the case to be handled under the legal expenses insurance without the risk of the panel solicitor trying to negotiate for too long and the claim potentially becoming stale. In these days of pre-action protocols, perhaps a maximum of six months would be reasonable in most cases.

If the before the event legal expenses insurer declined to provide such an undertaking or written agreement, it would seem reasonable that the insured should have the opportunity to choose not to use the before the event insurance product. They could instead opt for a Conditional Fee Agreement with an after the event insurance policy at the outset. This would guarantee that they would be able to obtain the benefit derived from insuring early when a lower premium would normally be available than would be available later.

So what should you do in those cases where the legal expenses insurer refuses to sanction the claimant's personal choice of lawyer? As the Court of Appeal indicated in *Sarwar v Alam*, in normal circumstances if a claimant is making a relatively small claim, in a relatively simple road traffic case and has access to pre-existing before the event legal expenses cover, it should be used. This is, of course, following proper examination of the policy, establishing that it provides cover for the type of injury involved and it appears to be satisfactory for a claim of it's size—that is to say, with a value of under £5,000.

Cases including those involving minors, bereavement, serious injuries and those injuries giving rise to permanent or long term disability, require the injured party and their lawyer to rely on a close relationship of trust and confidence. The starting point for that relationship must be the injured party's freedom to choose a representative they are happy to have acting on their behalf.

This shows up a major problem with before the event insurance products because of the tendency of the before the event legal expenses insurer to only instruct lawyers on a very restricted panel. Many cases are dealt with at considerable distance from the client who has little or no opportunity to meet the person representing them. In more serious cases, the decision to decline representation by a before the event panel lawyer many miles away from the home of the insured person is probably justified in any event. In such cases, ease of access to the lawyer and the building of a relationship of trust and confidence is essential.

Although not forming part of the *Sarwar v Alam* decision, the Court of Appeal recorded its concerns about the size of some before the event insurers' panels which are sometimes very small. They expressed this concern about "the possible inappropriateness in these post-Woolf days of a before the event claimant being denied freedom of choice of solicitor (at any event so far as the members of the Law Society's or some other reputable panel of approved personal injury solicitors are concerned) at the time the procedures in a pre-action protocol come to be activated".

The problem of the restricted choice of lawyers is very well recognised. This is illustrated by a quote from Tony Boorman, head of the insurance division of the Financial Ombudsman Service, in the February 2002 edition of *Litigation Funding*:

"There are good reasons why the customer should want to choose their lawyer. Perhaps the insurer's choice is a solicitor located at a distance, or simply someone not sufficiently skilled in a specialism."

An adjudication from the Financial Ombudsman Service handed down on June 17, 2002 on freedom of choice clarifies the position a good deal. The dispute was about the terms on which the insurer DAS would accept a claim under the legal expenses section of the complainant's household policy. DAS believed it was entitled to appoint panel solicitors of its own choosing to act for their insured's wife until such time as court proceedings were issued. The insured disputed this.

The insured's wife wished to claim damages for personal

injuries she sustained in an accident at a hotel. The insured and his wife approached a solicitor in their locality; they previously had dealings with her, were satisfied with her services, and wanted her to act for them again.

The solicitor asked whether they had legal expenses insurance; they replied they did not. On that basis the solicitor proceeded to take instructions. After carrying out a certain amount of preliminary work, she wrote again to the insured, recommending that he checked his policy documents to verify whether or not he actually did have legal expenses cover. The insured had to obtain these from his intermediary; it was only then that he realised for the first time that he did have such cover.

The insured submitted a claim to DAS, explaining what had happened, and seeking their consent for the case to continue to be handled by the solicitor he and his wife had already instructed. DAS was not prepared to agree to this, and would only accept the claim if the case was transferred to one of its panel solicitors.

DAS believed that its position was justified not only by the terms and conditions of the policy, but also the relevant provisions of the Insurance Companies (Legal Expenses Insurance) Regulations 1990 referred to above. The insured and his wife's solicitors argued that the policy did not in fact specifically prevent his wife from choosing her own lawyer. The insured and his wife preferred to continue to deal with a solicitor who was already familiar with the matter and in whom they had confidence. Given that most claims for damages are settled without the need for formal court proceedings, they believed their choice of solicitor had been unfairly limited by DAS.

The central issue for the adjudicator to consider was whether the position adopted by DAS was supported by the policy wording that it had produced. Judging by the terms he had seen amongst the many policies currently available, it seemed to the adjudicator that by no means every legal expenses insurer reserves the right to appoint the solicitor. Some policies provide little more than an indemnity for the reasonable legal costs incurred by a policyholder, with relatively little intervention by the insurer concerned.

The adjudicator felt this case appeared to be very different, however. The adjudicator felt that DAS itself contemplated playing an active role in the resolution of whatever legal problem was the subject of a claim. DAS anticipated being in a position to resolve most claims in-house, through its Legal Claims Centre. It appears to the adjudicator that DAS envisaged the involvement of an outside solicitor being the exception rather than the rule. Even then, DAS wished to reserve to itself the right to choose the solicitor concerned as far as circumstances permitted. DAS said that policyholders could instruct a solicitor of their choice to act for them only if legal proceedings become necessary—and even then, only if the firm itself agreed those proceedings were in fact necessary.

The adjudicator had to consider whether the policy wording was sufficiently clear to give effect to the insurer's intentions. The policy defined "appointed representative" as "the lawyer, accountant or other suitably qualified person who has been appointed to act for an insured person in accordance with the terms of this policy". This definition did not specify who did the appointing, or had the right to do so.

Those circumstances were governed by condition 2, the relevant parts of which provided as follows:

"(a) We can take over and conduct in the name of an insured person, any claim or legal proceedings at any time. We can negotiate any claim on behalf of an insured person.

(b) If we agree to start legal proceedings and it becomes mandatory for an insured person to be represented by a lawyer, or if there is a conflict of interest, an insured person can choose an appointed representative by sending us the suitably qualified person's name and address. We may choose not to accept the choice of representative, but only in exceptional circumstances.

(c) Before an insured person chooses a lawyer or an accountant, We can appoint an appointed representative.

(d) An appointed representative will be appointed by us and represent an insured person according to our standard terms of appointment. The appointed representative must co-operate fully with us at all times..."

Condition (b) basically confirmed the policyholder had the right of choice at the point in time when the insurer agreed that proceedings became necessary, and condition (c) gave the insurer the right to appoint a solicitor before the policyholder did without specifying whether this was when the insurer accepted the claim or at some other point.

In the adjudicator's view, the conditions were capable of being read independently of each other. He concluded that condition (b) merely described a couple of circumstances in which a policyholder "can" appoint a solicitor, without making it clear that those were in fact the *only* circumstances the insurer had in mind. He felt that It was quite possible to construe condition (c), independently, to mean that if a policyholder has already chosen a solicitor to act, it is too late for the firm to exercise that right of choice. In this case, of course, the insured had already appointed the solicitor his wife wanted to act for her at the time the claim was made.

The insurer's right to take over and conduct claims or proceedings in the name of the policyholder, as conferred by condition (a), was not clear enough in the adjudicator's view to be reasonably interpreted as giving the insurer the sole right to choose which lawyer acted prior to the issue of proceedings. The adjudicator believed that a much more explicit provision in the policy to that effect would have been necessary to confer that right on the insurer.

The adjudicator went on to say that they have consistently taken the approach that any doubts or ambiguities in the wording of a policy should be construed against the insurer who drafted it in favour of the policyholder concerned. However, he then went on to review the position overall saying:

> "More generally, some parties have put to us that the words 'inquiry or proceedings' in the 1990 Regulations should be considered from a fresh viewpoint. They point to the programme of reform set out by Lord Woolf as underlining the fact that proceedings should have a broader interpretation than a limitation to actual court action. The interpretation of the Regulations may have widespread ramifications beyond the Ombudsman's jurisdiction, and it may therefore be better for the courts to determine this issue.
>
> However, it seems to me that care needs to be exercised in interpreting the phrase 'legal proceedings' as used in the policy.

My general impression is that policyholders would tend to interpret this phrase more widely than the narrow interpretation favoured by the firm. Extensive work is now required before a case can proceed to court. I think it likely that most policyholders would tend to understand legal proceedings in a wide context of formal communication between lawyers representing the parties.

The distinction between policies such as the one presently under consideration, and others which do give real freedom of choice to the policyholder, is not always readily apparent: their layout or wording do not appear significantly to differ. Whilst the freedom to choose a solicitor from the very outset of a claim may be a feature of cover which matters for all legal expenses policyholders, it is clearly important for at least some. I have to say that I am troubled that this apparent lack of clarity may not assist their ability to evaluate the contract properly, to understand exactly what sort of cover it is that they are buying, and to ensure that it accords with their needs and expectations. Greater clarity would also ease the task of policyholders and their advisors in assessing the process they should best follow to progress a claim or make separate arrangements.''

Taking these factors into account, the adjudicator reached the conclusion that the wording of the policy in question was insufficiently clear, and that he should give the benefit of the doubt to the policyholder. He had no reason to believe that the solicitor appointed by the insured was other than well qualified to handle the dispute with the hotel. Accordingly, he concluded that DAS should confirm the solicitor selected by the insured to act as the appointed representative.

He upheld the complaint and required DAS to accept the claim under the terms and conditions of it's policy, allowing the matter to continue to be handled by the solicitor already acting for the insured's wife. The policy provided indemnity for reasonable legal fees charged by the solicitor "on the standard basis". The adjudicator held that this seemed to be a reasonable restriction, as was the requirement to co-operate with the insurer and confirm the prospects of success for the case.

On lawyer's charges another decision of an adjudicator from the Financial Ombudsman Service on May 3, 2002 helpfully clarifies the position further. Here the complaint was against Cornhill Insurance plc regarding a legal expenses policy the insured wished to call upon following a motorcycle accident. The insured was taking proceedings against the third party driver for compensation for injuries suffered in the accident. The insured instructed solicitors to act who were approved by Cornhill. However the insured was dissatisfied with them and later instructed alternative solicitors who were not on Cornhill's approved panel. Cornhill agreed in principle to the insured instructing alternative solicitors but would only agree to them acting on the basis that all costs be recovered from the third party if the insured won the case. The insured did not accept this and the new solicitor wrote to Cornhill stating that it would expect there to be a shortfall between the total costs incurred and those recovered from the losing party. The insured argued that the refusal to indemnify for these costs fettered their choice of solicitor.

Page 1 of the policy in question stated:

"Under this policy we will pay the following.

- The professional fees, and expenses reasonably and properly charged by the legal representative, up to the standard rates set by the courts."

Section 3g stated:

"At the end of the claim, [the insurer will] settle the costs covered by this policy, if there is no other way of getting those costs back."

It was the adjudicator's view that the policy did provide cover for all charges reasonably incurred in the course of authorised legal proceedings. The adjudicator said

"as it is usual in any court proceedings for there to be a shortfall between the costs incurred and those recovered from the third party, in my view, the firm is not entitled to refuse to provide indemnity for such costs. It is also my view that to refuse to allow you to instruct solicitors unless they agree to waive such costs or you agree to pay them privately does unfairly fetter your choice of legal representation."

The adjudicator recommended to Cornhill that it agreed to

meet the costs of their insured's chosen solicitor in accordance with the terms and conditions of their policy and they agreed with the recommendations.

The Cover Provided by the Before The Event Insurance Policy

1.017 Even if there is before the event legal expenses insurance available, you must look carefully at the cover provided by the policy. The quality and extent of the cover can vary immensely. Historically the population was less litigious and the likelihood of before the event insurance being called upon was less frequent. Before the event insurance was often perceived as a "bolt on" which gave the impression of added value but in reality provided little or none. Sometimes policies impose conditions which rendered the cover almost worthless. For example, policies with an excess potentially greater than the cost of an after the event insurance policy! In the past you might also have found that the policy had an exclusion which terminated it on commencement of court proceedings, or which had totally inadequate limits of indemnity.

Fortunately, the position has improved. However, it is still essential to fully examine the terms and conditions of the cover and any exclusions which may apply before electing to proceed with the before the event policy as the preferred method of funding.

Whilst indemnity limits have improved significantly, terms can often appear to contradict each other and sometimes time sanctions can be imposed. For example, where an injury occurs to the before the event insured person within the first three months of the period of insurance, then the policy may not respond and no legal expenses cover will be in effect to financially support the claim made by the insured. Further it may be that the injury is not reported to the before the event insurer promptly. When investigating the extent of the cover, it is essential to identify if a reporting condition is in place as some before the event policies may not respond if the claim is reported after a specified time period for example, as short as 120 days from the accident date.

It may be that the incident occurs outside specified territorial limits. Certain types of claim may be fully excluded such as injury by process or occupational disease.

Household policies frequently exclude road traffic accidents but some don't, there is no short-cut, policies need to be read and considered fully. A Conditional Fee Agreement with an after the event insurance policy is usually going to be the preferred funding option when the before the event policy does not provide the required protection.

If you believe that a Conditional Fee Agreement is clearly the correct way forward, you may wish to consider the Law Society Conditional Fees Checklist for use with Model Conditional Fee Agreement. It contains a non-exhaustive list of issues which should be considered *before* signing the Conditional Fee Agreement. A copy of it is to be found in Appendix 1—Essential Materials and Useful Precedents.

We have also included two other checklists on matters covered in this chapter. The first is designed to ensure that the correct funding option is selected and to provide a record to establish this. The second is specifically for situations where before the event legal expenses insurance exists but is not used. The checklists will often need to be used together to cover the position fully.

COLLECTIVE CONDITIONAL FEE AGREEMENTS

The Collective Conditional Fee Agreements Regulations 2000 **1.018** came into force on November 30, 2000. The Regulations apply only to agreements entered into on or after November 30, 2000. They are very similar to the Conditional Fee Agreement Regulations 2000. Funding on a CCFA is now a normal funding option used by trade unions.

Regulation 3 provides that a collective Conditional Fee Agreement is one which does not refer to specific proceedings, but provides for fees to be payable on a common basis in relation to a class of proceedings, or, if it refers to more than one class of proceedings, on a common basis in relation to each claim. The agreement may be a CCFA whether on not the funder is the client or any clients are named in the agreement.

- *Client*—person who will receive advocacy or litigation services.

- *Funder*—the party to a CCFA who is liable to pay the legal representative's fees.

The Requirements for a Collective Conditional Fee Agreement

1.019 It is no less important to meet the statutory requirements for a CCFA than it is for an individual CFA. Failure to do so will almost certainly render it unenforceable. Regulation 4 of the Collective Conditional Fee Agreements Regulations 2000 sets out the requirements for any CCFA. They are:

(1) The agreement must specify the circumstances in which the legal representative's fees and expenses, or part of the, are payable.

(2) The agreement must provide that, when accepting instructions in relation to any specific proceedings, the legal representative must inform the client as to the circumstances in which the client may be liable to pay the costs of the legal representative and if the client requires any further explanation, advice or other information about the above, give that explanation, etc.

(3) Para. (2) does not apply to the agreement with counsel.

(4) The CCFA must provide that, after accepting instructions in relation to any specific proceedings, the legal representative must confirm his acceptance of instructions in writing to his client.

Regulation 5 provides conditions for a CCFA with success fee:

(1) The agreement must provide that, when accepting

instructions in relation to any specific proceedings the legal representative must prepare and retain a written statement containing—

● his assessment of the probability of being successful in the proceedings
● his assessment of the percentage increase having regard to the risk assessment
● the reasons, by reference to the risk assessment, for setting the percentage increase at that level.

(2) The agreement must provide that solicitor client privilege is waived in the event of an assessment of the success fee. It also has to confirm that if the court disallows any part of the success fee, on the ground that the level at which the increase was set was unreasonable in view of facts which were or should have been known to the legal representative at the time it was set, then that amount ceases to be payable unless the court is satisfied that it should continue to be so payable. If a lower success fee is agreed with the other side, the amount payable under the CCFA shall be reduced accordingly unless the court orders that the full amount should continue to be payable.

Regulation 6 provides that a CCFA must be signed by the funder and the legal representative, but not if agreement is between legal representatives, in effect solicitor and counsel.

In essence the CCFA Regulations have tried to mirror the CFA Regulations as far as possible. A specimen model Collective Conditional Fee Agreement can be found in the Appendix 1—Essential Materials and Useful Precedents. However there is also another set of regulations to be considered if work is to be carried out on a CCFA basis.

Since April 1, 2000, when section 30 of the Access to Justice Act 1999 came into force, membership organisations with prescribed body status have been able to recover a sum as part of legal costs from unsuccessful opponents to reflect the provision of legal help for members and their families.

By virtue of the Access to Justice (Membership Organisations) Regulations 2000, which also came into force on April 1,

2000, bodies which were prescribed for the purpose of section 30 of the Act were those bodies which were approved by the Lord Chancellor. However, with effect from April 1, 2000 the Lord Chancellor approved all trade unions listed by the Certification Officer as at March 31, 2000 as prescribed bodies. Other membership organisations were required to apply for approval.

The Access to Justice (Membership Organisations) Regulations 2000 are quite short but they are important. There are two specific regulations of considerable significance. Those are regulations 3 and 4 which relate to the requirements for arrangements to meet costs liabilities and to recover an additional amount for insurance costs. These state:

"3.—(1) Section 30(1) of the Access to Justice Act 1999 applies to arrangements which satisfy the following conditions.

(2) The arrangements must be in writing.
(3) The arrangements must contain a statement specifying—
   (a) the circumstances in which the member or other party may be liable to pay costs of the proceedings,
   (b) whether such a liability arises—
       (i) if those circumstances only partly occur,
       (ii) irrespective of whether those circumstances occur, and
       (iii) on the termination of the arrangements for any reason,
   (c) the basis on which the amount of the liability is calculated, and
   (d) he procedure for seeking assessment of costs.

(4) A copy of the part of the arrangements containing the statement must be given to the member or other party to the proceedings whose liabilities the body is undertaking to meet as soon as possible after the undertaking is given.

4.—(1) Where an additional amount is included in costs by virtue of section 30(2) of the Access to Justice Act 1999 (costs payable to a member of a body or other person party to the proceedings to include an additional amount in respect of provision made by the body against the risk of having to meet the member's or other person's liabilities to pay other parties' costs), that additional amount must not exceed the following sum.

(2) That sum is the likely cost to the member of the body or, as the case may be, the other person who is a party to the proceedings in which the costs order is made of the premium of an insurance policy against the risk of incurring a liability to pay the costs of other parties to the proceedings."

It would seem that to enable the recoverability of additional liabilities by a prescribed "Membership Organisation" that both sets of Regulations should be complied with. The requirements of each is explicit and they do require different things. Only when the two sets of regulations are read together are the full obligations clear.

Changing funding to a CCFA in cases had benefited from old style full union funding was challenged by the paying party in *Brady v Liverpool CC* [2002] 5 C.L. 61. In this High Court matter at the hearing for the detailed assessment of costs, Liverpool CC challenged the right of Brady's solicitors to recover a success fee, to which they claimed to be entitled pursuant to a collective Conditional Fee Agreement dated December 1, 2000, which had superceded an earlier traditional solicitor and client agreement between Brady's trade union and Brady's solicitors.

Brady had brought a claim, relating to an occupational stress injury, which was settled just prior to trial. A large part of the costs were incurred in the period immediately prior to settlement and during the period covered by the Conditional Fee Agreement. Brady contended that the December 2000 agreement was a Conditional Fee Agreement and entitled his solicitors to recover a success fee of 100 per cent from Liverpool CC. Liverpool CC argued that by virtue of the Civil Procedure Rules 1998 Part 48 PD 48 paragraph 57(8)2 no second or subsequent arrangement entered into on or after April 1, 2000 could give rise to an additional liability recoverable from the paying party. Brady submitted that the court should look behind the wording of the practice direction and consider the Access to Justice Act 1999 (Transitional Provisions) Order 2000 which drew attention to section 58A(6) and section 58A(7) of the Courts and Legal Services Act 1990 into which were incorporated the relevant provisions of the Access to Justice Act 1999.

Giving judgment on December 20, 2001 District Judge Knopf held, finding in favour of Brady, that if the purpose of the practice direction was to prevent a Conditional Fee Agreement from being entered into if there was any sort of prior funding arrangement, whether a Conditional Fee Agreement or not, then the practice direction appeared to go beyond the wording of the 2000 Order. If the practice direction was given any other interpretation it would mean that in every case where a member of the trade union had been pursuing an action before April 2000, that member would not be able to take advantage of a Conditional Fee Agreement. On the facts, the initial agreement was not a Conditional Fee Agreement and section 58(7) of the 1990 Act applied; accordingly the success fee was recoverable.

2

Nuts & Bolts One—Getting the Conditional Fee Agreement Right

Nothing illustrates the need to get the Conditional Fee **2.001** Agreement (CFA) right better than the decision of Costs Judge Master Rodgers on April 30, 2002 in the case of *Woods v Chaleff* (High Court, Supreme Court Costs Office, SCCO Ref. PR0108754, 0108755). Solicitors Allen & Overy represented the claimant in a libel action. Close to trial on or about June 6, 1999 the case settled for £55,000 plus costs to be assessed on the standard basis if not agreed. On May 25, 1999 Allen & Overy had entered into a CFA with their client having entered into a CFA with counsel the previous December.

Allen & Overy's bill for the period covered by the CFA with their client was approximately £191,000. The defendants contended that neither CFA was enforceable because of breach of the relevant regulatory provisions, which were at the time the Conditional Fee Agreements Regulations 1995 (SI 1995/1675). The defendants alleged that the CFA did not comply with regulations 3(d) and 4. The agreement did not state the amount payable or the method to be used to calculate the amount payable; in particular, whether or not the amount payable was limited by reference to the amount of any damages which might be recovered on behalf of a client. Nor did it state that the matters listed in the regulations had been drawn to the client's attention.

The claimant argued that the Regulations should be construed in a benevolent way so as to allow them to be enforced rather than the reverse. They contended that mere technical breaches should not render them unenforceable.

The judge held that where a statutory instrument laid down express provisions which had to be complied with, failure to comply with those provisions had to make the agreement unenforceable, as regulation 2 of the Regulations made quite clear. The solicitor's CFA was unenforceable and there were no sums payable in respect of the solicitors' bill of costs.

That was not the end of it however. The judge held that unless the claimant's solicitors' CFA with counsel could be treated as a stand-alone agreement at common law that must be the end of the claimant's case for recovery of any of counsel's fees. He held that counsel's CFA was subject to the Regulations as well. Again there had been a clear failure to comply with the requirements if the regulations. The agreement between the solicitors and counsel was unenforceable. Counsel's fees were unrecoverable as well.

The current requirements for the content of a CFA are set out in the Conditional Fee Agreement Regulations 2000. To be valid a CFA must be in a form which complies fully. We see no reason to expect the current regulations to be construed in any more benevolent a fashion than the old regulations. Getting the wording of the CFA right is vital.

Using a reliable precedent is clearly sensible. The most commonly used precedent is the Law Society's Model Agreement, published in July 2000. A copy of this is reproduced in Appendix 1—Essential Materials and Useful Precedents. Some after the event insurers produce their own model version of a CFA and require those who use their insurance product to use that particular model. Many after the event insurers use the Law Society's Model Agreement as their starting point adding in changes to fit their individual needs. As an example the Law Society's Model Agreement in the Appendix 1—Essential Materials and Useful Precedents is followed by a copy of the Aftersure standard agreement.

If you modify any insurer's model agreement it may still comply with the regulations. However some insurers regard modification without their consent as a breach of their insurance policy conditions. You should always check with the insurer before making any modification. Failure may mean that your client is not insured.

These are the key sections of the regulations and the requirements for compliance with them.

GENERAL REQUIREMENTS (reg.2)

- Specify proceedings (or parts) to which agreements **2.002** relates.

- Specify when all or part of your fees and expenses become payable.

- Set out what payment is due:
  - If you only partly succeed.
  - In any event.
  - On termination of the agreement.

- Specify the amounts payable or the method used to calculate what is payable.

- Specify whether the amount is limited by reference to the recovered damages.

- Confirm that Regulation 4 has been complied with.

The requirement to specify whether the amount is limited by reference to the recovered damages has been the source of challenges in the courts. The problems developed in respect of the interim Law Society Model CFA (which preceded the July 2000 version). The defendants successfully argued in the case of *Barnard v Milburn* (see below) that the interim CFA failed to comply with regulation 3(d) of the 1995 regulations or 4(2)(e) of the 2000 regulations. Some district judges were declaring the agreements to be invalid and declaring that the successful claimant's lawyer was not entitled to any payment at all, as a consequence.

In *Barnard v Milburn* (unreported, Darlington County Court, August 8, 2002) the claimant had signed a CFA with his solicitor which followed the Law Society's May 2000 Model

Agreement, the interim agreement, often called "the running repair agreement".

Under regulation 2(1)(d) of the Conditional Fee Agreement Regulations 2000, the CFA must specify "in particular whether the amounts [of costs] are limited by reference to the damages which may be recovered on behalf of the client".

The court held that the CFA was invalid in that it was unenforceable as between the claimant and her solicitor. The basis of this decision was that the interim CFA did not comply with the 2000 regulations because (quoting the written reasons from the District Judge)

> "it simply provides under the section headed 'paying us' that the amount of the success fee is not calculated or limited by reference to the damages. A success fee is only part of the claimant's damages [sic] [should read 'costs']."

The reasons go on to say that "[u]nder the indemnity principle the defendant cannot be called upon to pay any costs for which the claimant is not liable to her own solicitor". The District Judge found that the CFA used was invalid because it only provided for the success fee to be limited by reference to the damages recovered. The claimant's costs were assessed at nil.

Not all judges have taken the same view. In *McCourt and McCourt v McCourt* (unreported, Liverpool County Court, November 8, 2001) the facts of the case were very similar to those in *Barnard v Milburn*. In *McCourt*, Part 8 proceedings were issued when costs could not be agreed at the conclusion of the case. Here the district judge held that the words "whether the amounts are limited by reference to the damages which may be recovered by the client" in regulation 2(1)(d) of the 2000 Regulations have a perfectly simple meaning. If the amount payable by the client is limited to a proportion of the damages the agreement must say so, but if they are not, there is no necessity for the agreement to say so.

Both decisions are currently subject to pending appeals.

Comparing the wording of the 1995 and 2000 regulations shows that they differ slightly on the relevant point. The Conditional Fee Agreements Regulations 1995 (SI 1995/1675) in regulation 3(d) sets out the requirements of a CFA including the requirement to specify

> "the method to be used to calculate the amount payable; and in particular *whether or not* the amount payable is limited by reference to the amount of any damages which may be recovered on behalf of the client."

The 2000 Regulations say in the corresponding regulation 2(1)(d):

> "[T]he amounts which are payable in all the circumstances and cases specified or the method to be used to calculate them and, in particular, *whether* the amounts are limited by reference to the damages which may be recovered on behalf of the client."

There has been a slight (but highly important) change in wording. In *Milburn* the District Judge seems to have imported into the 2000 Regulations words that were not there and had been removed. At paragraph 2 of his judgment the Judge stated:

> "I find no difficulty in understanding or interpreting this provision. It is mandatory in its terms and the word is 'whether' (*i.e.* whether or not) and not 'if'. I do not and should not look at Hansard or the Government's Consultation Papers as the Regulation in question is neither ambiguous or obscure."

Can the word "whether" mean "whether or not"? If this was the intention of the parliamentary draftsman then the extra words would have been left in. It cannot be presumed that this was an accidental omission, see the House of Lords decision *Wiseley v John Fulton* and *Wadey v Surrey County Council* (*The Times,* April 7, 2000).

If this is correct the only requirement of the CFA on this point, was to state whether the amounts were limited by reference to damages. There is no requirement to state whether "*or not*" the amounts are limited or those elements that are not limited. The CFA should therefore be valid.

A fundamental point of construction here is that the basic issue of law is that to succeed in an argument that the CFA is invalid a defendant would have to persuade a court that the claimant could take the point with her solicitors that the agreement was invalid. The observations of Lord Mustill in *Giles v Thompson* ([1994] A.C. 142 at 165) may well be pertinent. He said "the solicitude of the defendants and their insurers for the interests of their potential opponents may fairly merit a measured, if not sceptical regard".

The District Judge declined to look at parliamentary intention because, he held, the meaning of the statute was clear. Purposive interpretation must be relevant. The purpose of the provision was made clear by the then Lord Chancellor, Lord Mackay, when moving the approval of the Conditional Fee Order 1995 on June 12, 1995. He had been pressed to include in the regulations a mandatory cap into all CFAs. He declined but said (*Hansard*, col.1545):

> "It may well be that a cap such as the Law Society recommends in its model agreement will prove a useful tool. It certainly helps to focus attention on this aspect of the matter in discussion between lawyer and client. However, it is important for the client to be aware of the implications of this uplift and it is for this reason that I have included in the Regulations a requirement for the agreement to state whether or not there is to be a cap on the amount of damages to be taken by way of the uplift. This will ensure that the matter is addressed in all cases if the agreement is to be a conditional fee agreement obtaining the protection of the law and therefore enforceability."

This seems to make it clear that parliamentary intention was that the agreement should state whether or not there was a cap on the uplift and that was their only concern. However, it will ultimately be for a higher court to decide whether or not these CFAs are indeed invalid.

There are serious implications if they are. Not only for solicitors who have been using that version of the agreement but potentially in many cases for the after the event insurers linked to the individual CFAs. If the CFA was not valid on the wording of many policies, the insurance is not valid either. In a case where the claimant succeeded, he would be entitled to a refund of the premium he had paid. In essence if there was never any CFA, there was never any insurance.

The converse of this is that where the claimant is unsuccessful and loses, the after the event insurer upon examination of the CFA at presentation of the claim for payment, may determine that because of the unenforceability of the CFA, the after the event insurance is in fact void and the claim may be refused. This could lead to the losing claimant being responsible for the defendants costs with no means to pay.

Such a situation may lead to a negligence action against the solicitor by the claimant or a subrogated action against the solicitor by the after the event insurer if the insurer felt obliged to pay the claim rather than leaving the claimant personally exposed.

CFA WITH SUCCESS FEE (reg.3)

- Specify the reasons for setting the level of success fee. **2.003**

- Specify how much of success fee relates to delayed payment of fees and expenses.

- If the agreement relates to court proceedings specify that you may if required disclose to the court the reasons for setting the level of success fee.

- Specify that if the court disallows any part of the success fee it ceases to be payable under the agreement unless the court orders otherwise.

- Specify that if a lower fee is agreed with the other side, this overrides the agreement.

- Unless the court otherwise orders.

ADDITIONAL REQUIREMENTS (regs 5 and 6)

Regulation 5 requires that the conditional fee agreement must **2.004** be signed by both solicitor and client. If the CFA is not signed by both parties it is likely to be unenforceable.

Regulation 5 also confirms that a conditional fee agreement between solicitor and counsel does not need to be signed. However at the conclusion of the APIL/PIBA 5 Model Conditional Fee Agreement Between Solicitors and Counsel it states:

> "By signing and today returning to counsel the last page of this agreement by fax the solicitor agrees to instruct counsel under the terms of this agreement and undertakes to furnish counsel within 14 days of today with hard copies of the signed agreement together with any documents under paragraph 5 of this agreement which are not already in counsel's possession."

This means that notwithstanding the regulations normally the CFA between a solicitor and counsel will need to be signed. A copy of the APIL/PIBA 5 Model CFA can be found in Appendix 1—Essential Materials and Useful Precedents.

Amendment of the agreement is dealt with in regulation 6. Where an agreement is amended to cover further proceedings or parts of them you must comply with all of the requirements of regulations 2, 3 and 5 as if the amendment were a fresh agreement.

The Civil Procedure Rules mention that a cap on the total additional liability claimed linked to the level of damages recovered is a factor which a judge may take into account when assessing a success fee. There is no requirement in the regulations to have any such cap in a conditional fee agreement.

In the vast majority of cases any cap will be irrelevant. Indeed it seems illogical to use a cap when the payment of the success fee is not coming from damages recovered. However it is possible that in some cases the client may be left with a residual liability in respect of costs. A Solicitor may choose to include a cap at a low percentage of the damages simply for client security. In larger cases this would avoid any risk of seriously depleting their damages.

3

Nuts & Bolts Two—Providing the Right Information

Having cleared the hurdle of drafting a CFA which is valid, the next potential series of hurdles come from the various requirements to provide information. Any failure to provide the correct information to a client, an opponent or the court can mean that there will be a risk that you will fail to recover all or part of your costs in the action. This is a risk that can be eliminated completely by providing the right information at the right time. **3.001**

INFORMATION TO BE GIVEN TO THE CLIENT

The conditional Fee Agreements Regulations 2000 specify the information which a solicitor must provide to their client before a Conditional Fee Agreement is put into place. The task of complying with these requirements can be time consuming and sometimes frustrating. Even so, it is essential if you want to be sure you are not going to end up loosing out financially. The bulk of the requirements are set out in regulation 4. However you also need to cover regulations 2, 3, 5 and 6. **3.002**

Regulation 4(2)

This places an obligation on you to explain to the client: **3.003**

- the circumstances in which the client may be liable to pay the solicitor's costs;

- when and how the client may seek assessment of your fees and expenses;

- whether potential adverse costs are insured under an existing insurance policy;

- whether other methods of funding costs are available and if so to what extent;

- whether the legal representative considers that any particular method of funding costs is appropriate and if insurance is appropriate;

- if a particular insurance product is recommended;

- the reasons; and

- whether the legal representative has any interest in recommending this product.

Having fulfilled these requirements, regulation 4(3) obliges the legal representative to explain the conditional fee agreement to the client. It may be that the form of agreement they are using is drawn up in such a way that as they explain it they will in effect be complying with the requirements of regulations at the same time. This will depend on the wording used.

Regulation 4(1)

3.004 This requires that before making the conditional fee agreement the legal representative must inform the client of the matters in regulations 2 and 3 and having been through the entire explanation process if the client requires any further explanation, advice or information, the legal representative is obliged to give it. If the agreement is subsequently amended to cover further proceedings or parts of them, regulation 6 imposes a duty upon the legal representative to provide the client with any fresh information necessary. To comply the legal representative need to ensure that as far as the amendments are concerned they fulfil all of the obligations under regulation 4 where the amendments affect any of the matters mentioned in that regulation.

Regulation 4(5)

This requires that the information in regulation 2(a)–(e) and   **3.005**
regulation 3 must be given to the client orally. In addition, the information in regulation 2(e) and regulation 3 must also be given in writing. Providing it orally is important. Of course it does not need to be provided in a face-to-face meeting to satisfy the regulations. For example, providing it by telephone would also be acceptable. However, that may not be possible or practical in some cases. For example, there may be difficulties with a client who's first language is not English. Then it might be essential to have a face-to-face meeting and to work with an interpreter to ensure that the regulations are complied with. A failure to do this is likely to invalidate the CFA and leave the solicitor with no enforceable charging agreement at all.

A failure to provide oral informational at all, although offering the client the opportunity to seek it if required, is likely to be held to breach the regulations. In *Walters v Child* (Leicester County Court, May 21, 2002) this is what happened. The solicitor supplied a very good explanation by letter and made it clear that if the client wanted to discuss any aspect they had only to telephone. District Judge May held that was not good enough. The regulations had been breached and there was no valid charging agreement. As there was no agreement between solicitor and client, the indemnity principle had been breached and the claimant was unable to recover any costs from the defendant.

Use of an intermediary to provide the explanation has also been held to breach the regulations. In *English v Clipson* (Peterborough County Court, August 5, 2002)[1] District Judge Wharton held that an employee of a referral agency could not provide the required verbal advice. The thrust of the defen-

---

[1] Subject to appeal.

dant's submission was that the claimant's solicitor failed, as the client's legal representative, to provide to Mr. English with the information, and the further explanation, advice or other information, if sought, required by regulation 4. Since compliance with regulation 4 is mandatory, the CFA concluded between the solicitor and Mr. English was held to be unenforceable. As there was no liability between solicitor and client, there was no right to an indemnity for any of Mr. English's costs from the defendant, Mr. Clipson. Once more the claimant was unable to recover any costs from the defendant.

It is extremely easy to miss something when putting a conditional fee agreement in place with a client. To try to help practitioners to get it right, the Association of Personal Injury Lawyers (APIL) have provided their members with a useful conditional fee checklist produced by Counsel, Gordon Exall. The checklist should be signed by the client prior to entering into a conditional fee agreement. A copy of the checklist can be found in Appendix 1—Essential Materials and Useful Precedents.

Where the client is represented under a CCFA with a membership organisation the information requirements of the Access to Justice (Membership Organisations) Regulations 2000 and the Collective Conditional Fee Agreements Regulations 2000 must be complied with.

Under the CCFA Regulations the information to be given to the client is set out in regulation 4(2). The client must be informed as to the circumstances in which they may be liable to pay the costs of the legal representative and if the client requires any further explanation, advice or other information, then it must be provided to such extent as the client may reasonably require.

Under regulation 4 of the Access to Justice (Membership Organisations) Regulations 2000 there is a requirement that a copy of the part of the arrangements between the membership organisation and the lawyers containing "the statement" must be given to the member or other party to the proceedings, in other words the client, whose liabilities the body is undertaking to meet, as soon as possible after the undertaking is given.

The statement in question must include details of the circumstances in which the client may be liable to pay costs of the proceedings, detailing whether such a liability arises if those circumstances only partly occur, irrespective of whether those circumstances occur, and on the termination of the arrangements for any reason. It must also include details of the basis on which the amount of the costs liability is calculated, and the procedure for seeking assessment of costs.

These requirements are set out in more detail in Chapter 2.

PROVIDING INFORMATION TO THE OTHER PARTIES AND THE COURT

Notification Before Proceedings

There has been much confusion about what information should be supplied to all other potential parties before proceedings commence. The Civil Procedure Rules do not deal with this. They are concerned with what happens in litigation. The costs practice direction is not very helpful either. Section 19 deals with the providing of information generally. It simply states that "there is no requirement for the provision of information about funding arrangements before the commencement of proceedings". Such provision is however recommended and may be required by a pre-action protocol. **3.006**

This was followed up by a change to the Pre-Action Protocols Practice Direction being amended. The changes came into force from October 2, 2000. The relevant sections are 4A.1 and 4A.2. Section 4A.1 requires that where a person enters into a funding arrangement within the meaning of rule 43.2(1)(k) "He should inform other potential parties to the claim that he has done so". Section 4A.2 confirms that paragraph 4A.1 applies to all proceedings whether proceedings to which a pre-action protocol applies or otherwise.

Many liability insurance companies seem to have found this difficult to understand. Frequently they have been sending out standard form letters seeking much more information than they are entitled to. Examples of some companies' approach is reflected in the questions they have been asking such as:

- Please state the percentage of the success fee which you have set in this case.

- Please provide us with a copy of your client's CFA.

- Please provide us with a copy of the risk factors set out in your clients CFA.

- Please provide us with a copy of your CFA risk assessment.

- We require you supply us with a copy of your CFA risk assessment with details of the mechanism you have used to calculate the uplift.

- How much is the "after the event" insurance premium your client has paid in respect of this case?

In *Ashworth v Peterborough United Football Club Limited*[2] (see Chapter 5) the claimant's solicitors advised the defendant's solicitors that they were in the process of taking out an after the event legal expenses insurance policy. They pointed out that they were precluded from revealing the exact insurance premium figure but went on to say "we are sure you will be aware the figure will be substantial, given the costs estimated in our respective allocation questionnaires".

In their reply the defendant's solicitors wrote "if the premium quoted by the insurers is substantial then it indicates that the insurers do not think much of your client's case." This one sentence illustrates graphically the precise reason why the information to be provided is extremely limited, and rightly so.

We could provide many other examples all of which are equally inappropriate and where the liability insurer/lawyer has no right whatsoever to this information until the time for assessment of the additional liability or liabilities.

---

[2] *Ashworth v Peterborough United FC*, SCCO Ref: 0201106.

In the spring of 2001, in an effort to avoid these problems, the pre-action protocols working party agreed a change to the pre-action protocol for personal injury claims. This forms an addition to paragraph 3.2 saying:

"Where the case is funded by a conditional fee agreement, notification should be given of the existence of the agreement and where appropriate, that there is a success fee and insurance premium, although *not* the level of the success fee or premium."

The draft letter of claim has also been amended to show what should be included. This same approach has been incorporated in the requirements of the new pre-action protocol for illness and disease claims. The suggested wording to cover notification in both protocol claim letters is:

"Please note that we have entered into a conditional fee agreement with our client dated ****** in relation to this claim which provides for a success fee within the meaning of section 58(2) of the Courts and Legal Services Act 1990. Our client has taken out an insurance policy dated ***** with (name of insurance company) to which section 29 of the Access to Justice Act 1999 applies in respect of this claim."

Specimen copies of the full letters of claim appear in Appendix 1—Essential Materials and Useful Precedents. In any other type of litigation specifically covered by it's own pre-action protocol, such as clinical negligence, or in areas of litigation where there is no specific protocol in place, it would be sensible to use the same or a very similar form of words so as to avoid the risk of the court reducing the recoverable amount of an additional liability or disallowing it entirely as a recoverable item.

Perhaps one of the most surprising requests from insurers is for the provision of details of additional liabilities in cases where the claimant has not notified them that any such additional liabilities exist. Since failure to notify might well be a bar to recoverability of the additional liabilities, why would a liability insurer want to bring to the attention of a claimant that they had failed to provide notification? Nevertheless, a request for information of this type has appeared in correspondence from several major liability insurers on a regular basis.

Method of Giving Information in Proceedings

3.007 Both section 19 of the Costs Practice Direction and CPR Rule 44.15 deal with the requirements for providing information about funding arrangements. Any claimant who has entered into a funding arrangement before starting the proceedings to which that funding arrangement relates must provide information to the court by filing a notice using Form N251 when he issues the claim form. The notice of funding to be filed and subsequently served is set out in Form N251. A "claim form" includes petition and application notice.

Where a defendant has entered into a funding arrangement before filing any document, he must also provide information to the court by filing notice with his first document. A "first document" may be an acknowledgement of service, a defence, or any other document, such as an application to set aside a default judgment.

In all other circumstances any party must file and serve notice within seven days of entering into the funding arrangement concerned. Whenever there is a change of information, CPR Rule 44.15 imposes a duty on a party to give notice of change if the information he has previously provided is no longer accurate. In particular further notification needs to be given if the insurance cover is cancelled or if new cover is taken out with a different insurer. To comply, the party must file and serve a notice containing the information set out in Form N251. It should be remembered that CPR Rule 44.15(3) may impose other duties in relation to new estimates of costs.

The Information You Must Provide

3.008 You must state whether you have:

- entered into a conditional fee agreement which provides for a success fee within the meaning of section 58(2) of the Courts and Legal Services Act 1990;

● taken out an insurance policy to which section 29 of the Access to Justice Act 1999 applies;

● made an arrangement with a body which is prescribed for the purpose of section 30 of the Act. This relates to collective conditional fee agreements.

If a party has entered into more than one funding arrangement in respect of a claim, which is commonly the case, such as a conditional fee agreement with an after event insurance policy, a single notice containing the information set out in Form N251 may contain the required information about both or all of them. The information needed in relation to each of these is as follows:

Where the funding arrangement is a conditional fee agreement:

● you must state the date of the agreement;

● you must identify the claim or claims to which it relates;

● including Part 20 claims if any.

Where the funding arrangement is an insurance policy:

● you must state the name of the insurer;

● the date of the policy;

● you must identify the claim or claims to which it relates including any Part 20 claims if any.

Where the funding arrangement is an arrangement with a relevant body:

● you must state the name of the body;

● you must set out the date and terms of the undertaking it has given;

- you must identify the claim or claims to which it relates including any Part 20 claims.

The court will not assess any additional liability until the conclusion of the proceedings or the part of the proceedings to which the funding arrangement relates. There is absolutely no requirement to specify the amount of the additional liability separately nor to state how it is calculated until it falls to be assessed. This is confirmed in the Costs Practice Direction, section 2.3 and CPR Rule 43.2A(1). Indeed, to do so might be detrimental to your own client's position in that it would reveal information about your views in respect of the risks in the case and it's prospects of success.

Giving Information for Assessment of an Additional Liability

3.009   If you are proceeding with a detailed assessment in respect of an additional liability only, you must comply with the requirements of the Costs Practice Direction, section 32.4. The receiving party must serve the following documents on the paying party and all other relevant persons:

(a) a notice of commencement;

(b) a copy of the bill of costs;

(c) the relevant details of the additional liability;

(d) a statement giving the name and address of any person upon whom the receiving party intends to serve the notice of commencement.

The relevant details of an additional liability are as follows in the case of a conditional fee agreement with a success fee are set out in Costs Practice Direction section 32.5:

(a) a statement showing the amount of costs which have been summarily assessed or agreed, and the percentage increase which has been claimed in respect of those costs;

(b) a statement of the reasons for the percentage increase given in accordance with regulation 3 of the Conditional Fee Agreement Regulations 2000.

Section 32.5 also details the relevant details of an additional liability if the additional liability is an insurance premium. They are:

(a) a copy of the insurance certificate showing whether the policy covers the receiving party's own costs; his opponents costs; or his own costs and his opponent's costs;

(b) the maximum extent of that cover;

(c) the amount of the premium paid or payable.

If the receiving party claims an additional amount under section 30 of the Access of Justice Act 1999 the relevant details of an additional liability are also contained in section 32.5. They are:

(a) A statement setting out the basis upon which the receiving party's liability for the additional amount is calculated.

(b) For a membership organisation this must not exceed the likely cost of the premium of an insurance policy.

If you are proceeding with a detailed assessment in respect of both base costs and an additional liability you must comply with the requirements of the Costs Practice Direction, section 32.7. This requires the receiving party to serve on the paying party and all other relevant persons the documents giving relevant details of an additional liability listed above plus in addition they must also serve on the paying party and all other relevant persons the documents listed in section 32.3.

4

Recovery of a Success Fee

Recovery of the success fee depends on many factors. First of **4.001** all you must be able to show that a conditional fee agreement with success fee was a reasonable funding option. Secondly you must have complied with all of the rules and regulations relating to CFA funding including the form of the CFA and notice requirements. Finally you will need to show that your success fee was reasonable. All of these various elements are outlined in this Chapter and in some key aspects those elements are set out in detail in other individual Chapters.

The factors to be taken into account by the court in deciding the amount of costs in a case are to be found in CPR rule 44.5. The Costs Practice Direction section 11.4 covers the position where a party has entered into a funding arrangement confirming that the costs claimed may, subject to rule 44.3B include an additional liability. Section 11.5 sets the scene by stating that in deciding whether the costs claimed are reasonable and (on a standard basis assessment) proportionate, the court will consider the amount of any additional liability separately from the base costs. In other words the base costs need to be dealt with as one item, normally followed by consideration of "additional liabilities".

Section 11.9 of the Costs Practice Direction section makes it clear that a percentage increase will not be reduced simply on the ground that, when added to base costs which are reasonable and (where relevant) proportionate, the total appears disproportionate. There should be no proportionality test on uplifts as they are about risk. They are in effect a multiplier to the base costs' multiplicand, which when applied, one to the other, produces the total costs figure.

In section 11.7 of the Costs Practice Direction it is made clear that when the court is considering the factors to be taken into account in assessing an additional liability, it will have regard to the facts and circumstances as they reasonably appeared to the solicitor or counsel when the funding arrangement was entered into and at the time of any variation of the arrangement. This clearly means that there should be no hindsight on the part of the court when assessing the additional liability. To ensure that this is the case it is wise to have clear records showing exactly what information was available when the case was risk assessed and taken on.

4.002   There is one possible exception to be found. It is in paragraph Costs Practice Direction section 17.8(2). This provides that in cases in which an additional liability is claimed, the costs judge or district judge should have regard to the time when and the extent to which the claim has been settled and to the fact that the claim has been settled without the need to commence proceedings. This provides scope to allow the judge to reduce the success fee when there has been an early settlement *without* proceeding but *in no other circumstances*. Clearly this means that if a case does settle pre litigation there is a need to consider negotiating a settlement of costs by agreeing to accept a lower success fee than the original assessment produced. The Conditional Fee Agreement Regulations 2000 regulation 3 anticipates this with the requirement that a CFA includes a term specifying that if a lower fee is agreed with the other side, it overrides the agreement unless the court otherwise orders.

The court does have the power, under the Costs Practice Direction section 11.8(2), when considering whether a percentage increase is reasonable, to allow different percentages for different items of costs or for different periods during which costs were incurred. This suggests that uplifts may vary. However this is an odd concept which flies in the face of not only Costs Practice Direction section 11.7 but all risk assessment and insurance principles. It is very difficult to see how this could be justified in all but the most unusual circumstances without a risk of the entire CFA system being undermined.

Perhaps if counsel has a different uplift to that of his instructing solicitor this section could have some use although it should not be needed for that. We are not able to imagine what such circumstances might be. Even so some liability insurers and some of those who act for them suggest that it is perfectly reasonable. The basis is the argument that if liability is admitted then the risk is significantly reduced and the success fee should be reduced accordingly. Of course if it is acceptable in such a situation then it would also have to be applicable if a case became more difficult. That would have to mean that a success fee could go *up as well as down*. The potential uncertainty created by this sort of approach could do nothing other than cause massive problems is sustaining the CFA system and the access to justice it is intended to provide.

Perhaps the power provided by section 11.7 was what the Court of Appeal had in mind with their ideas on split success fees set out in their first *Callery v Gray* judgment. In a lengthy section of the first judgement the Court of Appeal floated and then shot down the idea of using a two-stage success fee. By way of example, they said the uplift might be agreed at 100 per cent, subject to a reduction to 5 per cent should the claim settle before the end of the pre-action protocol period. Please note the words "by way of example". You could of course have any two figures. **4.003**

They said that the logic behind a two-stage success fee was that, in calculating the success fee, it could properly be assumed that if, notwithstanding the compliance with the pre-action protocol, the other party was not prepared to settle, or not prepared to settle upon reasonable terms, there was a serious defence. By the end of the protocol period, both parties should have decided upon their positions. If they were prepared to settle, they should make an offer setting out their position clearly and providing the level of costs protection which they determine is appropriate. In other words to make use of CPR Part 36 to the benefit of and for the protection of their client.

They also said that a further advantage of a two-stage success fee would be the knowledge that if a claim was not settled, the full success fee would be payable. "The full success fee would be payable"? Clearly this cannot have been their intention as it cannot be correct. A practitioner's risk assessment would be obsolete if this was correct. The decision has not changed the requirements of the CPR or the Costs Practice Direction in this area.

There does in any event seem to be a "fatal flaw" in the court's approach. First of all they said that by using a staged uplift the risk would more accurately reflect the risk in individual cases. Then they appeared to contradict themselves. Later in the judgment they said that the determination of the reasonable figures for the full uplift and the rebated uplift would have to be based on overall claims experience, with the proportion of contested cases which succeed, and the costs earned from such cases, being particularly significant. In other words not a case specific risk assessment at all. It simply cannot be both.

4.004 The crucial point came where the judgment says:

> "While the exercise involved in determining a reasonable two-stage fee would be more complex, we suggest that, once the necessary data is available, consideration will need to be given to the question whether, where fees are agreed at the outset, the requirement to act reasonably mandates the agreement of a two-stage success fee."

"Once the necessary data is available" means that it was not available, then and at best will not be for some considerable time. That in effect must mean that fluctuating success fees, even on the simplest basis such as the two-stage idea proposed and rejected by the Court of Appeal is currently a non starter. When looking at the setting of success fee and considering insurance principles, in later Chapters, we shall consider the sort of information which might be collected over time to enable actuarial data to be used in as support for the level of a success fee. Similar information *could* be used to give serious consideration to split success fees.

The split success fee concept has been brought to the fore again by the Court of Appeal's decision in *Halloran v Delaney* [2002] EWCA Civ 1258 (see Chapter 8) and may yet become a requirement rather than an option. We hope however that this is never a requirement, with changes to the regulations to make clear how it should work.

As things stand now when deciding whether a percentage increase is reasonable the relevant factors to be taken into account by the Court may include three things. They are set out in Costs Practice Direction section 11.8(1).

- The risk that the circumstances in which the costs, fees or expenses would be payable might or might not occur;

- The legal representative's liability for any disbursements;

- What other methods of financing the costs were available to the receiving party.

The risk that the circumstances in which the costs, fees or expenses would be payable might or might not occur is of course the risk linked to your *assessment of risks in the case.* The risk of failure in all its various forms. These are explored in detail in Chapters 8 and 9. The other two factors speak for themselves. We have already explored other funding options and emphasised the need to ensure that a CFA is the appropriate route before entering into an agreement with the client. However there are other things to consider too as was illustrated by the Court of Appeal's decision in *Sarwar v Alam* which we consider in detail in Chapter 5 dealing with recoverability of insurance premiums.

The court however gave some guidance generally on the subject of when a CFA with success fee and after the event insurance might or might not be justified when there was before the event legal expenses insurance available as a suitable means of funding an action.

In normal circumstances if a claimant making a relatively **4.005** small (*i.e.* under £5,000) claim in a road traffic case had access to pre-existing before the event legal expenses insurance cover which appeared to be satisfactory for a claim of that size, then it should be used. The argument that it was reasonable for claimants in small RTA cases to sign CFAs and to take out

ATE policies even if reasonable BTE cover was available were rejected. Perhaps even more importantly the argument that it was reasonable for trade unions to offer CCFAs with ATE or section 30 cover in such cases was also rejected in *Sarwar v Alam*. The Court accepted that it was not in the interests of motorists or the general public that motor liability insurers should have to make unnecessary payments which raise premium costs.

They suggested that a solicitor should normally invite a client, using a standard form letter (see Precedent in Appendix 1—Essential Materials and Useful Precedents), to bring to the first interview any relevant motor and household insurance policy, as well as any stand-alone legal expenses insurance policy belonging to the client and/or spouse or partner. They recognised that regard had always to be had to the amount at stake, and said that a solicitor was not obliged to embark upon a "treasure hunt". This does not just apply to *driver's* making a claim. They indicated that given the frequency with which motor insurance policies now provide legal expenses cover for a claim by any passenger of the insured, the solicitor ought ordinarily to ask his client to obtain a copy of the driver's insurance policy, if reasonably practicable. The question of practicability is necessarily fact-sensitive but that does not mean that the solicitor can simply ignore the fact that potential cover may be there to be used.

The final and perhaps most important thing of all is to have a proper risk assessment available to comply with the needs of Costs Practice Direction section 14.9(3). This requires that in order to facilitate the court in making a summary assessment of any additional liability at the conclusion of the proceedings the party seeking such costs must prepare and have available for the court a bundle of documents which must include a copy of the risk assessment prepared at the time any relevant funding arrangement was entered into and on the basis of which the amount of the additional liability was fixed. How that might be produced and what it might contain we shall look at in later Chapters.

4.006   An uplift is of course just one of a number of additional liabilities that may be recovered by a successful party from his or her opponent. It should not matter who that opponent is.

The Motor Insurers Bureau have however tried to argue that they should not be required to make such a payment. In the Costs Practice Direction section 2 (CPR Part 43.2) it states in paragraph 2.1 that where the court makes an order for costs and the receiving party has entered into a funding arrangement as defined in rule 43.2, the costs payable by the paying party include any additional liability (also defined in rule 43.2) unless the court orders otherwise. In effect if the MIB have to satisfy a judgment with costs there should be no reason why those costs should not include an uplift or other additional liability.

Even so in many cases including *Lunt v Coran & MIB* [2002] J.P.I.L. the MIB have contested their requirement to pay the success fee. In *Lunt* they argued that by reason of clause 6 of the Uninsured Driver's Agreement 1999, it was not obliged to pay it. In the agreement clause 5 sets out the MIB's obligation to satisfy compensation claims including costs. Clause 6 provides for exceptions.

The exception that mattered for the purpose of this case was sub-paragraph 6(c):

"A claim by, or for the benefit of a person, (the beneficiary) other than the person suffering death, injury or other damage which is made...
(ii) Pursuant to a right of subrogation or contractual or other right belonging to the beneficiary".

The MIB argued that the success fee was a subrogated claim and unrecoverable. They lost before DJ Simpson in the Oldham County Court on December 19, 2001 when he held that the MIB were liable to pay the success fee.

On appeal HH Judge Tetlow found that the exception under clause 6 did not apply if a conditional fee agreement is appropriate. If it did apply it would mean that if the claimant had not entered into a conditional fee agreement he could not have obtained proper legal help otherwise. Accordingly if there was no before the event insurance then the claimant could recover whatever uplift was found to be reasonable. That was the important point of this decision.

Obviously this could not change the fact that if a conditional fee agreement was not the proper means of funding the case then the uplift would be unrecoverable. In fact in the *Lunt* case the claimant's solicitor was held to have either ignored the existence of before event insurance or to have failed to make proper enquiry. The solicitor had therefore breached his duty to his client and was not entitled to recover the uplift. He was still able to recover base costs although the Motor Insurers Bureau tried unsuccessfully to convince the judge that the claimant should recover no costs at all.

5

Recovering an After The Event Insurance Premium

ESTABLISHING AN ENTITLEMENT TO RECOVER AN INSURANCE PREMIUM

Many practitioners are concerned about whether they will be **5.001** able to recover all of an insurance premium paid for an after the event policy. That should not be the starting point. The key question is can your client establish an entitlement to recover an after event insurance premium at all? Indeed, if the case is funded by a membership organisation the same applies. There are those who argue that, for example, once liability is admitted there is no longer any risk to insure. Once again the sensible approach is to follow best advice principles. Again it is necessary to look for assistance to the Costs Practice Direction. Sections 11.10 and 11.11 apply.

Practice Direction Section 11.10

In deciding whether the cost of insurance cover is reasonable, **5.002** relevant factors to be taken into account include:

(1) Where the insurance cover is not purchased in support of a conditional fee agreement with a success fee, how its cost compares with the likely cost of funding the case

with a conditional fee agreement with a success fee and
supporting insurance cover;

(2) the level and extent of the cover provided;

(3) the availability of any pre-existing insurance cover;

(4) whether any part of the premium would be rebated in
the event of early settlement;

(5) the amount of commission payable to the receiving
party or his legal representatives or other agents.

Practice Direction section 11.11 looks at cases where the court
is considering a provision made by a membership organisation [rule 44.3B(1) (b)]. It states that any provision which
exceeds the likely cost of the premium of an insurance policy
against the risk of having to pay the costs of other parties is
not recoverable. It confirms that in such circumstances the
court will, when assessing the additional liability, have regard
to the factors set out in paragraph 11.10 above, in addition to
the factors set out in rule 44.5.

Obviously this means that whether we are dealing with an
after the event insurance policy or a provision made by a
membership organisation, exactly the same tests will be
applied by the court with regard to reasonableness and
recoverability. Regulation 4(2)(e) of the Conditional Fee
Agreement Regulations 2000, imposes a duty on you as a
practitioner to advise the client on whether you consider that
any particular method of funding costs is appropriate and if
insurance is appropriate. Best advice must mean that where
the client can be protected from a financial exposure to pay
adverse costs they must be given this protection. Such protection is provided by after event insurance in conjunction
with a CFA. Faiure to advise the client to insure against such a
risk exposes the lawyer to a potential negligence action. It is
therefore essential to offer the client the opportunity to insure
in every case and to try to convince them that it is a vital
element of CFA funding. Accordingly in our view in every
case, it should be possible to justify the fact the after the event
insurance was taken out if a CFA was the appropriate method
of funding.

There is considerable debate about whether there is always an insurable risk and in particular whether following an admission of liability, there is a continuing need for after the event insurance. Some liability insurance companies regularly contend that if they admit liability, this negates the need for after the event insurance as in their view, there is no risk. This ignores totally the potential for a dispute on the value of the case or a dispute on causation.

The statutory definition contained in section 29 of the Access to Justice Act 1999 makes it clear that "an insurance policy against the risk of incurring a liability in those proceedings" is recoverable from the paying party. If Parliament wished to limit the insurable risk to that of losing on liability alone, it would have said so. The Government's policy is that premium paid is for cover against the risk of having to pay legal costs and that premium should be recoverable from the losing opponent. This ensures that damages paid to claimants are not unreasonably eroded. That must be the effect of the Access to Justice Act 1999. Therefore, if a claimant succeeds in part perhaps by obtaining an award of damages below the level of a Part 36 payment into court made by the defendant, to protect their damages from erosion, they still need insurance to protect against the potential financial exposure to pay adverse costs. The simplistic idea that an admission of liability removes completely the insurable risk to the client is not just naïve but totally wrong.

There can be no better confirmation that the previous statement is correct than the claims history experienced by the after the event Insurance industry during its first seven years of existence. Far fewer cases resulted in claims for the settlement of adverse costs orders where a case failed on liability than in those cases where the lack of success arose through a causation or quantum issue.

With an admission of liability, in order for the claimant to have no insurable risk, the defendant would need to:

(1) Agree that the claimant may "name their price" in respect of damages;

(2) Waive any right to dispute causation;

(3) Waive any right to dispute quantum in any respect;

(4) Provide a guarantee that under no circumstances will they seek to obtain any costs from the claimant;

The reality is that no liability insurer would ever, agree to such terms in order to negate their obligation to pay an after the event premium.

There is another reason why the no risk argument after an admission is flawed. Best practice must be for the claimant to enter into a conditional fee agreement with after the event insurance at the earliest possible time. This will mean they can obtain the most favourable insurance terms to contain the potential financial exposure from adverse costs at the best possible price.

ESTABLISHING FULL RECOVERY OF THE PREMIUM

5.003   Having clearly established that realistically, no case is without risk, and therefore all cases need to be insured, the second consideration can be examined. How can you endeavour to make sure that the full premium will be recovered? Again it is necessary to look for guidance to the Costs Practice Direction where it states what the court must take into account in deciding whether the cost of insurance cover is reasonable. Sections 11.10 and 11.10(1) once more apply with section 11.11 confirming that where the court is considering a provision made by a membership organisation they must have regard to the five factors set out in section 11.10 which relate to an after the event insurance policy. There are five factors to consider.

Section 11.10(1) where the insurance cover is not purchased in support of a conditional fee agreement with a success fee, how its cost compares with the likely cost of funding the case with a conditional fee agreement with a success fee and supporting insurance cover.

An after the event insurance premium may entitle the insured to cover for payment of their own costs in addition to any adverse costs. This type of policy may be linked to a conditional fee agreement but a success fee will not be recoverable. An additional liability in the form of a both sides' costs after the event insurance premium may be used without being linked to a conditional fee agreement at all. In most circumstances, the insurance premium paid for a "both sides" policy will be higher because of the additional cover provided.

There seems to be little doubt that "both sides' costs insurance" is within the ambit of section 29 of the Access to Justice Act. In June 2000, the Government published a consultation paper on collective conditional fees. It included the following statement:

> "Section 29 of the [Access to Justice] Act allows the court to include in any costs order, any premium paid for an insurance policy against the risk of incurring a liability in those proceedings. The recovery of the insurance premium is not limited to polices backing conditional fee agreements, but covers all after the event policies. The way in which recovery operates is subject to rule of court".

The well established principle of purposive interpretation makes if difficult to understand how the Court of Appeal in *Callery v Gray* were able to conclude that this document and the quotation referred to were not admissible when they were considering this subject. However, they nevertheless concluded that section 29 should be interpreted so as to treat the words "insurance against the risk of incurring a costs liability" as meaning "insurance against the risk of incurring a liability that cannot be passed on to the opposing party".

In simple terms premiums paid on both sides after the event insurance policies are recoverable. Insurance cover may provide a party with indemnity against their own costs in the event their claim fails. There are many circumstances under CPR 44.3 which may lead a court to exercise its discretion not to award a successful party all of their costs and this may be covered under such a policy as well. This is an option with obvious attractions.

The test cases supported by Claims Direct Plc (*Re: Claims Direct Test Cases* Supreme Court Costs Office (Chief Master Hurst) 19/7/2002) to determine issues of principle relating to payments by various claimants to them throws some light on the court's views on both sides costs insurance. The most important issue was whether the money paid by the claimant in each case was a premium within the meaning of section 29 of the Access to Justice Act 1999 and therefore recoverable as costs in litigation. Secondary to that was the question of the extent to which it was a premium, and thirdly whether or not it was reasonable.

The claimants' position was that the money paid by them was all insurance premium. They argued that it was not susceptible to further breakdown and that the amount payable was reasonable and proportionate when compared with other cases conducted under conditional fee agreements. The defendants argued that the recoverable premium was only the risk-bearing element. By that they meant that part of the money paid which was directly referable to the amount paid to underwriters. The premium claimed in all but one case was £1,250 plus £62.50, insurance premium tax totaling £1312.50.

5.004   The court held that the only costs of funding litigation that were recoverable were those permitted by statute, in this case section 29 of the Access to Justice Act. Anything falling outside the scope of that section was not recoverable. It was also held that when a claimant entered into a contract with Claims Direct he was not exclusively taking out an insurance policy, insurance being only part of the package purchased. The claimant was entitled to recover the insurance element only. The money paid was not all premium. The elements that could be considered part of the premium were payment to underwriters, Claims Direct commission, money for insurance services and insurance premium tax on those elements. This gave a total recoverable premium of £621.13. That sum was held to be reasonable and proportionate.

Two other issues of general importance were considered. First whether it was reasonable for a claimant in a road traffic accident case to take out insurance costed on a block rating basis, that is all cases have the same insurance premium. The argument against block rating was that although block rating is not itself objectionable, applying it across the board would lead to disproportionate premiums.

At paragraph 23 of *Callery v Gray (No.2)* the master of the

Rolls referred to Master O'Hare's report on after the event insurance. Master O'Hare had been told that had Mr Callery been issued with a block rated policy he would have been charged a premium of £997.50 including insurance premium tax.

Lord Scott, in his dissenting judgment in the House of Lords, paragraphs 124 and 125, said:

> "The factual basis, therefore, on which the Court of Appeal concluded that the £350 premium was reasonable in amount was erroneous. The Court of Appeal did not address the question whether in a case, like the present, where the percentage prospect of success is at the least in the mid 90s, it was reasonable to charge a premium calculated on a block basis for all cases with a percentage prospect of success of better than 50. Your Lordships do not know what answer the Court of Appeal would have given ... The injunction in CPR 44.4(2)(b) that requires the court to resolve doubts about reasonableness or proportionality in favour of the paying party does not mean that in every case where a decision as to reasonableness or as to proportionality is a difficult one to reach, with something to be said on each side, the paying party must win. The costs judge must endeavour to reach a conclusion on the issue, taking account of all the circumstances and of the factors that the rules and practice directions require to be taken into account. If, having done so, the costs judge remains uncertain whether the item of costs under review is reasonable and proportionate, then the paying party should win ... The issue of whether it would have been reasonable for Mr Callery to take out insurance for his claim at a much higher premium than £350, costed on a block rating basis, does not arise for determination on this appeal. On the face of it, adoption of such an option would seem hard to justify."

Both Lord Hoffman, at paragraph 35, and Lord Scott at paragraph 114, expressed the view that the correct approach for costs assessment purposes to the question whether an item of expenditure by the receiving party has been reasonably incurred is to look at the circumstances of the particular case. In other words it is a case specific decision.

Here the court looked at the evidence and concluded that such evidence as there was on the topic of block rating suggested that it had little effect on the recoverable premium altering it only to a minimal effect. On the evidence the court held that there would be no deduction in respect of block rating.

5.005 The second was what premium would be reasonable in circumstances where liability was admitted before a policy was taken out? Here the court held that where an incident occurred, particularly a minor road traffic accident, causing slight injury and where liability was accepted at the outset it would generally be disproportionate and unreasonable to take out an ATE policy. However, it was accepted that there may however be circumstances surrounding the incident, particularly if there is likely to be a live issue on causation, which would make it reasonable to take out an after the event policy.

Before we move away from the "both sides cover" option the case of *Ashworth v Peterborough United Football Club Limited* merits detailed consideration. The claimant was awarded £66,000 damages and costs to be the subject of detailed assessment on the standard basis if not agreed. The issue before the court was whether the claimant was entitled to be reimbursed for all or part of the premium he paid for an after the event legal expenses insurance policy. A premium of around £46,000 was paid by the claimant in December 2000, during the course of proceedings. At that time it was expected that damages would be in the region of £75,000. The defendant argued that the claimant could have taken out the insurance at the outset, rather than when the proceedings were well advanced and the amount of the premium was disproportionate and excessive, given the risks applicable in this case. The defendant also argued that the risks included a risk that was outside the risk of incurring a costs liability and that could not be passed on, namely a deficiency of damages.

The judge referred to Master O'Hare's report annexed to *Callery v Gray (No.2)* in which he said "In run of the mill cases it was not appropriate for the Court to delve into how the premium was calculated". The test was simply whether the receiving party had made an adequate search at reasonable rates. However, where as in the Ashworth case, a "bespoke" policy had been purchased the Court should enquire further. Even if there was very little evidence which could be put before it, the Court should not be deterred from taking a view having regard to market forces even without the benefit of direct evidence.

In the Court of Appeal's Judgment *Callery v Gray (No.2)* the Court said at paragraph 11:

> "It was common ground, and rightly so, that the Court, when considering whether to award an insurance premium by way of costs, has to consider whether the premium is reasonable. It was also common ground that, insofar as the court finds that the premium is not reasonable, it can and should reduce it."

The mechanism for dealing with this comes from *Callery v Gray (No.2)* where they said at paragraph 16 "In the meantime, where an insurance premium is challenged it must open to the insurer, whose position is akin to a subrogated underwriter, to place evidence before the court in an attempt to demonstrate that a premium is reasonable having regard for the costs that have to be covered. Satellite litigation involving such an exercise is, however, unsatisfactory. The Judge can only be expected to give broad consideration to such evidence, for it is not part of the function of a Judge assessing costs to carry out an audit of an insurers business."

If this means that you are working with an insurer who can an will justify and support their premium, the prospects of recovering the premium in full will be greatly enhanced.

In *Ashworth*, the case had been listed for a six day trial. As **5.006** Master Wright put it at paragraph 94, "There were therefore substantial risks at the time the policy was taken out that the situation could 'blow up' in the claimants face at any time." The claimant had submitted that when the chances of success had been assessed initially the picture and the predictability of the risk had not been clear. At the time the claimant was looking for insurance, insurers were very reluctant to grant cover. Greystoke had declined to give a quotation. Saturn Professional Risks were then approached. Here we had a claimant funding a case on a private client basis. The risks in the matter were such that it could not be funded under a conditional fee agreement. The claimant had to consider some other method of funding because to continue to be represented on a normal fee paying basis was not an option for him. A CFA is not always appropriate however, where cover obtained is greater than adverse costs only, the premium will inevitably increase. A conditional fee agreement is only one method backed by after the event insurance. In fact after the event insurance funding on its own can do almost anything. This case would have merited a high uplift if the CFA route had been viable. The success fee is and must be directly proportional to the risk. It is likely that the cost of the additional liabilities on a CFA with success fee and ATE would not have been much different from the premium paid on the "both sides costs".

The argument that the insurance should have been taken out earlier, thus securing a lower premium, failed. Initially insurance was declined. Whilst the argument to insure early and spread the risk amongst large number of cases does work for the "run of the mill" cases in more complex litigation such as clinical negligence or commercial cases it does not. Often there is insufficient evidence upon which any risk assessment can be executed by an insurer and therefore the premium cannot be calculated. It must be remembered that there is no obligation on any insurance underwriter to accept a given risk. Since insurance is the mechanism for the transfer of risk, then the underwriter needs to identify what they are taking on before they can quote and they always retain the right to decline to quote if the risk is unattractive, unquantifiable or unacceptable.

In *Ashworth*, evidence was put before the court from the underwriters. An important section of a letter before the court said. "We do not consider the premium disproportionate and would not have provided a policy for any less, particularly since we were providing cover for both sides costs."

Master Wright reached these conclusions:

(a) On the evidence before him insurance would probably not have been available at the outset and the ground of dispute failed.

(b) The premium was not disproportionate when measured against the total sum insured. For the defendant to have succeeded on this point, they would have had to show the premium was not proportionate "to the matters in issue" (see CPR 44.4.2).

(c) The insurer would not have provided cover for any less sum so therefore it would be necessary to conclude that the claimant should not have taken the policy out at all if recoverability of the premium was not to be allowed.

The court of Appeal in *Callery v Gray (No.2)* said at paragraph 14: "unfortunately, Master O'Hare concluded that the market in ATE insurance was not yet sufficiently developed to enable him to identify standard or average rates of premium for different categories of ATE insurance. He expressed doubt as to whether market forces were yet sufficiently compelling. He received a considerable body of evidence of the costs of individual at insurers, proffered in confidence, in an endeavour to form a view of the level of premium that was reasonably needed to cover costs."

Again at paragraph 68 the court of appeal said:

"Paragraph 68: Master O'Hare did his best to investigate premium rates in the market. He found that is was not possible to state standard or average premiums for different classes of business. He also found that results over several years had been uniformly poor, leading to several major increases in premium rates over those years"

Master Wright considered two paragraphs from Master O'Hare's report to be very relevant.

"Paragraph 17: As well as noting the different categories and classes of insurance it is necessary to observe that there are two different schemes, standard off the peg policies issued to all cases within the same class (see for example Abbey and The Accident Group); and one off insurance policies (e.g. policies issued by more specialist ATE providers such as Saturn). Premiums are lower in standard policies than they are in one off policies. This is because the most difficult cases and therefore the higher risk cases are likely to gravitate towards one off insurance policies (although it was not proven before me to what extent this is true of RTA cases). The most difficult cases are also the ones in which the solicitor will be reasonably to a higher than average success fee."

5.007 In paragraph 19 Master O'Hare says:

> "for several reasons it is not possible to state standard or average premiums for different classes or average premiums for different classes or categories of ATE insurance. The insurance is still immature and its results over several years have been uniformly poor. Premiums have undergone several major increases over those years. The range of products offered by the industry and the details of profit costs and disbursements they cover are both extremely varied."

This is not unique to ATE. Different insurers will rate what appears to be the same risk sometimes at quite different premium levels. However, what is currently lacking, is a known typical standard range of premium rates for ATE insurance likely to be found in the market. The calculation of insurance premium is routinely based on actuarial analysis of the past in order to predict the losses likely to be incurred in the future. Where there is no history or a very unstable and evidentially poor history, insurers will be cautious when determining the premiums to be charged if cover is available at all.

The ATE insurance market in terms of underwriters willing to insure this type of business is small. The history so far is poor with some of the larger schemes suffering heavy losses. This does not form a good basis for attracting more insurance companies into the ATE market or for supporting low premium levels.

Section 11.10(2)—The Level and Extent of the Cover Provided

5.008 Clearly the court will want to know what the level and extent of cover provided was and whether looking at the market place as a whole, the premium paid was a reasonable rate for that cover. In *Callery v Gray (No.2)*, the Court of Appeal held that the paying party must establish that a premium is unreasonable, the presumption being that it is reasonable unless shown to be to the contrary. When assessing costs on the standard basis, CPR Part 44.5 requires the Court to have regard to whether costs were proportionate and reasonable in amount. This rule will impact on the after the event insurance premium as with any additional liability it is an item of costs.

In theory, a paying party might argue that if the level and extent of cover provided would have been insufficient to meet an adverse costs order, that the after the event insurance premium claimed from them as an additional liability, should be disallowed. In essence the argument would be that if it was insufficient to provide indemnity to the after the event insured person, in the event of a claim upon it, it did not fulfil the requirements of section 29 of the Access to Justice Act 1999.

Consideration needs to be given to the terms, conditions, exclusions and insurance indemnity limits when advising the client on utilising after the event insurance.

Section 11.10(3)—The Availability of Any Pre-existing Insurance Cover

The Court will want to know whether the client was eligible **5.009** for cover under a pre-event legal expenses insurance policy.

If such a policy was in existence and was not used, then consideration by the court will need to be given to the following five points:

(1) Was client eligible to use the policy?

(2) Was the policy viable in the long term?

(3) Did the policy cover the type of claim?

(4) Was the level of indemnity adequate?

(5) Were the terms reasonable for the needs of the client?

These five points should all have been considered by you with your client before a decision was made to support the claim with an after the event policy. Proper consideration should mean that even if there was a pre-existing legal expenses insurance policy, it was reasonable not to use it and therefore, the additional liability should be recoverable. Good records will need to be kept to enable you to show how the decision to use a conditional fee agreement with after the event insurance in preference was reached.

The Court of Appeal gave guidance on these matters in *Sarwar v Alam* [CA (Lord Phillips M.R., Brooke L.J., Longmore L.J.) September 19, 2001]. This was an appeal in costs-only proceedings concerned with the arrangements for financing the cost of Mr. Sarwar's personal injury litigation. The claimant Mr. Sarwar was the passenger in a car being driven by the defendant Mr. Alam. It was in a collision with another vehicle. Sarwar made a claim backed by an after the event policy. The claim was settled for £2,250 together with reasonable costs.

In the subsequent costs-only proceedings, Alam's insurers disclosed for the first time that Alam's motor insurance policy included legal expenses insurance, which would have covered a claim by Sarwar against Alam as a passenger in the vehicle being driven by Alam. Both the district judge and circuit judge held that because this insurance was available to Sarwar it was unreasonable for him to have incurred the cost of an after the event insurance premium and the recovery was consequently disallowed. In particular, the judge below held that Sarwar and/or his solicitors ought to have made inquiries of Alam and/or his insurers about the existence of the before the event legal expenses policy.

The Court of Appeal held that the premium in this case was recoverable. Primarily because of the conflict point it was not incumbent on Sarwar to use Alam's legal expenses policy. The policy provided for legal representation to be arranged by Alam's insurers, who were, of course, the insurers for Sarwar's opposing party. Furthermore, the policy provided for those insurers to retain full conduct and control of the claim. That was not, in the circumstances, a reasonable alternative to representation by a lawyer of Sarwar s own choosing.

The Court of Appeal did say that the position might well be different, however, if before the event legal expenses insurers generally were to finance some transparently independent organisation to handle claims such as Sarwar's, and made it plain in the policy that they were so doing. That was no the position here.

The Court gave some guidance on the subject generally

which is of considerable assistance to practitioners. Their view was that in normal circumstances if a claimant in a road traffic case is making a relatively small claim, which means under £5,000 in value, and had access to pre-existing before the event legal expenses cover that appeared to be satisfactory for a claim of that size, then it should be used. The argument put to the court that it was reasonable for claimants in small road traffic cases to sign CFAs and to take out after the event policies even if reasonable before the event cover was available was rejected.

Perhaps even more importantly the argument that it was reasonable for trade unions to offer CCFAs with ATE or section 30 cover in such cases was also rejected. Their solicitors too need to investigate the before the event options.

The Court accepted "that it is not in the interests of motorists or the general public that motor liability insurers should have to make unnecessary disbursements which raise premium costs".

They suggested that a solicitor should normally invite a client, using a standard form letter, to bring to the first interview any relevant motor and household insurance policy, as well as any stand-alone legal expenses insurance policy belonging to the client and/or spouse or partner. Regard had, of course, always to be given to the amount at stake, and a solicitor was not obliged to embark upon a "treasure hunt".

They emphasised that given the frequency with which motor insurance policies now provided legal expenses cover for a claim by any passenger of the insured, the solicitor ought ordinarily to ask his client to obtain a copy of the driver's insurance policy, if reasonably practicable. The question of practicability is of course necessarily fact-sensitive.

Section 11.10(4)—Whether Any Part of the Premium would be Rebated in the Event of Early Settlement

In any case where an after the event insurance policy was **5.010** purchased where the premium level was slightly higher than average it might still be fully recoverable if part of the premium was to be rebated in the event of early settlement. Such an insurance product would carry an incentive for the paying party to try to reach an early settlement and therefore to limit their exposure with regard to that part of the additional liability. Any product like this should be attractive to the court as the encouragement to settle early and save costs, fits with the modern approach to litigation. The attraction of this type of policy should not in any way encourage premature or under-settlement of claims.

Section 11.10(5)—The Amount of Commission Payable to the Receiving Party or his Legal Representatives or Other Agents

5.011   In *Callery v Gray*, before the Court of Appeal, no objection was taken to the parts of the premium that covered risk/profit costs, administrative cost or commission payments. The court commented that in the longer term market forces would prevent premiums being unreasonably inflated by extravagant commission payments. It would be difficult in our view to for a lawyer to justify receiving a commission payment for placing a client's case with any particular after the event insurer.

It should remembered under regulation 4(2)(e) of the Conditional Fee Agreement Regulations 2000, if a particular insurance product is recommended you must not only state your reasons for recommending it but also whether you have an interest in doing so. Clearly the payment of a commission would be "an interest". If such a commission was payable, the court might well conclude, when assessing an additional liability, that the sum may be "hidden" within the premium quoted and reduce the recoverable premium by an equal amount.

6

Applying Insurance Risk Principles

The study and analysis of insurance principles are a con-   **6.001**
siderable and extensive subject and it is not the intention of
this work to relate these fully as this is not a reference book on
insurance. We will instead be selective in the elements we are
applying. That is, those simple general principles related and
then applied to the specific area—Conditional Fee Agreements (CFA) and after the event insurance.

A lot of time has been spent since the inception of CFAs in
1995, discussing risk. There is no doubt that for some, the
impact on day to day legal business brought about by the
removal of legal aid for personal injury is yet to be felt. Many
still have cases which are funded in this way and are not yet
fully reliant on conditional fee agreements underwritten by
after the event insurance cases. The new regime brings a new
type of business. It brings business which is not only risk
dependent for you, but risk dependent for your client as well.
Understanding that risk attaches to all conditional fee cases
will be essential for the survival of your business. Understanding that risk exists for all clients is essential in order for
you to ensure that all you clients receive best advice.

What exactly do we mean by risk? The word is used frequently in everyday conversation and most recognise what it
means in general terms. However, how does it apply in reality
to CFAs? How does it interact with after the event insurance
and then how does it apply to the firm as a business?

In this chapter, we will examine some simple insurance

principles and apply them to risk dependent CFA personal injury business.

What Do We Mean by Risk?

6.002   The concept of risk is not new, the entire insurance industry has evolved based upon the management and analysis of risk which has often been converted into a profitable operation and thereby achieving business survival. The development from risk management to profitable business has grown over many years utilising detailed analysis of historic and accrued evidence, projecting the results of that analysis forward to produce some sophisticated profitable business models.

Uncertainty surrounds all of us in everything we do, every day.

At a personal level, making a career choice, considering whether to marry are possible risks. We can experience risk when considering a course of medical treatment, or a business decision to re-locate or expand a department.

Uncertainty is the very essence of risk.

We have observed the manifestation of risk over and over again during recent history through a collection of terrible incidents ranging from natural disasters, to industrial accidents, the emergence of work related diseases, acts of terrorism and mass cause of injury and destruction of life. Such incidents translate risk from uncertainty into certainty, from unlikely possibility into reality, the physical manifestation of what was thought would never happen.

Within our own recent knowledge, we will all know of incidents which by mention or thought of the name alone, signifies huge tragedy. Hillsborough, Kings Cross, Lockerbie, Dunblane, Zeebrugge and during the development of this book, September 11, 2001, the tragedy of the World Trade Centre by act of terrorism.

The enormity and scale of such tragedy, capture news headlines, are, quire rightly, promoted by extensive television and media coverage and through the power of communication and the response of united shock, reach the attention of the world.

At an every day, ordinary level, the manifestation and the toll of risk borne by individuals continues, unrelenting.

In the United Kingdom alone, in excess of 3,500 people are killed on the roads every year, there are in excess of 1,650 fires every day, over 27 road accidents occur every hour of every day, the list goes on and on.

No matter how carefully a car is driven or how fire conscious we are, we can never eliminate risk. We can however, identify the obvious more likely risks and prepare a contingency plan for those less likely risks. We may have all dealt with the tragedy of debilitating or catastrophic injury, and if we are honest, we all hope that such an eventuality will never happen to us. In real terms, whilst we all recognise that catastrophe could befall us at any time when placed into context, the possibility of such an eventuality actually occurring is ideally remote. However, there is no doubt that such risk increases considerably if the car we drive for example is unfamiliar, very powerful, not what we are used to or in an environment which is outside of our normal experience.

The likelihood of catastrophe occurring is acknowledged, recognised and historically demonstrated. However the likelihood of such eventuality occurring relies on an unforeseen combination of circumstances or hazards which ultimately lead to the manifestation of the catastrophe.

WHAT EXACTLY IS RISK—HOW IS IT DEFINED?

There is no simple easy to identify complete definition. Risk **6.003** has often been the subject of intellectual debate and analysis. We can however, identify some key elements of what risk means:

- Risk *implies and suggests* **uncertainty** about an outcome of a particular situation.

- Risk *implies and suggests* **doubt** about the future.

- Risk *implies and suggests* a **worse position** than at present.

Overall, risk *implies and suggests* an **unfavourable** outcome for our purposes, the risk of injury leading to exclusion from the life currently enjoyed confirms this.

In situations where there is uncertainty, we can also find use of the word **chance**. How many times for example, do we see the word **chance** used by Counsel in relation to the chance of success? What do we mean by **chance**?

Chance also implies uncertainty.

SO, is risk the same as chance?

Chance implies and suggests doubt about the future BUT with a possible **favourable** outcome—overall a more optimistic impression. We may think and consider the chance of recovery as a far more optimistic outcome.

When risk is compared with chance we see:

- The **RISK** of losing as **UNFAVOURABLE** *but*

- The **CHANCE** of winning as **FAVOURABLE**

In simple terms, we would see the **RISK** of an individual sustaining a personal injury and suffering pain and loss as an **unfavourable** outcome rather than the **CHANCE** of an individual sustaining personal injury and suffering pain and loss as representing a **favourable** outcome!

However, we may also say that following a personal injury and suffering pain and loss which is clearly unfortunate, there is a **CHANCE** of achieving an award of damages, an amount of compensation for the injured victim in a form recognition of the loss suffered, a **favourable** outcome. This translates an unfavourable incident, from a financial point of view at least, into a favourable outcome.

It is therefore vital that when applying any risk assessment process to the conduct of a case by way of CFA that the distinction is made between RISK and CHANCE when applied to a potential outcome of any particular or overall aspect of a personal injury claim.

When assessing what we routinely refer to as the prospects

of success, what we really mean is what are the chances of us winning?

From the claimant perspective, routinely, the chances of winning are generally higher than the risk of losing. However, whilst the risk of failure may be smaller, the consequences of such failure are significant—not only to the client but to your business.

Failure for a claimant represents financial loss, uncertainty, anxiety, a definite unfavourable outcome. Fortunately, this can be mitigated most of the time by after the event insurance. However, this class of insurance is comparatively new and in some areas of CFA work, not yet readily available.

From a business point of view, what we really should be thinking about is "WHAT ARE THE RISKS OF FAILURE?" What impact will that failure have on this business? Your duty to the client to protect them from the possibility of failure by providing advice on funding options is now part of everyday practice and indeed the subject of detailed scrutiny by opponents. However, the duty to restrict the impact of failure and consequential loss to the business is just as important. Strategic planning for this eventuality and acknowledgement of the possibility must be a factor in the business budget and forecasting process and the consequences of such possible loss on the cashflow.

As the business is now reliant on CFA income—a long term risk based income, balancing the cash flow during this development period is essential.

This means in practice that you may have to be more selective about the type of work you take on if some of that work represents an increased risk of failure. This risk of failure being related not only to the inherent risks of the case itself but also to the skills of those dealing with it. Additionally, consider the implications of the volume of work undertaken, the level of staff undertaking that work, and the infrastructure to support it.

It may be that you have a 98 per cent success rate. Do you know that for certain or are you adopting the general statistic? Do you monitor the type of cases that you have historically conducted? Do you know whether the expertise of the firm is good enough? Do you know the type of cases which have been unsuccessful and why? One case with an unforeseen or understated risk can irradicate business income, turning profit to breakeven or worse, business loss.

Do you review the effectiveness of individual fee earners? Do you recognise that one of the easiest risks to remove is the risk of not knowing the law?

Often, in the absence of definite experience, knowledge, evidence or actuarial information, the acceptance of risk is determined by "judgement"—the gut feel method.

This utilises the basic concepts of:

- Familiarity—"I've done this sort of thing before"

- Ability to control and manage the risk—"I will be cautious, and monitor very closely"

- Skill in recognising the changes to that risk—"I will stop before it's too late"

- It will never happen to me—"head in the sand"

Good judgement in uncertain circumstances can often be the basis for unforeseen success and catalyst for the translation of uncertain cases into landmark law. However, the key skill is the ability to judge the levels of actual risk when compared to the perception of that risk and the severity should it occur.

The reaction to acceptance of a given risk is not always influenced by how often a loss occurs—the frequency, but the severity should it occur—the level of cost—the amount of the loss.

The continual argument that in personal injury, the RTA is the zenith of risk free litigation. Whilst it can be agreed that of all the types of injury, the RTA carries the least risk of failure, when an RTA fails, the cost of that failure is often more severe when it occurs than is perceived. In simple terms when an RTA fails, the actual cost of that failure is more than another type of accident which may lose more often but costs less when it does.

Applying that directly to the impact of risk to your business, it is important that you understand the profile of cases which you have the skills to undertake and be selective about those which represent an increased risk or higher prospects of unforeseen risk.

Again applying insurance principles, for general mainstream insurance not all insurers are prepared to accept the transfer and to carry certain classes of risk. As an illustration, some of the direct motor insurers are seen to be less expensive in terms of insurance premium, however, some of the types of business they underwrite are excluded or carry a higher premium. This is primarily because they represent an increased risk within the portfolio of insurance business carried by that underwriter.

We can demonstrate this very simply in that whilst there are many hundreds, if not thousands of insurance companies, very few of them will underwrite after the event insurance business primarily because it is an unknown market, its short history is unstable, and the development of this class is uncertain. Therefore, if an insurer is not able to determine the risk profile being carried, a cautious approach will be adopted when entering new areas of business or accepting new risks.

If the CFA and ATE risk based regime is to work for the client, the after the event insurer and you, risk identification is essential. However, knowing what the risks are, is not enough alone, CFA risk must be measured or rated and systems put in place for control and management.

We have included some useful precedents in this book which are found in Appendix 1. Among them you will find some important checklists. Use them, modify them, tailor them to your own needs. They are essential and used widely in the insurance industry.

Use a checklist for every case. The list should be easy to understand, include all the relevant points you need to consider and easy to complete. It should be precise, accurately completed and unambiguous. Keep it short and focussed.

Analyse the results, if the list identifies issues, clarify them. If the list indicates an adverse risk, rate the outcome. As we describe in Chapter 8, careful management and understanding of your capabilities and skills coupled with training, communication and knowledge of the law should lead to a more certain CFA future.

INSURANCE AND RISK

What is Insurance?

6.004 Insurance is a mechanism that offers protection against risk.

- Insurance is, in simple terms, the transfer of risk.

Out of preference we would all rather transfer the uncertainty of whether or not we may suffer a financial loss to someone else—an insurer. An insurer may then accept that risk transfer and the subsequent acknowledged likelihood of them suffering a loss in return for an insurance premium, which, should be calculated to represent the likelihood of that loss occurring. The core of insurance is therefore, the analysis and acceptance of risk in return for payment of money—a premium.

This principle operates on the fact that risk does occur. There is something to insure—something to transfer. In the event there is an allegation that risk does not occur, that in fact there is no risk, this, it has been argued, must negate the requirement for insurance.

It must always be remembered that an insurer will want to examine the risk being considered for insurance and request information where necessary to enhance the understanding of the risk. In turn this will form the basis for assessment of the premium to be paid for acceptance of the risk.

Insurers work on the basis of the LAW OF LARGE NUMBERS. It supports the concept that the risk of the many pay for the claim of the few. This leads to predictability of the number of size of claims that will be made on the indemnity provided. The premiums paid for a known and identified class of risk form what is referred to as a COMMON POOL. The calculation of premium factors equitable premiums which cover losses as well as costs and profit from the common pool.

Insurers are established to provide insurance for specific classes of insurance business.

Higher risk categories are often placed among lower risk cases to ensure a stable and predictable range of business—sometimes referred to as a "book" of business.

Equitable premiums are derived from the concepts of severity and frequency and compared to the typical exposure and claims which an insurer may have experienced.

The analysis of past evidence or actual experience by actuarial analysis enables prediction and forecast for the future. Where a particular type of "book" has shown good results, then this will assist in keeping premium levels consistent. Where a "book" has given adverse results and cause losses resulting say in lack of profit, then there is every likelihood that premium levels will rise to allow for future adverse performance.

It is important to remember that an insurer has the right to refuse to underwrite a risk or where there is little past evidence or actual experience to estimate a premium based on that risk alone. We can begin to see the emergence of the way a scheme or "block" facility exists when compared to a "bespoke" risk. That is the grouping of a large number of risks with a common or predictable profile against those which stand out from this pool or do not have sufficient numbers to form a pool. In CFA terms typical personal injury compared to clinical negligence.

RISK, ATE AND CFA

Within the total term of CFAs and ATE insurance, only, we **6.005** must not forget, a period of seven years, the continual cry that "there is no risk—insurance is not needed" has become almost a mantra. Initially heard from what were the plaintiff lawyers, who then became claimant lawyers and more recently the defendant lawyers, their instructing liability insurers and their costs negotiators!

The typical issue that a passenger in a rear end collision has no risk of failure has been the subject of argument throughout this time. The view has been that ATE insurance is not required as these cases never fail. Because of this, the claimant or defendant should not have to pay a premium in return for the transfer of risk of failure and subsequent adverse liability for disbursements or costs to an after the event insurer. After all, it is alleged, rear end shunts carry no risk!

To follow this argument, by applying insurance principles, if there is no likelihood of failure, there must be no insurable risk for these type of cases. The outcome of these incidents, all rear end shunts, MUST therefore, be CERTAIN. This in turn would as we discussed previously in Chapter 2, require advance agreement from all parties that no risk exists and unconditional guarantees given by opponents that there would be no possibility whatsoever under any circumstances, of any adverse costs award being made against the other party. An ultimate total risk free case.

Rear end passenger cases can fail. They can fail from the obvious risk, a Part 36 payment. Many have done so. They can fail from other risk. What if you are faced with an allegation that there was a gradient at the site of the accident and in fact the driver in front rolled back but claims that he is the innocent party? What if the driver in front selected the wrong gear accidentally or otherwise and caused the collision? In either of these simple situations, the likelihood of resolution being achieved during the protocol is uncertain. If both parties hold their argument, proceedings will probably need to be commenced. Limitation may become a critical factor. The case will progress to trial and may turn ultimately on who the judge believes, especially if witness or expert performance on the day is less than anticipated. How easy is it to predict the likelihood by this stage of how the judge will react? What will happen if our expert evidence is vague or the site of the accident has changed radically from the date it was examined? This now produces a situation where the outcome of the case without risk is in reality, no better than 50:50.

Even with a passenger, the ultimate risk free case, they may not always be "a totally innocent victim". They may be alleged to have "distracted" or "interfered" with the driver. There may be arguments about contributory negligence in relation the wearing of a safety belt. There may be pre-existing or unrelated problems on the medical side of the claim. There are many possibilities. What will you do after you have invested considerable time and money investigating a case, you may have taken the initiative, taken the bull by the horns and commenced proceedings and you are faced with a cast iron no risk case deteriorating to at best a 50:50 prospect? Not only are you in a **worse** position than before you started, so is your client.

However certain you are of a case, however convinced you are that you will not fail, you can never **guarantee** to your client, who after all, carries the ultimate liability for failure, that there is never going to be a risk. However hard you try you will not obtain from any liability underwriter an unconditional guarantee that there will never be any risk of an adverse outcome however small.

Risk can never be totally eliminated.

Risk of failure for CFA cases can, however, be managed **6.006** from both your clients perspective and yours. The failure of a CFA case carries a cost. That cost is your time, your money and the adverse exposure to your client. CFA risk issues can be identified. They can be assessed and quantified in terms of the likelihood of loss, and the possible cost of that loss and importantly, the risk carried by the client can be transferred to an after the event insurer in return for an insurance premium. We will deal with identification of risk issues and their management in Chapter 8—Carrying Out a Risk Assessment.

Because there will always be a degree of uncertainty and that represents the possibility that the client could end up in a worse position than before, paying an after the event insurance premium is replacing *uncertainty* with *certainty*. The variety of cover offered by after the event insurers continually develops and more comprehensive cover is available. Often, this will include the insurance of the premium itself, protection from loss in the event of a failure to beat a Part 36 payment. Therefore, from a clients perspective, the provision by an after the event insurer of certainty, is far better than the uncertainty of how much they would have to pay in costs if they lost. There can be absolutely no excuse for the argument that after the event insurance in not necessary,

DOES RISK IMPACT ON THE DEFENDANTS?

6.007   The removal of legal aid for personal injury not only changed the environment for claimant lawyers, it altered the outlook significantly for defendants as well.

The position from the claimant side is that all cases must be viewed by taking into account the possibility of failure however small or remote that might be.

There will be analysis, identification and management of the **risk** of an **unfortunate** outcome. The element of that risk which would ultimately be the liability of the claimant can, using insurance as a risk transfer mechanism, be passed over to an after the event insurer.

BUT, how is it from the defendant side?

As we move away from legal aid and rely on CFAs as the main method of deriving business income and ATE insurance as the method of risk limitation for the client, the way defendants conduct cases will evolve. We have already seen this in practice.

The spirit of co-operation, early mitigation, dealing with cases justly, expedited settlement where possible, the use of pre-action protocols, proportionality, the whole approach of the Civil Procedure Rules to give a level playing field are designed to "even up the odds" between the parties. Lines of communication are to be, at least in theory, more open.

There is no doubt that recoverability and the requirement for defendants to have to pay additional liabilities, has provoked an immediate response. Represented at this stage by *Callery v Gray* [2002] 3 All E.R. 417, *Sarwar v Alam* [2001] 4 All E.R. 541 and *Halloran v Delaney* [2002] EWCA Civ. 1258.

Defendants can, should and will utilise the opportunities afforded to them.

6.008   As claimants, we have historically afforded the luxury of legal aid. The safe and certain knowledge that where a Legal Aid Certificate existed, then work in progress was certain at least, for the duration of the certificate. The clients position was secure with regard to adverse costs. This however, was not quite so attractive form the defendant point of view. In the event they were successful, what good did it do? There was nothing to be gained, no big fees to win, no large sums of money to be recovered from the funding Legal Aid Board for the victory. Quite disappointing after all the hard work. Sometimes the fight was not really worth having.

The regular use of conditional fee agreements backed by after the event insurance has already changed all that and will continue to alter the way defendants themselves will react.

The burden for the defendant to pay the additional liability of a success fee and after the event insurance premium on a case will impact considerably upon the financial position of liability insurers. Recoverability should not be a licence to print money for the claimants. Proportionality must apply to success fees and they must represent the risk that the case itself carries. ATE insurance premium should follow the insurance industry principles and practice by calculating the premium to represent the risk being transferred having regard for the circumstances which will give rise to a loss and the likely cost, frequency and severity of that loss.

However, there is an opportunity in this environment for the defendants.

We have identified earlier in this chapter, the difference **6.009** between RISK and CHANCE and we have emphasised that when considering the risk issues we must be careful to differentiate between these two adjectives and how they are applied to risk assessment.

Remember:

- Risk *implies* and *suggests* **uncertainty** about an outcome of a particular situation.

- Risk *implies* and *suggests* **doubt** about the future.

- Risk *implies* and *suggests* a **worse position** than at present.

Overall, risk implies and suggests an **unfavourable** outcome.

SO WE KNOW:

- The **RISK** of losing is **UNFAVOURABLE** *but*

- The **CHANCE** of winning is **FAVOURABLE**

We have previously in this chapter, examined the so called "cases without risk" the "rear end shunt" the "dead cert passenger". We have stated that risk can never be totally eliminated. We can say that whilst risk can never be completely removed, some risk is greater, more likely to occur, more probable than another. We can support this by saying that whilst a "passenger" is not totally without risk, on the general rules of probability a Fast Track "passenger" is less likely to fail than a Fast Track "deafness" claim. We can over time devise a method or assessing these risks and rating them. Defendants can also do this.

6.010   Let us look at a case scenario that starts off as an excellent claimant CFA prospect and think about it from the defendant point of view:

The client is a professional who is involved in a rear end collision whilst stationary at a set of traffic light which are fully operational and indicating red. The accident happens outside of rush hour traffic, it is daylight and it is not raining. Fortunately to help support the version of events given by the client, there are several credible witnesses at the scene including a police officer who is off duty but standing at the crossing within full view of the incident.

The impact is quite severe. The client is the insured driver and registered keeper of a two year old Mercedes C200 four door saloon. After the impact, the Mercedes is not road worthy and unable to be driven. In fact, examination by motor vehicle engineers subsequently confirms that the floor pans have sustained severe distortion, the chassis is very badly damaged and although the vehicle is comparatively new, it does have very high mileage and it is deemed to be beyond economical repair. We know that the vehicle behind the Mercedes is a large Ford Cargo utility services vehicle.

6.011   When the client comes to see you, what is your immediate response?

It is probably going to be—"this is a dead cert". So certain is it, you can almost visualise the costs schedule you will present the opponent when you win. Dare you consider the option of "self-insuring" that is to say not effecting an ATE insurance policy?

Consideration must be given to funding options. Chapter 1—Selecting the right Funding Option is the point of reference for this.

Consideration of all possible funding options available must be fully undertaken and in particular, the examination of any before the event insurance policy. In this case, after investigation, due to the time delay between the accident and the time the client consults you, the pre-existing legal expenses insurance cannot be used. Correctly, the client is advised that the best method of progressing this case is by conduct and funding by way of CFA backed by ATE insurance.

A full and detailed risk assessment is undertaken to establish the risk profile of the case and a success fee is determined. Chapter 8—Carrying out a Risk Assessment is the reference for this. This will be the point where *Halloran v Delaney* ([2002] EWCA Civ. 1258) will impact most. Consider very carefully at this point the issues which may affect a case such as this in the longer term. Whilst initially it would appear to be a "dead cert" this cannot be guaranteed to the client at this stage.

The CFA is signed, the ATE insurance premium is paid and the case formally commences.

From examination of the hospital records, it is determined that an ambulance was called. Further, hospital evidence supports the clients version of events that upon examination cervical whiplash was diagnosed. Examination indicates at this stage that there is no suggestion of any lower back injuries.

Evidence gathered from witnesses and the police report confirm the initial belief that—based on the evidence and the professional status of the client, this case will win.

Typically in cases such as these, the opponents admit liability only, they do however, do it early. In this particular case it is in response to the Letter of Claim which includes an offer to settle. There is likely to be a dispute over quantum, again, this is not uncommon.

The client says that more recently whilst working, and particularly while standing for prolonged periods, which is necessary for the course of work, lower lumber pain is experienced which is not eased particularly by painkillers. The client alleges that working capacity is definitely reduced and that because of the nature of work, substantial past and future losses are confirmed by you as having been suffered.

Expert medical evidence supports the clients story and does confirm the presence of an injury to the lower back. The client is a professional and credible.

Utilising fully the overriding objective and the scope of the CPR a claimant offer is made in accordance with CPR Part 36. There is a counter offer made from the opponent in return.

An unrelenting campaign continues against the opponent. They in turn continue to argue that the injuries sustained do not support the general damages we believe this case is worth.

6.012   The client maintains that symptoms are not improving.

At this stage does the claimant have cause for concern?

Evidentially the case is strong. However, the opponent is clearly not inclined to settle at an acceptable level, therefore, the presence of ATE empowers the client with the ultimate ability to follow through with this claim and commence court proceedings.

Now, from the defendant point of view, they see a potentially large claim from a professional who due to the injury sustained from the significant impact, is not able to realise the earning capacity the profession entitles. After consideration by them of the medical evidence, a Part 36 payment is made at the earliest opportunity after issue. This payment represents 55 per cent of the value the claimants general damages claim.

What is the clients position now?

At the outset the **risk** of an **unfavourable** outcome from a case such as this is perceived as a low level of risk. Has that changed now?

At this point, the defendants see a **chance** of a **favourable** outcome. They see the **chance** that despite the **risk**, there could be an opportunity to win. More to the point, they know the claimant is funding the case by way of conditional fee agreement backed by after the event insurance. If they take this **chance**, make the most of the **opportunity,** they can recover their costs and as an added "bonus", possibly, a success fee. What have they got to lose? They enter into a conditional fee agreement themselves.

Is it because the client has after the event insurance that the case proceeds to trial? Or is it because of the likelihood that the final award will be greater than the 55 per cent paid into court?

If it is decided that the Part 36 payment even though it is a possible acceptable amount is not sufficient, in effect the risk now being taken is that the money in court will be beaten even though the payment was made early and subsequent to an offer made at the time of admission on liability in response to your letter of claim.

Surely the risk has now become based around who the judge will believe, what will the reaction be? What award will be made? What will happen when the case reaches trial?

On the day, the matter has in terms of prospects of success **6.013** the likelihood of winning become no more than a 50:50 prospect.

If judgment is given in favour of the claimant for more than the amount in court under Part 36, then notwithstanding the arguments on recoverability and given that the CFA does not fall foul of defendants scrutiny, significant fees in respect of work in progress, the recovery of the success fee and ATE insurance premium will be achieved. The defendants will leave with nothing. We are justified in our belief that the **risk** of an **unfavourable** outcome was small and did not materialise.

If however, the final award of damages is less than the amount in court under Part 36, then the defendants will themselves achieve significant success. A claim will be made from the claimant after the event insurance policy. This ATE claim will be subject to investigation. The claimant will, if the ATE insurance policy makes provision for failure to beat Part 36 payments, receive all of the awarded damages. As claimant solicitors, you will receive significantly reduced amounts. The victory predicted, is minimised. The defendant **chance** of a **favourable** outcome was an opportunity well taken.

This case is based on a general scenario which has been common for ATE insurers and which we have all experienced.

However only a fraction of our caseload is made up of cases like this one.

The point here is that at the outset, it is not possible to determine *which* of the RTAs this could happen to. Therefore to say RTA cases carry no risk and therefore do not need ATE is wrong. It is the inability for anyone to predict the forseeability of where and when the loss will occur which is the need for insurance.

Think about how this works in cases carrying higher levels of **risk,** those cases, those types of injury which in every day practice fail more often.

ADDITIONAL LIABILITIES—THE DEFENDANT PERSPECTIVE

6.014 Recoverability, whilst the subject of continued argument and controversy focused at this stage on RTA cases, does, in real terms, impact on the opponent.

We have identified that from an insurance perspective, the frequency, the severity and the likelihood of a risk occurring are areas considered by insurers when deciding to accept a risk and applied to determine an equitable premium for that risk.

Within the typical classes of general insurance which responds to the liability claims we make on behalf of our claimant clients, we will make road traffic act claims, employers liability claims, product defect claims, and claims for disease, etc.

Because liability insurers have been providing insurance cover in these areas historically, they will have collected large amounts of data to assist in determining their likely exposure in a give period. Their potential losses have been forecast based on actual tangible experience.

They will for example know the level and range of damages they will be paying for a typical profile of claims with a specific injury type in a specific area, the anticipated number of claims they will be likely to have to consider and the level of costs they will pay as an opponent/defendant and this will depend on levels of fee earner, pre- or post-proceedings, the firm acting and the appointed court. Allowances are then made for inflation, predicted increase—we are experiencing a market shift towards a "compensation culture" and importantly, elements for provision of profit.

Additional liabilities alter this.

Whilst it can be argued that the circumstances we now operate in were "on the cards" for some time, as is typical with most organisations, the likely effect is often ignored until the impact is upon us. Let us not forget that many claimant solicitors themselves ignored the impact of conditional fees until legal aid was actually removed.

Removing legal aid for personal injury was clearly a step taken to mitigate government expenditure and it is not the intention of this work to rehearse that decision making process. However, given the perceived success rate of personal injury the introduction of CFAs with ATE insurance as a method of funding was seen as a potentially attractive proposition for the insurance industry. Significant difficulties and losses occurred with some of the early ATE insurance schemes demonstrating evidentially that the personal injury "market" was perhaps not as glittering as first thought. Some radical restructuring of this market was called for. The Woolf reforms assisted greatly in standardising time scales and procedure but did little to alter the losses experienced by the ATE insurance market. From initial observation evidence seemed to suggest the inability to manage risk by practitioners could seriously undermine the whole ATE insurance concept.

However, the presence of CFAs and ATE insurance may protect the client from adverse outcome and unforeseen loss, the requirement for the client to pay a success fee out of awarded damages and often having to take out large consumer credit loans to pay for an insurance premium was seen as unsatisfactory.

It seemed eminently sensible to transfer the liability for success fees and ATE premiums, now classified together as additional liabilities and pass these for payment to the opponent.

What impact does this actually have?

The exposure to additional liabilities which the opponent

under access to justice must pay significantly increases the average claims cost by this amount. As we become more compensation orientated not only does the likely cost increase, *i.e.* the severity, but so does the frequency.

Such is the apparent differential between additional liabilities that in practical terms the opponents are exposed to unknown, and therefore uncontained, claims payments, the response to which will be to challenge.

To an extent opponents are justified in mounting a challenge against additional liabilities primarily because historically practitioners have resisted the concept of risk, its analysis and management and have often presented an inconsistent approach. The ATE insurance market has had some areas of doubt and market entrance with lack of experience and understanding.

As with all insurance there will be a fundamental objective to mitigate, contain and predict likely exposure. The knock on effect is that the average claim will increase by the ATE premium and the success fee which because of recent market history creates a hornet's nest.

However the fact remains that additional liabilities are a fact of life and the protracted litigation seems only to create even more uncertainty. This cannot be access to justice.

IN SUMMARY

6.015 In a situation where there is a **chance**, however small of a **favourable** outcome, the **chance** of winning, defendants will take it. The presence of a conditional fee agreement underwritten by ATE insurance, means that where a defendant has an opportunity for success, it is far more likely now than previously under the legal aid regime that this case will be vigorously pursued. Why? Because in these circumstances, the defendant is the recipient of the funds paid out by the ATE insurer. This is stipulated in the insurance contract and providing that no breach of that insurance contract has occurred, the liability for defendant costs and disbursements will be discharged. Reward for victory now exists for defendants.

We must always keep in our minds that CFAs, with a success fee and possibly an ATE insurance, can also be operated by defendants. They can claim additional liabilities in exactly the same way and under exactly the same rules as we operate. At the time of writing this book, so much remains uncertain with regard to the extent of recoverability. It will remain to be seen just how likely it will be that defendants will operate on a CFA with success fee perhaps with their own ATE insurance. We will watch with interest how this in turn impacts on claimants. How will we respond when defendants claim additional liabilities? Will there be the same challenge we have seen from the defendants? It will certainly impact on the way you assess, contain and manage risk.

Far greater emphasis will now be paid to the depth of risk assessment undertaken when selecting the correct funding option. Opponents will continue to scrutinise the structure of the CFA itself, how the success fee is derived and the level of ATE insurance required for a given case.

Therefore, the relationship which exists between claimant and their chosen ATE insurance provider will be pivotal for the future success of CFA and ATE insurance cases.

LEARNING FROM THE INSURANCE INDUSTRY

The entire insurance industry has developed based upon the **6.016** ability to identify, assess, manage and evaluate risk. Its success has evolved from the collection and analysis of data, learning from this historic experience, projecting it forward and then planning for the likelihood of the manifestation of the risk itself.

Risk in general terms, from an insurance perspective is:

- **POSSIBILITY** of an unfortunate occurrence leading to loss

- **COMBINATION of ADVERSE EVENTS** leading to loss

- **UNPREDICTABILITY** results differ from predicted, leading to loss

- **UNCERTAINTY** of loss—when it will and will not happen and when it will occur

This gives us some of the essential elements an insurance business examines and plans for when considering the impact of the acceptance of risk. It considers how these basic factors can combine and effect the risk carried by them so that they can plan for the likely loss which could be suffered in a given situation. Consideration of these factors takes place before an insurance company will accept the risk—before the risk is transferred to them and agreement given with regard to the basis upon which the risk is transferred. That is, the price an insurance company places upon acceptance of the risk—the insurance premium.

So, do any of these considerations relate to CFA business?

YES!

Let us examine each basic risk element applied directly to conditional fee business in turn:

- **POSSIBILITY** of an unfortunate occurrence leading to loss

6.017   From the claimant perspective: the possibility of the accident itself. The environment in which we live impacts on the possibility of the incident occurring which ultimately leads to loss. Typically, the possibility of a person with a dangerous occupation sustaining personal injury during the course of work is higher and more likely than an office worker.

The driver who achieves very high mileage each year, such as a person working in sales based out on the road, represents a higher possibility of road traffic accident than the driver who achieves low mileage, simply because of the increased frequency of road use. Thereby we can see the increased likelihood of accident and the greater the possibility of accident occurring and leading to loss.

From your perspective, the possibility of an unfortunate occurrence leading to loss can occur at any stage during the conduct of the conditional fee case.

* the scene of an incident can be altered significantly before you have gathered enough evidence from it;
* you unfortunately select an unreliable expert;
* you discover at trial your client is a liar;
* you make a mistake.

The possibilities are in fact, endless. It is because of the uncertainty surrounding these possibilities that careful risk assessment and management is essential. However, we shall see more in Chapter 7—Identifying Case Risk Factors, Chapter 8—Carrying Out A Risk Assessment and Chapter 9—Control and Management of Risk.

- **COMBINATION of ADVERSE EVENTS** leading to loss

From the claimant perspective it is the combination of events which by their unfortunate nature lead to the accident. Because of geographic location and high levels of unemployment the claimant may well work in an environment which in itself is unsafe and through the continued negligence of the environment operator gives rise to a series of adverse events causing the accident. Thereafter, the claimants inability to work leads in turn to domestic difficulties, financial difficulties and consequential loss. **6.018**

From your perspective the combination of adverse events leading to loss can arise from not investigating funding options correctly, incorrect risk assessment, overestimating success fees, and they are before we deal with control and managing possible adverse events such as experts, fee earners, case loads, etc.

The combinations again are endless. It is because the potential combination of adverse events is unforeseen, the continual review and risk management process becomes pivotal.

- **UNPREDICTABILITY** results differ from predicted, leading to loss

6.019   From the claimant perspective, the unpredictability and thereby the results differing from predicted and therefore consequential loss are illustrated completely by the rear end collision and Part 36 payment scenario. Here, whilst we may be certain in theory that we will win, where a final award of damages is less than predicted, loss can occur. Similarly, the emergence of a pre-existing medical condition can significantly cause predicted results to differ.

From your perspective the unpredictability that results may differ from those expected can occur at any stage during the progress of a case. For example, you may be progressing a matter where you are part way through collecting evidence from your client which is *insufficient* at that time to produce a convincing argument to the opponent and thereby settlement of the matter.

You have invested a considerable amount of time, you have accrued a considerable amount of disbursements and additional liabilities.

Your client dies suddenly.

Again, the unpredictability may be mitigated by identifying known areas that can give rise to loss, thereby reducing elements of a case which can give results which differ from those predicted.

- **UNCERTAINTY** of loss—when it will and will not happen and when it will occur

6.020   From the clients perspective, it is often as simple as will the case win? In real terms what are the consequences to the client when the case loses. The essential mechanism to contain the uncertainty of loss is to eliminate as far as possible that risk from the client. In simple terms identifying the most effective funding method is containing the largest area of uncertainty which the client faces. The enforcement of an adverse costs order by a defendant against a claimant conjures up images of seizure of possessions, county court judgements, and loss of home. Utilising the risk transfer option via ATE insurance removes uncertainty.

From your perspective, uncertainty of loss can be mitigated by thorough and detailed risk assessment of the case at outset followed by strategic review procedures. Whilst the client may fear enforcement of adverse costs orders, your concerns must be focused on the possibility of failure and not achieving costs recovery at all. In risk terms, there is a significant difference between loss arising through case failure and loss arising because, upon scrutiny, your CFA is found to be unenforceable by the opponent. It may simply be that the case takes longer than anticipated only to fail.

Again, the uncertainty of loss must be factored into the portfolio of CFA/ATE cases undertaken and the impact this may have upon business financial planning.

It is essential not to underestimate the length of time—the longer it takes the higher the cost of that loss is likely to be.

So What Does This all Mean?

There is a remarkable similarity between all of these general **6.021** terms. It could be said that each of them could be applied to all of the potential risk factors we consider for a particular case.

We are seeking here to introduce some basic insurance principles and develop the idea of commonality between those well established insurance principles and the operation of a CFA business portfolio.

This leads us to begin to understand that there is **a common thread** to the application of risk.

That is:

(1) The underlying idea of UNCERTAINTY.

(2) The implication that there are DIFFERING LEVELS or DEGREES OF RISK.

(3) The result is brought about by a CAUSE.

Therefore, put simply, there will always be uncertainty about a given situation.

The Common Thread—the Three Main Components of Risk

(1) Uncertainty

6.022 The concept of uncertainty implies and suggests doubt about the future based on a lack of knowledge or imperfection of knowledge.

Insurers seek to perfect their knowledge by looking at the past and adjusting for either an UPWARD, DOWNWARD or STATIC **TREND**.

Once a TREND is established adjustment can then be made for other factors which can influence the number of losses in the future.

(2) Level of risk

6.023 There are different **levels** of risk.

We can not assume that all risks are equal or equally likely to occur, some will be more or less risky than others.

(3) Cause of risk

6.024 The acknowledgement and recognition that certain factors will cause risk to manifest. That is identifying those known, likely factors and planning for the eventuality should they arise. This in turn indicates those events most likely to cause a risk and its subsequential loss.

TO CONCLUDE

In this chapter we have identified the basic principles of **6.025** insurance to reinforce the interaction between risk and CFAs.

The concepts of risk may, with the benefit of hindsight, appear obvious, however the CFA/ATE insurance relationship has demonstrated quite clearly during the last seven years that what might be obvious here has not necessarily been obvious in practice. There is a fine balance between effective risk management and becoming risk averse. Further, there is a fragile relationship between the presence of ATE insurance in the market place and the reliance of the legal profession upon it.

ATE insurance must apply insurance risk principles to it's business methods in order to achieve longevity and market stability supported by fairly calculated insurance premiums.

Practitioners, need to understand the relationship that risk now has with their business and that the principles applied by insurers for decades can be applied directly to their own business models.

We should now see the emergence of claimant solicitors and ATE insurers building a stable funding mechanism which must not be abused if it is to fully achieve the working replacement for legal aid.

There is a danger that adverse selection where only the likely "losers" are insured and the "dead certs" are not, as demonstrated in some of the early ATE insurance schemes, if continued will destabilise insurance facilities and result in significant premium increase or withdrawal in entirety from the market.

The principle of insurance which works on the principle that the premium paid by the many affords the claims made by the few operates only with the law of large numbers. We have illustrated within this chapter that every case carries a degree of risk, if only those high risk case are insured, the frequency and severity of claims upon an ATE insurer will result in business profit loss and the demise of such an insurance facility.

CFAs and ATE insurance operate in tandem and firms

practising adverse selection will inevitably find themselves isolated from ATE insurance facilities and in turn witness a significant reduction in the amount of work they are able to undertake.

Whilst the opponents may challenge ATE insurance and the premium levels which it attracts, this is, as with other classes of insurance, directly proportional to the levels of underwriting profit or loss which the ATE insurer has suffered.

With market maturity comes more sophisticated methods of quantifying and calculating ATE insurance premium and thereby measuring the true risk associated with personal injury.

Abuse of the system can only lead to reduced availability for the profession of ATE insurance and ultimately "restricted access to justice".

7

Working with an After The Event Insurer

We discussed in Chapter 6 the basic insurance principles   **7.001**
whereby when an insurer is considering accepting transfer of
a risk in order for decisions regarding premium levels and
acceptance criteria to be made, analysis is undertaken of history in order to assist in predicting the future and thereby
identify the likelihood of losses, the likely frequency with
which they will occur, and the severity should they do so.

When "After The Event" (ATE) was first introduced in 1995,
it was introduced in the absence of any historical actuarial
evidence. The main form of funding had been legal aid, some
legal expenses insurance, private funding, union funding and
in many cases, "spec'd". When the first CFA after the event
insurance product was launched into the market in August
1995 the criteria given to it was that the premium should be
inexpensive, preferably less than £100, and underwriters were
expected to provide ATE insurance on a personal injury book
of business about which very little was really known. It was
almost a foregone conclusion that personal injury was a
completely successful class of business and cases rarely lost,
and if they did they didn't cost much. With the benefit of
hindsight, that was indeed naïve.

Personal injury cases do lose, and they do lose very often in
circumstances which are totally unforeseen. Because there
was such little evidence and in reality personal injury is
routinely quite successful, ATE kicked off with premiums of
less than £100.

The profession began to experience it's own learning curve and in the early days perhaps did not fully recognise the reliance upon ATE insurance that would become an essential ingredient in every day practice life. Additionally, from an ATE insurance perspective it became apparent that risk was bigger and more unpredictable than originally thought and therefore schemes began to develop and be tailored to represent the type of risk that insurers were being asked to take. It became apparent that different types of injury collect different types of risk and that some firms do have better processes than others, which in turn makes them a better "risk" from an underwriting perspective.

During the early evolution, the profession was generally uncertain as to whether ATE would be a viable funding mechanism. During this time an opportunity was identified within the market; we witnessed the emergence of the claims management company, or "claims farmers".

The reliance upon ATE insurance as the main form of funding for personal injury was underpinned by the removal of legal aid for personal injury.

7.002　This then gave rise to two fundamental dilemmas. First, were there going to be enough ATE insurers to take up what would have been the legal aid market? Secondly, were practitioners expert enough as risk managers to be able to run CFA cases at an acceptable level, not only for themselves to operate profitable business but at an acceptable level to their ATE insurance underwriter.

From an ATE insurance perspective, because there was initially no information to determine the exact risk that the insurance industry was being asked to take, premium levels were significantly underestimated.

This gave rise to what seemed to be unrealistic premium increases and the development of the common theory that insurance was not needed and that whatever premium was set was unrealistic compared to the case it was insuring.

The continual bombardment by opponent's to the level of insurance premium reinforces this.

The principles of insurance apply directly to ATE insurance. The primary function of ATE insurance is to act as risk transfer mechanism to replace uncertainty with certainty relating to containment of adverse outcome in exchange for a premium. The sixty four million dollar question is what should the premium be? As the ATE insurance market begins to develop, new insurance providers will enter the arena. They may, however, enter with caution given the market reputation so far and the acknowledged uncertainty and volatility of this class.

The essential ingredient for the success of ATE insurance as **7.003** the main form of funding must be the relationship between the insurer and the firm of solicitors who are utilising that specific insurance product.

It is essential that the arrangements between the two need to be open, frank and flexible. If ATE insurers are viewed as "the enemy" then their enthusiasm to develop and expand their levels and capacity of underwriting will be restricted. Conversely, if firms do not respect the presence of ATE insurance, then their own ability to establish flexible access to a facility will be reduced. This will have a direct impact on business profitability.

When assessing an ATE premium, the stage at which the premium is to be paid is directly related to the risk the underwriter is being asked to accept. We have seen in *Ashworth v Peterborough United Football Club* the discussions regarding the level of the premium and it's recoverability. We have seen how the stage at which the premium was taken out did impact upon the level of the premium, but also that there is a point at which without sufficient evidence a premium cannot be assessed at all which is closely linked to the stage at which a premium is too expensive to be paid.

We have established that because insurance works on the principle of large numbers, in order for an underwriter to fully spread his risk a large range of cases needs to be considered. The common thought is that insuring early gives an insurer the opportunity to spread risk and by virtue of the volume of cases carried is increased, giving the opportunity for profitable business and sufficient premium to deal with the claims should they arise. Insuring early enables the maximum certainty to be provided by an underwriter in return for the minimum premium. Given that it is the client who ultimately has the responsibility to bear the ATE insurance principle, it must follow that the opportunity to take advantage of this should be available to a client.

If the defendant objection is that the cost for the premium is too high, then the converse argument is that where the cases are insured at a later stage, the likelihood of loss is greater, the volume smaller, the cost higher and therefore the larger the premium will be. It cannot be ignored that if proportionality is to be applied, there will be circumstances where a premium is prohibitive in that respect. If consideration is given to clinical negligence cases, where the volume is lower and the risk is higher, it can be seen that premiums are routinely high. Sometimes (certainly within our experience) the premium has in certain circumstances actually been greater than the damages attempting to be recovered.

Therefore, an ATE insurer will want to achieve a large number of cases with considerable premiums coming in, in order to ensure that there is sufficient funds to pay the claims and keep stable premium levels.

7.004   As the ATE insurance market becomes more sophisticated a far more structured approach will no doubt be implemented using risk identification as an integral part of the firms operation and acknowledged techniques available by which such risks can be easily identified. It is already known that there are specific risks attached to different types of cases and that there is a common thread which follows such risks. Whilst the risk of liability is common to all, causation for example attaches to some risks over and above others. The skill will evolve whereby each aspect of the case will be risk rated—we suggest an approach for this within this book. Risk rating is a method used generally in insurance.

Currently there are large gaps in the ATE market. Some providers will adopt a comprehensive approach to the analysis of cases whilst others will shy away from everything apart from RTAs.

If ATE is to stand the test of time then the relationships between firms and insurers must relate to trust. and commonality and recognition of the "mutual" interest in the case.

We see more and more the decision taken by firms to offer an array of insurance products to their clients believing that having more than one provider means that they can spread their cases. Whilst there is logic to this, the inevitability will be that RTAs will go to the provider who likes them most and the complicated cases will end up having been touted round the market in the hope that somebody might take them.

The reverse of this is that if certain insurers only see your high risk, high cost cases then they will not have the opportunity to spread their own risk and will become more reluctant to take such risky cases.

An ATE insurer will no doubt develop a specific taste for **7.005** certain types of litigation. In an ideal world, we would probably all like to see RTAs. However, there are reasons to consider the long term position.

It is very likely that we will see an increase in the presence of before the event for RTA cases and therefore the RTA ATE book may significantly reduce.

Given that in the absence of legal aid the vast majority of personal injury cases will need to be funded by way of ATE, firms need to carefully consider, when selecting which ATE insurer to work with, whether or not that ATE insurer will be able to provide them with a comprehensive range of insurance products to actually deal with the case loads which the firm has.

Some products may offer low indemnity limits at the beginning with the possibility of increasing them as the case progresses. Whilst these may initially suggest lower and more attractive premiums because the indemnity is lower, the question must be asked, in the event that more is required what will the additional premiums be? Further, will continuation of cover actually be available?

One of the very great dangers with staged indemnity limits is that cases are under insured, which then, in the event that cover runs out, are not able to go the full distance, that is, to trial.

From an ATE insurer's perspective, if the only time cases are seen for insurance is at the post proceedings going to trial stage, then premiums will become higher and higher and this will compound the issues surrounding how these premiums are funded and indeed how they are subsequently recovered.

ATE insurers and firms must work as a co-operative.

Since the emergence onto the market of ATE there have been many different approaches implemented. In this chapter we will examine how some of those have worked and we will consider what will be required in order to achieve stability and longevity and lasting relationships.

ATE INSURANCE SCHEMES

7.006 Some ATE insurers will implement a scheme type facility whereby a standard range of premiums are offered in return for a standard range of accepted risks. Often these will deal with pre letter of claim cases for fast track or pre letter of claim cases for multi track and will be further subdivided into different injury types. The insurer is able to identify fairly readily the risk which they are prepared to accept and the premium to be charged in return for this.

There will be reporting requirements implemented to the firm and these form part of the scheme and the responsibility the firm has to the insurer to comply with these.

Each insurer will have it's own thoughts with regards to the key information which it will need to know and when it will need to know it.

Because personal injury has for each case a different length of time from start to finish, when an insurer goes on risk he does not necessarily know the time at which the risk will end, that is, how long from start to finish. With most types of insurance, such as car insurance or house insurance, the insurer will commence the risk at day one of the policy and the policy stays in place for a period of one year. At the end of this time, the policy may be renewed or, in the event that it is not renewed, the insurer does not stay on risk for that car or that specific property. With ATE for personal injury, an insurer may go on risk at day one of the policy, but does not necessarily know the date at which the policy will end. This means that the premium cannot be deemed as "in the bank" until the policy ends.

It is a basic insurance principle for any underwriter to review the risk that he is being asked to take at the outset and may review this during the time that the policy is on risk. To put it simply, an underwriter needs to continually review the likelihood of a claim being made upon the insurance policy or more generally within a facility which is in place.

There is no mystery as to why this happens. It is simply a question of insuring that there are enough funds to meet claims and what the likely cost of a claim will be should it arise. It also makes provision for the operation of the facility and hopefully a profit element. Preparing for the eventuality of claims payment is known as reserving. It follows exactly the basic insurance principles we have discussed in Chapter 6.

Therefore, for most insurance schemes, there will be a routine reporting procedure. In actual fact, it is not that far removed from the reporting requirements originally required by the Legal Aid Board.

In some circumstances, the policy taken out at the begin- **7.007** ning of the case will provide cover for that case for it's duration. Other schemes may work on an indemnity basis whereby at the outset a limit of indemnity will be put in place which will make provision for the maximum claim that could be made and at the point at which that indemnity expires the case may need to be reviewed with an extension perhaps made for that particular case.

Different ATE providers have different procedures. It is vital that during your work with an ATE insurer, you fully understand and implement the reporting requirements which they stipulate.

The longevity of the insurance facility which is available is related directly to the efficiency of those using it.

Different providers will have different processes in place to deal with the payment of the insurance premium. For schemes, the premiums will usually be at pre determined levels. There will be certain requirements for the payment of this premium and one of the essential factors to remember is that where a policy has a specific provision for payment, *i.e.* at the outset, where the premium is not paid within the time frame given the cover will not be in place.

Within our experience we have seen circumstances where practitioners have thought policies have been in place but in the event cases have concluded unsuccessfully and a claim has been made, the underwriter has no record of the policy because the premium has never been transacted. This leaves the client in a very difficult position.

It is essential to remember that the premium must pass to the underwriter in the way defined by the underwriter in order for the policy and the cover it provides to be in effect. If a provider requests payment within a given number of days from the issue date or in advance of the issue date, then the premium must be transacted within that time frame or otherwise the policy does not exist.

7.008   For schemes where payment of a premium is organised in a different way, such as staged payments or deferred payments, then it is essential that the practitioner has fully determined exactly what is required for premium payment so that their client's position is not prejudiced in the event of an unsuccessful outcome.

It is not professionally acceptable to fail to meet an insurer's premium payment requirements and then face the likely negligence of a claim from your client because the ATE insurance premium was not correctly transacted.

Schemes usually provide for standard cases following a standard pattern with a standard limit of indemnity that is following the time provisions of the CPR for fast track for example. They are usually fairly easy to operate and if the prescribed reporting requirements are followed, and established within the practice, then they are relatively efficient. Schemes will usually follow the theory that all cases are insured before a certain event. Traditionally, it has been a pre letter of claim, all cases approach.

Some schemes will make provision for cases which insure later with separate schedules of premium payments for these and the scope of insurance available. In any event, it is essential that every practitioner who is transacting CFA with ATE insurance understands the reporting requirements placed upon him.

ATE insurance is now an essential practice tool. If this form of funding is to survive and to become economic and viable, insurance schemes need to be implemented and operated correctly in accordance with prescribed procedures.

Make sure that you have evaluated the mechanisms within

the facility which you have elected to use and everyone using it is fully aware of their responsibilities.

Ensure that where an ATE provider issues operational manuals or procedural guidelines that these are distributed correctly and that where updates are issued and where amendments are made these are implemented efficiently and speedily.

Make sure that accounts departments understand how premium payments are to be made. Make sure that policy documentation is distributed properly.

Make certain that you understand the cover which is in operation.

Make sure you understand and are aware of the provisions the policy makes when there is more than one opponent, where there is any offer or payment in accordance with CPR Part 36, where the client dies, where the case may be in the next friend, or the simple provisions for abandonment before proceedings commence and discontinuance after proceedings have commenced.

The ATE market has, in it's very short life, experienced a significant degree of turbulence—many insurers have come and gone.

As a mechanism for funding it has proved itself from a clients perspective to be valuable. There have been circumstances where clients have been able to bring litigation which otherwise they would not have done and for those whose cases have been unsuccessful, ATE insurance has prevented County Court judgments, enforcement proceedings, seizure of goods, etc.

In very simple terms, the more ATE insurance is used regularly the better it will become.

BESPOKE FACILITIES

Despite the misapprehension that all personal injury is simple, **7.009** straight forward and certain, in practice we all know that some cases are difficult, complicated, develop twisting and tight turns and often do not end up as they started out.

There will be cases which have started out with one form of funding and end up with another; there will be circumstances where before the event legal expenses insurance may have been present but ends because of case circumstances or indemnity limits, or quite simply the case is too difficult for a general scheme to facilitate. In these circumstances, a more bespoke policy will be required. This may be because the case itself has complexities which causes it to fall outside of a scheme or it may simply be of a value whereby the indemnity limit provided within a general scheme facility is not adequate for the case in hand. Here a policy may need to be written specifically.

7.010 Not all ATE insurance providers will write bespoke policies. Do some homework.

Think about the type of cases which as a firm you do. Think about the apportionment between injury types and tracks and whether you do have cases which are outside of typical scheme parameters.

Identify in advance providers who can facilitate bespoke policies for individual cases which are of an unusual or higher risk category.

When dealing with a bespoke policy indemnity limits can be flexible, premium payments can be flexible. The policy can be tailored to the specific requirements of the case. However, whilst it is possible to insure almost anything, the premium will be proportional to the risk the underwriter is being asked to take. In the absence of history, premium levels may be more than anticipated.

If a case has had several forms of funding before an ATE provider sees it, then that will impact upon the premium level because the reasons for previous funding being removed or ended will need to be identified. This may impact on the ability of that case being transferred to yet another insurer.

It may well be that where previous Legal Services Commission support has been in place and that ends, the reasons for it ending will need to be examined.

The stage at which the case actually is will impact upon the desirability of it from an insurance perspective.

The essential thing for bespoke policies is to identify as soon as possible that the case is likely to require such a facility and make provision in advance.

Do not wait until the last possible moment to arrange cover. This will require you having to explore many, many different options and in some cases not being able to obtain cover at all.

Keep a pro-active approach for bespoke policies and identify who you will go to for such cover in such circumstances should it arise.

Remember also that ATE insurers are commercial organisations. They offer insurance products in return for premiums and intend for ATE insurance to be profitable business.

Remember, there is no requirement for any ATE insurer to take any case at all.

For bespoke policies premiums will be higher—before you enter into negotiations think about how the premium will be paid.

Do you have facilities to ensure the premium can be paid?

It will be your responsibility to ensure that the client is adequately protected.

It will be your responsibility to disclose all the information necessary for an ATE insurer to make an informed decision.

Most ATE providers will request detailed information in relation to specific cases.

Make sure that you have all the necessary information to expedite the decision making process.

REPORTING REQUIREMENTS

We have already illustrated that ATE insurers will require **7.011** certain information to be disclosed at the outset and at specific times during the course of the case. The reason that ATE insurance providers require regular updates is so that the risk they are carrying can be reviewed and where necessary financial provision made for the payment of claims.

Some of the more regular reporting requirements will be where any offer or payment is made in accordance with CPR Part 36. The reason behind this is generally that as opponents offers and payments become more accurate the risk of failing to beat any offer or payment must be recognised and the decision to accept or reject will become a focused objective.

We have seen cases of Part 36 payments being beaten by amounts as small as £5. We have also seen cases where Part 36 payments have failed to be beaten by as little as £10. The risk to an ATE underwriter will alter upon a Part 36 offer or payment and each provider will determine what impact that has upon their own underwriting capacity.

Commencement of proceedings is an essential reporting requirement for ATE insurance. It significantly alters the exposure the underwriter carries as in the event of adverse outcome, the cost of a claim will now include a provision for defendants costs. It will also impact on the longevity of the case and likelihood of an underwriter having to stay on risk until the case concludes. Further, the number of opponents and where proceedings are commenced defendants, will impact upon an underwriter and again may be a reporting requirement. Make sure that you report when you are supposed to in the format prescribed.

When selecting an ATE provider make sure you have identified from them the requirement which they will impose. It is much easier to implement a reporting regime at the outset than to not do this and have large bulky administration procedures to have to deal with retrospectively at a later stage.

It is essential that cases are sensibly reviewed and objective decisions made with regards to progress of a case where risks significantly alter. In the event that case prospects changes it is our view that where a risk materially reduces and is more likely to result in loss than initially thought, we would strongly recommend that irrespective of whether it is a reporting requirement or not that your ATE provider is advised.

Ensure that you have kept the insurer fully advised at all times so that in the event a claim is made it is able to be dealt with on a fully informed basis.

Do not allow your failure to disclose essential information to an ATE provider to prejudice your client's position in the event of an adverse outcome and subsequent claim.

MAKING AN ATE CLAIM

Each provider will advise as to their own specific require-   **7.012**
ments when making a claim for a case with an adverse outcome. It is essential that you are aware at the outset what this
provision would be. If in any doubt, ask.

Obtain in writing from your provider what requirements
they have and what you will need to do.

When making a claim, consider in the background whether
there is a funding arrangement in place.

Regardless of how a case is funded, if it is through a
financial organisation on a commercial basis then interest will
be running. This interest is usually chargeable to the client or
may be supported by the firm.

If you delay unnecessarily and additional interest accrues,
then this may again prejudice your client's position.

When making a claim ensure that you understand the
procedure. Make sure that you have the full documentation
available to you in order to present to your ATE insurer in
order that they may deal with the claim and expedite the
payment.

In the event that there are any shared costs orders, costs
apportionment between various funders any form of costs
negotiation, make sure that the ATE provider is aware. There
may be circumstances where your provider wishes to dispute
the costs or indeed challenge any costs claim. It may be that
you are not authorised to agree any amounts to be paid by the
ATE indemnity at all.

Determine at the outset whether it is your responsibility to
deal with adverse costs on behalf of your provider or whether
they intend to deal directly or through a third party.

The reason you need to understand the provisions is simply
to mitigate any additional financial costs because of delayed
settlement.

Make sure that the claim you are making is actually covered
by the policy. This means that you should review the cover
the policy provides and make sure that nothing has happened
during the course of the case which has prejudiced that cover
or breached the insurance contract.

For circumstances where there is more than one funder, the ATE provider will only be liable for the period of cover for which they have been on risk. In the event there is more than one funder then the adverse outcome will need to be apportioned accordingly.

Essentially make sure that the premium payment requirements have been complied with so that the claim can, once it has been established that it falls within the policy terms and conditions, be made.

Be efficient. Make sure that you can submit disbursement payments that you have costs schedules, that you have copies of the order readily available to expedite the settlement of the claim.

Where funding arrangements are in place through commercial funding organisations, make sure that you have understood fully the requirements for repayment of such loans. It may be that the ATE insurance provider discharges the loans directly from the commercial funding organisation or through you.

If it is through you then ensure that your accounts department understand the process for repayment. The longer it takes to repay the commercial funder, the higher the interest is likely to be.

If the delay occurs between you and the funder, then it is likely that you will become liable for any additional interest charges which have accrued during that period.

Make sure that where there is any restriction on the claim when related to a Part 36 payment that you are aware of this, you understand the requirements, and most importantly that your client understands that there may be a recovery from his damages in relation to the claim if the policy does not protect.

PAYING INSURANCE PREMIUMS

7.013   We have dealt with earlier the requirement upon you to understand the premium payment mechanism which your ATE provider has implemented.

But how do premiums get paid?

Since the inception of ATE insurance in 1995, there has been the never-ending question of how to pay the insurance premium which has now escalated given the increase in typical premium payments. No matter how sophisticated an insurance solution is, it is of little use if it can't be paid for.

When premiums were routinely less than £100 funding them may have been difficult, but far less difficult when the average premium now sits somewhere between £700 to £1500.

There are two main options available.

Consumer Credit Act funding

With this form of funding, a commercial provider will operate through you a mechanism where a Consumer Credit Act loan (which should be regulated under the Consumer Credit Act 1974) is extended to your client in respect of the premium and / or disbursements as and when required. **7.014**

Generally these facilities are operated on a delegated authority basis where you have the decision to make regarding offering funding and you simply execute agreements for your clients by your funding provider.

It is essential to consider in these circumstances the interest rates which accrue and whether there is any service payments to be made in respect of the loan during the life of the case by the client or by you.

Further, identify what your position is going to be with regards how interest schedules are obtained and the advice that you are giving your client at the outset with regards to the likely cost of interest payments. This is effected by the duration of the case which can be influenced by how efficient your own case management process is.

Most of the Consumer Credit Act facilities are flexible with regards to credit checks and often do not require these to be made.

This is just as well as given some of the socio-economic groups which ATE insurance must now include, the presence of an adverse credit history is more likely. When selecting a funding provider make sure that you understand any provisions with regards to credit checks and what the provisions would be in the event the client is bankrupt, insolvent or dies.

You would need to consider these for example should you undertake mesothelioma cases where there is a fairly high likelihood that your client would die. Should this happen, what provision is there for the repayment of the Consumer Credit Act loan or the continuance of it in the event that the case carries on beyond the death of your client?

You will need to identify whether the ATE insurance which you intend to use is recognised by the Consumer Credit Act funder and whether loans can then be made in respect of those issued policies.

Not all policies are recognised and approved by all CCA funders.

Make sure that you understand and have identified in advance any reporting requirements which your Consumer Credit Act funder has implemented and that you have recognised and comply with repayment requirements at the end of cases.

Where you use more than one Consumer Credit Act funder, make sure that everybody knows within the firm which funders are used for which type of cases and in conjunction with which ATE policies.

Where a Consumer Credit Act agreement is in place, make sure that if the ATE insurance policy makes provision for repayment of interest, that the policy does cover the interest levels charged by a Consumer Credit Act funding provider. It is essential to understand this simply because CCA interest rates can often be higher than global interest rates and some ATE policies make restrictions with regards to interest levels.

Global funding facilities

7.015 The global funding facility provides funding at pre-agreed limits to each individual firm which they subsequently offer to their clients when required. These facilities deal with premium, disbursements and do not require individual Consumer Credit Act documentation to be placed with each individual client. Usually there will be a limit for each case which may be linked to the injury type and track.

Interest rates for global facilities are often lower than those prescribed for Consumer Credit Act arrangements and where the funding element is insured within the ATE insurance policy, may more accurately represent a true "no win no fee" rather than a Consumer Credit Act alternative.

Ensure that you are aware of the reporting procedures required and that early mitigation of any claim reduces the exposure with regards to increased interest which accrues with delay in claims payment.

Make sure that you have understood fully the repayment procedures which are required. Again, your global facility may not operate with your chosen ATE provider.

Hopefully you will be successful more often than otherwise. Remember that the longer the opponent takes to pay the claim, the higher the interest charges may be – this will need to be considered when explaining to the client why the damages deduction if applicable is higher than originally planned.

Some ATE providers will operate in tandem with a funding mechanism which is offered to you as a complete package. The commercial funding providers will need to identify from you a realistic limit with regard to your global funding arrangement. This will be relative to the likely range of cases you will need to fund and the average loan for each one.

Global funding facilities are relatively new to the market and are very effective but will require efficient operation if they are to be cost effective.

Funding facilities in general

There is no doubt that with the increased reliance upon ATE **7.016** insurance as the main form of funding for personal injury that sophisticated insurance solutions will begin to develop as market forces change with time.

Whilst there is a continued cry to the effect that "Before The Event" (BTE) insurance will negate the need for ATE, that of course will require BTE to be effected by most of the population.

Whilst liability insurers may be able to reduce the need for ATE in road traffic cases, there will still be a large percentage of the population who suffer personal injury which is either not a road traffic act claim or is not a claim eligible for cover under a pre-existing BTE, or that the victim does not actually have any BTE insurance.

Therefore, ATE solutions will grow and evolve. However, regardless of how sophisticated these solutions become, whether by more accurate actuarial analysis or by market growth, there will still be a need to pay for them. Therefore, methods of funding must grow and develop and the reliance upon funding for insurance solutions will become more important. It may be that as the market reliance upon funding becomes greater, more funders are prepared to enter into the market. We shall have to wait and see.

In the early days, let us not forget that there were few ATE providers – although in reality that position has not grown that much, there are still very few commercial funding providers.

Whichever funding arrangement you choose, whether global or Consumer Credit Act, there will be criteria that funding organisations must, because of there own professional and regulatory rules, implement and with which you will need to comply.

Where CCA funding is utilised and where this is not effected through a claims management company, you will have an individual arrangement with the CCA funder. They loan the money to the client on the basis that where the case wins such a loan is recovered from the opponent, and in the event of loss recovered from the ATE provider. However, it must not be forgotten that this is unsecured borrowing and ultimately the Consumer Credit Act funder will take security from the firm for the eventuality of shortfall.

So whilst on the surface it appears to be a loan to the client, in actual fact it is a loan to the client through the firm and secured against the firm in the event of failure by recovery from the opponent or from the ATE policy. Because of this, when offering funding solutions a CCA funder is likely to need, because of professional regulations, to determine the financial security of the firm and those within the firm who will be utilising such a facility.

It would not therefore be uncommon for such a service to want to look at a financial history of the firm and require analysis of accounts and profit and loss statements, etc., together with confirmation of identification of partners specifically responsible for that area of funding.

Claims management companies tend to operate on a different basis, whereby the Consumer Credit Act loan is tied in through them with their ATE insurance. There is often less reliance upon the firm than there is in standalone facilities. However, it cannot be forgotten that where the agreement occurs between the firm and the claims management company there will usually be provision somewhere in the agreement for shortfalls on loans and undertakings to repay such shortfalls.

With regard to global facilities, where a pre-agreed amount of money is allocated to the firm for use on ATE CFA cases, the commercial funding provider again has professional rules and regulations with which it must comply. Specifically, money laundering investigations will need to be undertaken and that will require confirmation of the identities of those partners effecting personal injury within the practice at least, and again verification that the organisation with which the bank would be dealing is solvent and operational.

Increasingly, banks are becoming more stringent in the **7.017** application of these rules. Primarily, because of the general increase in money laundering or fraudulent activity, and given that ATE CFA funding is unsecured, this gives concern. In any event, if you look at the routine opening of new bank accounts with new banks, you will see that more paperwork is required in terms of verification of identity and financial security.

In real terms, whilst it may appear painful or indeed the disclosure of confidential financial information may appear invasive, it is really a question of speculating to accumulate.

Once a funding organisation has confirmed identities and that there is not an insolvency difficulty, provision of funding gives greater flexibility with regards to the ability to take on and conduct increased volumes of work. Further, it also makes the whole issue of purchasing ATE insurance and then purchasing subsequently any disbursements required to support the case, a much easier proposition.

When selecting which option may be best for you, the CCA process of passing the loan to the client is of course attractive from the point of view that such loans do not appear attached to the firm or on the firms balance sheets. However, undertakings are still often in place to deal with default on the part of the client or the cover any shortfall in the ATE insurance.

Global facilities, however, can appear to be more in keeping with the no win no fee philosophy and do not require the cooling off periods prescribed by the Consumer Credit Act.

Consideration needs to be given to the provisions of agreements with regards to servicing of any loans which may exist under them. There may be circumstances where interest payments are required to be made either by the firm or by the client and these need to be factored into any advice being given or decisions being made. Further, there may be periods of time attached to loans which are restrictive, there may be interest charges which are excessive or unattractive from a clients point of view.

In any event, it is essential that consideration is given to funding provisions, and the relationship between the funder, the ATE insurer and the firm is an equally important one.

THE ATE POLICY AND THE CFA

7.018   When working with an ATE insurer identify the relationship which exists between the CFA and the ATE insurance. In some schemes, in the event that the CFA ends or for some reason were to be found unenforceable, it may negate the effect of the cover attached to the CFA. Conversely, there may be circumstances where the insurance policy can exist in it's own right in the absence of a valid CFA.

It is essential when working with your ATE provider to identify the relationship between the two essential documents. With the CFA becoming increasingly under the microscope of the opponent, and the whole enforceability issue becoming more contentious on a daily basis, it would be prudent to confirm the position with regards to the ATE insurance in the event a flaw is found in the CFA.

When working with an ATE provider, understand the relationship between the policy and the CFA where counsel is concerned. If you use counsel on all of your cases and counsel is happy to work on a CFA, then you perhaps do not require cover which includes counsel as part of the ATE policy. However, for larger cases or bespoke cases it may be that counsel is required and when negotiating policy cover or obtaining policy cover it is a provision for which you would need to negotiate.

As the ATE market becomes more competitive, you may take a view that the cheapest is the best and most likely to be recoverable.

That is, of course, not the case. Historic analysis of insurance generally indicates that cheapest may appear to be best from a pricing point of view, but may contain restrictions in terms of types of policy issued and the cover included. From an ATE perspective, if an ATE provider insures only rear-end passenger RTAs then it is more likely the premiums will be considerably less than a provider that is able to grant a facility to you making provision for all of your case types.

In any event, from an evidential point of view and in support of the recoverability argument, there are few facilities which have been able to devise it's premiums in an actuarial way.

In order to assist with recoverability arguments, where a **7.019** premium can be confirmed by an underwriter as having been actuarially analysed and in the event of dispute such actuarial evidence is produced, these may be options which are more attractive when selecting which provider to use.

You, of course, have a choice with regards to the type of cover you may want but consider very carefully that as the argument with recoverability becomes more contentious and is unlikely to be an argument that is not going to go away, you would need to consider how, in the event your premiums are being challenged, how, if at all, your ATE insurer can assist you in the recovery of the same premium which they have set.

If you are searching for a new provider as the market grows and develops and becomes more sophisticated there is an increased likelihood that ATE underwriters themselves will be looking to analyse your own success rates when considering offering you a facility of any sort.

From our experience, we are keen when assessing the

provision of capacity to a firm to identify the likely amounts of insurance they would require and just how successful they are.

It may appear on the surface that firms are in a position to pick and choose who they insure with, but in actual fact what they are selecting is a product which not only fits the profile of cases which they conduct, but also provides adequate cover for the clients who ultimately have the responsibility for the ATE policy and the capacity which that underwriter is able to provide.

As the CFA is examined and rules and regulations surrounding them are revised and altered, ATE insurance will alter and grow. ATE providers may become themselves more selective about the firms with whom they are prepared to work and wish to actuarially examine your own results.

When considering funding provisions and giving advice on funding provisions to clients, be equipped with information about the product you are providing.

Do you know the provision your ATE insurer has with regards to the death of your client?

It may be that during the course of the case your client dies, either of the injuries sustained as a consequence of the accident or through other causes.

The case may be strong enough evidentially to continue. What provision do you have for this?

It is possible to enter into a new CFA with the personal representatives of the deceased, and it may well be that the original policy attaching to the original CFA can continue.

If you routinely conduct disease cases such as mesothelioma you may well require the policy to continue after the death of your client. Make sure you have identified from your ATE provider what their requirements is for these circumstances. Are further premiums payable? If so, how will they be paid? What happens to any CCA loans?

The other essential question is whether you actually know the identity of your ATE insurer. If you don't, who does? Who is dealing with the cover and importantly who deals with the claims?

SUMMARY

Communication between the ATE insurer and the firm is vital. **7.020**
These are new relationships and it is essential to identify
specific areas of responsibility within the firm and have clear
lines of communication through the firms to the ATE insurer
so that everybody knows their responsibility with regards to
reporting, to whom and when. If there is a problem with a
case, don't wait until it becomes a big issue—pre-empt the
problem by communication with your ATE provider. Ensure
that someone within your firm has the responsibility to deal
with the management of problems and the line of communication to the ATE provider centralised reporting if need be.
Make sure that you know the requirements of your ATE
provider in terms of reporting and premium payments and
claims procedures and, importantly, when you are successful.
This is essential information to allow insurers to review their
own risk and ensure adequate financial provisions. It also
reflects on your firm and how you are rated as a risk to an
insurer.

If in doubt, ask. Obtain a clear answer in writing and revise
your internal procedures accordingly.

Because a planned structured approach to risk identification
is an integral part of the insurance process, adoption by this
within the firm will ensure that there is a commonality of
approach and that longevity for funding options can be
established. That means longevity for your business.

DATA ANALYSIS

This book deals with some of the key elements required for **7.021**
effective risk assessment and endeavours to bring together in
simple terms the commonality between risk assessment
within a firm for CFA cases and process of risk assessment as
a general principle of insurance.

We have given risk assessment forms and we have identified the concept of historic actuarial analysis by insurers of

data in order to determine risk and this is done essentially through effective data capture.

As funding solutions become more sophisticated and as your reliance on CFA as a form of funding becomes more pivotal to the financial viability of your firm as a business, the ability to determine problems giving rise to loss will become more important.

Data capture enables you to understand the profile of cases which you conduct and whether there are any factors which are common to the losses which you sustain. From collection and analysis of data, you should be able to identify the profile of cases which you conduct, the type of cases which you lose, the stage at which you lose, the cost of the loss and whether there is any particular fee earner or area of law which represents the risk of loss.

Success is equally important—record when you win, at what stage, the level of recovered costs, success fees and how long from the date of submission to the opponent until receipt. This will assist with case flow projections and management, particularly if overdraft facilities are in operation.

By recording such data ultimately you will be able to actuarially determine how successful you are as an organisation and importantly, how profitable the PI work is.

Therefore, you should consider establishing CFA databases—we have been involved in the detailed design and build of such data structures and are able to confirm the important role they play.

Where a case is unsuccessful it is absolutely essential that there is a post mortem. The exact circumstances of the failure need to be fully recorded and understood. It is our recommendation that information is retained in relation not only to the losses but for the victories as well. From this projections on overall success and profitability can be based.

We have referred previously to experience, knowledge, information, and we will now consider actuarial information. The recognition of data recording as an essential risk management tool cannot be underestimated. The entire insurance industry operates on this basis.

Therefore, when building a database, whether this be in comprehensive data programming form or in simple spreadsheet design, think about what you will want to know and then work backwards to ensure the correct data is captured at the outset. Remember, if the data is not captured in the first place you cannot analyse it at a later stage.

If you consider the risk assessment checklists which are included within this book, you may wish to include them as part of a database design.

The client personal injury questionnaire which you may adopt at the initial stages of your case also forms part of a database.

Having read this book you may conclude that this is obvious. However, from our experience there are considerably large numbers of firms who do not capture data, who do not have any way of identifying how successful their cases are, the profile of their cases, which funders they used, the apportionment between BTE, ATE LSC funding, private funding, specific funding arrangements, bespoke policies, and scheme policies.

Your business is reliant now upon CFA and ATE insurance. Therefore, you will need to know the amount of risk you are carrying at any given time.

Your accounts function will specifically, when providing **7.022** cashflow forecasts, profit and loss statements or simple end of year reviews, need to determine the obvious point of how much work in progress has been incurred which remains outstanding. In practice, this must be related to the likely number of cases to be lost and the amount of work in progress to be lost and cost that represents to the firm together with the lost success fees.

It may be that routinely these observations are already being done. However, whilst the information has perhaps been recorded already, is there a reporting process to review it?

If you review your current PI case load, do you know the apportionment between funders, ATE insurers, tracks, injury types? Do you know which case referral sources are most successful, or which advertising and marketing campaigns produce the best results?

Are you able to determine from the data which you have already captured, those cases which lose more often than those which don't? Do you know accurately how many cases conclude without the need for proceedings? Do you know what your average success fee has been? Do you know which insurer you routinely have difficulty with on costs or recoverability of additional liabilities? Do you know how long you wait to be paid?

Each firm will have it's own individual requirement with regard to the information for management purposes. If you do not already do it, then start. If you do, build in regular reviews—case and payment profiles change.

One thing is certain, as the reliance upon CFAs develops, the cashflow through the practice itself will become more dependant on accurate interpretation of management information.

If your overdraft facilities become more integral in the funding of your CFA cases whilst you wait for your work in progress to come, the ability to predict the average length of case from start to conclusion together with the average recovered cost and recovered ATE and success fee will become absolutely essential for the budgeting process.

7.023   Analysis of recorded data could for example confirm the viability from a cost benefit point of view of a large RTA book, when compared perhaps to a smaller disease book on the basis that whilst disease cases take longer, the cost recovery is larger when compared to the number of RTA cases required in order to achieve the same financial result.

To develop the risk assessment process to the next stage, you can, through effective data capture, easily implement strategic changes to your own risk assessment processes.

Further, capture of specific data can be achieved by working in conjunction with your ATE provider.

Where there is commonality of data capture between your ATE provider and you, this in turn assists in efficient reporting processes.

Where you are aware of specific information which the ATE insurer requires and the frequency with which such information is required, then reports can be routinely run to provide such information either on paper form or electronic form, whichever is required. Such reviews are beneficial to your management process.

Payment of premium can be recorded and confirmed together with the funding provider and reports can be implemented to ensure accurate information, again beneficial to the firm, for internal management purposes. ATE providers may wish to examine firms success rates, or funders may wish to determine the kind of facilities which a firm may require obtaining facilities will be much easier if assessment information is available to promote your funding requirements.

Whatever the level of your own IT facility, data capture is essential and will become an important tool in the entire risk management process.

8

Risk Assessment

CARRYING OUT A RISK ASSESSMENT

To understand risk assessment and use it well in conditional **8.001**
fee funded cases, an overall understanding of risk assessment
is required. This is not a new concept invented as justification
of a success fee. Far from it, even ignoring the world of
insurance, risk assessment is not new at all. In recent years
there has been a gradual move towards more risk assessment
and control based duties imposed by law. For example, the
cornerstone of all UK employer's liability and health and
safety law is risk assessment and control.

Risk assessment has a long history dating at least from the
1920s. At that time there was a dramatic increase in air travel.
This was mirrored by a significant rise in the number of plane
crashes. As a result, particularly in the USA, insurers began to
evaluate the accident rate for different types of aircraft based
on their operational records. This was an early form of risk
assessment. Risk assessment led directly to risk management
being used as a hazard control mechanism.

On June 1, 1974 a vapor cloud explosion destroyed the
Nypro Cyclohexane Oxidation plant at Flixborough. The
explosion was devastating, killing 28 people. Other plants on
the site were seriously damaged or destroyed and the site
presented a scene of utter devastation.

The plant was a stage in the production of nylon. It man-
ufactured a mixture of Cyclohexanone and Cyclohexanol
(known as KA, or ketone/alcohol mixture) by oxidising

cyclohexane, a hydrocarbon similar to petrol in its physical properties, with air in a series of reactors. One of them developed a leak and had to be removed for repair and a temporary pipe was constructed to replace it. There was no professional mechanical engineer on site at the time as the works engineer had left and his replacement had not arrived. The men who were asked to design and install the temporary pipe had very considerable practical experience and they had the plant back on line within a few days.

Unfortunately they did not realise that designing large pipes (20 inch bore) to operate at high temperature (150°C) and pressure (10 bar) was a job for experts. Their only drawing was a full-size sketch in chalk on the workshop floor; the only support was scaffolding on which the pipe rested.

They cannot be blamed for what happened as they were asked to do a job beyond their professional capabilities. They simply did not know that it was beyond them. This is perhaps the first message about risk assessment. If you do not have the right combination of knowledge, experience and expertise you may well not even recognise the risks you are taking. Exactly the same applies to a lawyer accepting instructions from a client. Risk management controls are needed to stop your firm from taking on cases if you do not have the required combination of knowledge, experience and expertise to identify the risks involved.

Carrying out a conditional fee risk assessment involves the same process as carrying out a risk assessment in any other activity. The key is to remember that this is not just about success fees, it is about staying in business. In fact the funding should not be the driving force at all. Risk assessment is about best practice. Good risk assessment means a successful lawyer, be it solicitor or barrister.

RISK ASSESSMENT FOR CFA WORK

8.002 There are three elements in all risk assessments. They are the separate elements of hazard, harm and risk. Each needs to be considered on its own and then they need to be reviewed together. A hazard is quite simply anything with the potential to cause harm. When you look for risk factors you are in fact looking for the hazards in a case. The terms hazard and risk factor are interchangeable.

Harm is the damage from the hazard. The effect caused by the risk factor becoming a reality. The damage to all of the people involved in the case—the client—counsel—the solicitor—the funding insurer. The financial hit resulting from the risk factor becoming a reality hits the lawyers by their loss of profit. Many thousands of pounds worth of work is thown away. The financial hit impacts on the client through loss of their damages or reduction in their damages. On the other side of the coin the financial hit impacts the client who has to pay out the damages. The financial hit impacts on the funding insurer. They have to pay damages and costs as a losing liability insurer. They have to bear the costs of a claim as an after event insurer paying the cost of indemnifying their insured by settling the bill for the winning party's costs and all the loosing party's disbursements.

In the longer term there may be a more serious impact in terms of harm. The loss of reputation of the lawyers involved. The individual solicitors and their firms. Barristers' chambers and individual counsel. Loss of reputation as a competent lawyer could have the most catastrophic of consequences well beyond a drop in the number of new sets of instructions. Loss of reputation may well lead to loss of insurer backing. Without insurance to back cases there is no long term prospect of survival as a personal injury practitioner under our current funding systems.

So what about risk? Risk is the chance that a risk factor will cause the harm you have identified as it's outcome if it becomes a reality. Risks may be large or small. Clearly we are looking for the more serious risks as those are the ones that matter most.

Risk assessment is the process of identifying the risk factors. Then identifying the potential damage they may cause. Next risk assessment means assessing what the chance is of each of the factors becoming a reality and causing the damage. This is followed by evaluating the consequences of those risk factors becoming a reality.

Risk assessment should always be completed by using risk reduction and control measures to minimise the chances of things going wrong. This final element is all too often overlooked. This is however about risk management *after* accepting instructions on a CFA, *not* about reviewing the success fee.

IDENTIFYING CASE RISK FACTORS

8.003 Identifying case risk factors is not carrying out a risk assessment. That is a much more complex process which we shall consider in detail later in this Chapter. The process of identifying factors is phase one of the risk assessment process. It allows a practitioner to focus both on those common recurring risks sometimes called "generic risks", and case specific facts. Generic risks are not necessarily specific to the detailed facts of the case in question. These are risks based on those factors that keep turning up in case after case or those which recur in cases of the same or broadly similar type. Frequently, they can be categorised and check lists used to help make sure that they are not missed. Case specific risks speak for themselves.

It is important to recognise that there at least six are areas of risk which need to be considered in all cases. Those areas are:

- Facts. The risk that your client will fail to establish what happened.

- Liability. The risk that your client will fail to establish breach of duty.

- Delay and Limitation. The risk that a time factor will undermine the case.

- The Opponent—The risk that your opponent will not prove to be viable.

- Causation—The risk that the claim will not prove to be sound on a causation issue.

- Quantum—The risk that damages will prove to be lower than expected.

Here are some examples in each area:

Facts—There may have been witnesses to the accident but they may not prove to be traceable, or reliable or prepared to assist. Your client may be a poor witness or have a poor recollection or may simply not be believed. There are many more.

Liability—Contemporaneous documents may not prove to have been completed or when you see them may not say what you expected them to say. Even if you win there may be a finding of contributory negligence. If there is a risk of a finding of contributory negligence there will be a risk of failing to better a Part 36 offer on liability. The law itself can cause problems. For example you may be faced with a difficult area of law or a changing area of law.

Delay & Limitation—The date of the accident may not be known. The date of the accident may be unclear. There may be a date of knowledge issue. There may be an unusual limitation period. The limitation period may simply be close to the expiry date.

The Opponent—Your client may not know who they are or who they are may be unclear. There may potentially be more than one. They may not have the ability to pay. They may not be insured. The insurer may repudiate or not be solvent themselves. The indemnity may be too low or have been used up on other claims.

Causation—Does your client have a recurrent injury? Is your client suffering from a disease or illness rather than an injury? Is there a risk of an incorrect diagnosis? Is the injury of a type where causation is often in dispute such as a back or neck injury or perhaps an upper limb disorder? Is there a risk of underlying factors playing a part?

Quantum—Are there complex heads of damage? Some heads of damage are much more difficult to prove than others. Even a straightforward head of damage such as loss of earnings may often become complex if you have a self employed client. How many heads of damage are there? The more there are the greater the potential for a failure to better a Part 36 offer. The trial judge is only going to award a global sum and just failing to recover what was hoped for on a single head of damage can mean failure overall.

Time can be a problem too. Is there an uncertain prognosis? Will the prognosis be slow to clarify? These can be matters that make a claimant vulnerable to an early Part 36 offer. Sometimes it is simply impossible to give advice on an offer without waiting for the medical picture to clear.

How many medical specialists and other expert witnesses on quantum will you need? Some cases are made risky by the simple fact that you need a number of experts. Only one has to change an opinion late in the case or to fail to come up to scratch in court and once again that Part 36 offer may not be bettered.

Finally, there is the risk that the claimant will be considered to have exaggerated or worse still been dishonest. Is there potential for exaggeration? Some injuries carry a much higher risk than others. Classically back and neck injuries fall into this category.

Quantum is often a badly neglected area of risk. There is often a totally incorrect belief that quantum is not a problem. It is. The history of claims on after the event insurance policies shows that relatively few cases fail at trial on liability. Far more fail on quantum by failing to better a payment into court or Part 36 offer.

In these six are areas of risk which need to be considered in all cases there is clearly room for overlap. A factor may be relevant in more than one area in the same case. It is better to have identified it twice that to have missed it all together.

It is a good idea to prepare your own lists of risk factors for the different types of cases that you regularly deal with. Keep them up to date by adding new factors when you have the misfortune to come across them. Risk is never static.

Identifying the risk factors is however just the beginning of the process. Risk assessment should follow on from it. We shall now move on to consider exactly what is involved.

RISK ASSESSMENTS

Undertaking a suitable and sufficient risk assessment on a **8.004** case by case basis involves three key aspects. These are:

(1) Reviewing all the aspects of the case.

(2) Evaluating the law, facts and evidence.

(3) Deciding what you can do to try to control of risks.

There are five basic steps to any risk assessment process. You should treat all risk factors as a hazard to the case and by implication to yourself and everyone else involved in the case. Step one is to look for the risk factors. Try to identify them all. Do not consider anything else other than to ask yourself what the factors are or may be on the basis of what you know.

Now move on to step two. Categorise the risk factors you **8.005** have identified on the basis of the impact they will have on the outcome of the case if they become a reality.

This principle of assessing a success fee is not very far removed from the risk analysis utilised by insurers themselves when assessing insurance based risk. In general terms the provision of insurance and the calculation of the premium due for acceptance and subsequent transfer of that risk is based on identifying and quantifying the known of forseeable potential hazards which give rise to the risk. The risk is influenced by the combination of those identified potential hazards, the likelihood of them occurring, the severity or impact should they occur, how often they are likely to happen and at what stage they will occur.

Premium in essence equates to uplift. Clearly to put all of this into an individual case risk assessment would be both extremely time consuming and difficult to achieve. It needs to be simplified. A good system is to adopt a low medium and high tariff approach to the risk factors and their impact. How this influences the overall risk assessment is explained below.

You may need to do more investigation or research at this **8.006** point before completing the risk assessment. If so take step three. This requires you to prepare an "action list" of things to do. The action list may be short or long. It will depend on the case and it's facts. Some cases will inevitably need more information than others to enable you to risk assess them adequately. You may feel that you need to see a police report or medical records or to contact a witness. You may want to visit the scene of the accident. Your action list will always be case specific.

After completing the tasks on your action list you will need to review steps one and two before moving to step four by re-evaluating the risk factors. You will need a format for the evaluation and one is explained below. There are many approaches but the key thing is to make sure you remember to assess what the chance is of each of the factors becoming a reality and causing the damage. That is the only way to ensure that you concentrate on the factors which are really important and that you are not simply ticking a list of factors without any real thought.

8.007   Step four is recording your findings in a suitable form. This written risk assessment is required to ensure that you can justify and recover your uplift. Specific information should be set out set out in the risk assessment sufficient to ensure that you can do this. By making sure that you explain the thinking behind the assessment you should have no difficulty in showing that it was indeed justified. This of course means that you should be in a very strong position to recover the success fee in full. If you link facts to risk factors and back that up with reasoning to show why you think these factors matter any reasonable Judge should be able to follow your reasoning and reward you accordingly in costs via the success fee.

There are those who advocate the generalist approach. Keep your risk assessment simple. Keep it woolly. Leave yourself the maximum room for manoeuvre and argument. They simply do not understand what risk assessment is about at all. Following their approach is a potential road to financial ruin. Unless you are only running very simple cases specific risk assessment is essential.

This was confirmed by the Court of Appeal in the first *Callery v Gray* judgment when they said:

"The solicitor carrying on litigation business on a large scale may have regard to similar considerations. He may seek to ensure that the uplifts agreed result in a reasonable return overall, having regard to his experience of the work done and the likelihood of success or failure of the particular class of litigation. This will not mean that he does not consider the merits of the particular case, where he is aware of facts which call for individual assessment. But there may be categories of claim that have, so far as he is aware, sufficient common characteristics to justify a standard approach to determining uplift."

Step five requires you to calculate your success fee. The **8.008** familiar chart used by so many in the early years of CFA work is not the answer. It ignores one of the core elements behind the purpose of success fees. The purpose of success fees is to make the CFA system operable. To achieve this the success fee recovered on winning cases must compensate for the losses on losing cases. In other words you put your success fees from your winning cases to one side so that when the inevitable loss happens you have enough in the kitty to be able to afford to take the loss and survive.

Of course if success fees are set too high that is unfair to defendants, as claimant's lawyers are over-compensated. However if they are set too low that is just as unfair to the claimant's lawyers. The key is to remember that the success fee on the case that you win does *not* compensate for losses on that case as there are none. The success fee on that winning case compensates for losses on another quite separate loosing case. The success fee you collect across a series of cases compensate for the loss of one or more of that series. You can never start at a zero success fee as even in the lowest risk cases you need to be preparing for the failures to come by storing up recovered success fees to cope with it. It is very important to remember that there is no room for a zero success fee even if it could be successfully argued (which it cannot) that there is such a thing as a totally risk free case.

The secondary point is that most cases settle. They settle early. They settle when costs are low so success fees are low too. Many success fees need to be collected in these cases to compensate for one case lost at trial. This too is ignored by the chart approach. Using the chart means that you will loose out both ways and end up with success fees that are simply too low to sustain a conditional fee based practice.

The final part of step five is to set dates and stages in the case for Review and Revision. On Review—check that the risk remains unchanged. If not—indicate the action required. Cases may get better in that the risk reduces. Clearly that means no action is needed if your opponent does not settle or abandon the case (depending on who you represent—claimant or defendant). If the risks become higher then it may be time to call a halt. It depends on the level of risk. Reassessment is vital for risk control purposes. There is no case for altering your risk assessment. This is management of risk.

Some liability insurers, on an admission of liability, ask the claimant to reassess the success fee (no doubt in a downwards direction). This may well be based on a misunderstanding of the Court of Appeal's decision in *Callery v Gray* and in particular their comments on split success fees (see Chapter 4 on recoverability of success fees).

Some liability insurers even argue that there is no risk at all following an admission. This flies totally in the face of all of the evidence from the world of insurance. If you have any doubt about this "fact" you will only need to have read chapter six on applying insurance risk principles to be convinced that risk is everywhere.

Format for Risk Assessments

8.009 As a minimum the risk assessment record form should contain the following information—

- Details of the case
- Assessment of risks
- Risk level for risks

When recording risk assessments, trivial risks can normally be ignored. Also, risks associated with life in general can be ignored unless the case substantially increases these risks. For example, death of a client could normally be ignored unless age, medical history or case type (terminal illness) indicated otherwise. Those risks regarded as greater than trivial need to be ranked. To do this involves a four part approach. First, of all list the hazards associated with the case. Secondly, decide on the likelihood of them happening. Thirdly, decide on the seriousness of the outcome if they do actually happen. Then complete the process by working out the risk ranking. This is calculated by multiplying the likelihood by the severity of outcome. A simple points system is sufficient to make the calculations. On the likelihood that the risk will materialise you can make an assessment based on low medium and high categories. If you choose low then your belief is that the risk is unlikely to materialise at all. If you consider the risk is medium your view will be that there is a fair chance that it may materialise. If your assessment if high then there is a serious risk that it will happen.

By way of example consider the risk that the client will not be believed by the judge at trial is a risk in all cases. There may be many reasons to form a view on likelihood of this happening. If the facts of a case were identical there may still be a considerable difference in the chance or likelihood of the judge not believing the client. You might conclude that, for example, a clergyman was a low risk but that a client with a criminal record was a high risk. The risk factor is the same but the outcome of the assessment of the risk very different.

That is where severity of risk needs to be added to the equation. If a risk factor does become a reality sometimes it will have catastrophic consequences for the case while in other circumstances it will have very little impact at all. To evaluate severity the same low, medium and high approach can be taken. If the impact were to be low there would only be minor damage to the case and it would have very little effect. If the impact were to be of medium severity it would cause moderate damage to the case but usually short of total failure. There might, for example, be a reduction in the damages recovered. With a high severity effect on the case it might be a total loss. It might fail on quantum or liability by not bettering a well pitched CPR Part 36 offer or payment. That is the sort of risk that simply cannot be ignored.

To marry up both sides of the equation and arrive at the risk level the likelihood should be multiplied by the severity. If you score one point for low, two points for medium and three points for high in each part of the risk level calculation process you should simply multiply the two numbers together and reach the risk level for each risk identified. The outcome will produce a figure that can be categorised as low, medium or high. A figure of 1, 2 or 3 would be a low risk level. All identified risk should be recorded as there is no such thing as a risk free case. Figures of 4 or 6 would represent medium level risks. They are risks that are clearly significant in the case. Where the outcome is the figure 9, that is a high risk level and must be taken very seriously. In some cases a single score of 9 properly calculated might justify a maximum uplift of 100 per cent on its own. That would not by any means be automatic however.

Using the example above of the clergyman and criminal it is easy to see how calculating the risk level adds significantly to simply identifying that a risk is present. Doing this with all identified risks will allow you to produce a risk profile for the case.

Client	Risk Factor	Likelihood	Severity	Risk Level
Clergyman	Not believed	1	3	3
Criminal	Not believed	3	3	9

If you score a 9 in your assessment of your prospective client it would not be surprising if you did not take the case on at all. Consider another situation. Your client seems honest to you. He and the potential defendant blame each other for the accident. The case will turn on whom the judge believes. You are in a 50/50 situation.

Client	Risk Factor	Likelihood	Severity	Risk Level
Mr 50/50	Not believed	2	3	6

The risk factor is the same in all three examples. The severity of outcome does not change either. What changes is the risk level rate and that is why it is important to try to assess it in relation to all risk factors. Without it the risk assessment is flawed. The numbers can differ. The chance and severity options can be increased but in essence the outcome is basically the same.

It is very important to remember that all cases needs to be monitored regularly and reassessed after any change of significance such as a Part 36 payment. Good risk assessment is an ongoing process throughout the life of the case. It is of course the key to risk management and control addressed in the following chapter.

To carry out a risk assessment on the basis we advocate, a **8.010** relatively simple pro-forma can be used for your assessment and ranking of risk. You will find a precedent in Appendix 1. That is not however designed to be the formal risk assessment record document to be kept as a record for the court. This type of form could be used by a fee earner as preparation for presentation of a case to the office or department committee.

It lists areas of risk to insert your own risk factors. Your own list of factors should be added to it. It may be changed or replaced in its entirety to suit the needs of the user and the type of work being vetted.

At the conclusion of the risk ranking task the fee earner should be able to evaluate the case and conclude whether it is a low, medium or high risk case. Then the rest of the document should be completed and the case submitted to the committee.

Ideally the fee earner should discuss the case with the committee, in effect pitching it to them as a case to take on a CFA. If the committee agrees that the case should be taken on then a formal risk assessment record should be completed and kept on the file. A *pro forma* for this purpose follows in Appendix 1.

The object is to ensure that all risks are covered and all are categorised. There should be no difficulty in justifying the risk assessment as it will be case specific. It should be enough to satisfy most judges that your risk assessment exercise was a genuine and realistic one.

You will note that the suggestion is that cases should only be rated as low, medium or high risk. We believe that such assessments merit a success fee of 50 per cent for low, 75 per cent for medium and 100 per cent for high. These assessments are prepared on the basis that the case will not settle during the protocol period. It they do then obviously in many cases it will be necessary to agree to accept a reduced level of success fee. We suggest that 50 per cent of the original uplift level will be reasonable in most cases.

8.011   The reason for this approach comes from the recognition by the Court of Appeal in *Callery v Gray (No.1)* [2001] EWCA Civ. 1117 that cases which do not settle during the protocol period carry real risk. They considered a two stage success fee but rejected that approach for the time being (paragraph 115) on the basis that suitable data was not available. However, their thinking is consistent with the need to set a success fee at a level properly reflecting the risks of the case in litigation, not on the basis that there is a *hope* that it will settle.

In paragraph 108 they say "the logic behind a two-stage success fee is that, in calculating the success fee, it can properly be assumed that if, notwithstanding the compliance with the protocol, the other party is not prepared to settle, or not prepared to settle upon reasonable terms, there is a serious defence. By the end of the protocol period, both parties should have decided upon their positions. If they are prepared to settle, they should make an offer setting out their position clearly and providing the level of costs protection which they determine is appropriate. They continue in paragraph 110:

"If a claim is settled before the end of the protocol period, it would be reasonable that there should still be a success fee payable since:

(i)   The lawyers are entitled to be compensated for accepting a retainer on a no-fee-no-win basis with the inevitable risk that this involves, however small this risk may appear in many cases.

(ii)   An appropriate success fee would contribute towards those cases where no fees are payable because they end unsuccessfully."

This is also important as it makes it clear that a success fee covers two elements. Risk merits reward. It is not just a matter of breaking even. If running a risk base enterprise breaking even was all that could be hoped for there would be no incentive at all for acceptance of the risk.

A further point to remember is the power of the court set **8.012** out in the Costs Practice Direction in section 17.8(2). It states:

> "In cases in which an additional liability is claimed, the costs judge or district judge should have regard to the time when and the extent to which the claim has been settled and to the fact that the claim has been settled without the need to commence proceedings."

This provides scope for reduction for an early settlement *without* proceedings. There is no such power post proceedings. Post proceedings Costs Practice Direction section 11.7 is the relevant section stating:

> "Subject to paragraph 17.8(2), when the court is considering the factors to be taken into account in assessing an additional liability, it will have regard to the facts and circumstances as they reasonably appeared to the solicitor or counsel when the funding arrangement was entered into and at the time of any variation of the arrangement."

This clearly means not only that hindsight should not be used by a judge on assessment of an uplift but also that after issue judges have no power to make a reduction because there was an early settlement *after proceedings* were issued when assessing the additional liability.

There are of course many other methods used by law firms to calculate their uplifts. For example according the House of Lords judgment in *Callery*, Amelans (Mr Callery's solicitors) assessed the success fee by reference to a "matrix" under which points were allocated between 0 (no success fee) and 20 (100 per cent). The Lords said that the effect of the matrix was that virtually no personal injury cases could score less than 7 (35 per cent) and Mr Callery's scored another six because there were no witnesses, Amelans were funding the case and it was expected to take over 6 months to settle. It is difficult to see why the absence of witnesses would matter at all when the claimant was a passenger in a car. It may have been a "risk factor" but the failure to "assess" that factor shows the weakness of the "factors only" approach.

The Lord Hoffman said at paragraph 46 "No doubt some kind of point system like this is essential in a firm in which large numbers of claims are processed. But it can hardly be regarded as a rational calculation and I do not think that the judge took much notice. What in fact determines the success fee solicitors charge is what costs judges have been willing to allow in more or less comparable cases, the fee being set at the level regarded as optimistic but hopefully not so optimistic as to provoke the liability insurers into contesting the amount. I shall in due course come back to the question of whether this is a sensible system." We know that the outcome was that on the question of what success fee could be regarded as reasonable in a simple road accident claim, the Court of Appeal said in its view 20 per cent was the maximum which a costs judge should allow in a "modest and straightforward claim" which had no special features to suggest that the claim might not be sound.

8.013   The decision of the Court of Appeal in *Halloran v Delaney* [2002] EWCA Civ. 1258 illustrates well that success fees will not be recovered without proper risk assessments being carried out and made available to the court to back them up. It also shows that the Court of Appeal has no sympathy for solicitors who seek to recover success fees set at unjustifiable levels. It is however an unfortunate decision as there appears to have been little or no evidence before the court on which to give a fresh ruling on success fees.

The claimant had instructed solicitors to act for him as a passenger in a simple road traffic accident claim under a Conditional Fee Agreement. The claim was settled without court proceedings. Part 8 proceedings were issued to deal with costs. The district judge ruled that the claimant had acted reasonably in issuing the costs the only proceedings and that he was entitled to recover the costs of those proceedings. She was also satisfied that the CFA covered the Part 8 proceedings. The substantial disputed question was whether the claimant should be able to recover a success fee on the Part 8 proceedings themselves. The defendant argued that the district judge should not have allowed any success fee on the costs of the costs only proceedings because there was no risk to the lawyer of not recovering his reasonable costs. The Court of Appeal upheld the circuit judge's decision that the CFA covered the Part 8 proceedings and that any uplift recovered should include the costs only proceedings.

The figure of 20 per cent had been allowed as the level of the recoverable uplift by the district judge. This was in line with *Callery v Gray* [2001] 3 All E.R. 833 (CA); [2002] 3 All E.R. 417 (HL). Even so the defendants argued that this was excessive given the minimal amount of risk involved. They contended that a figure of 5 per cent was more appropriate. The Court of Appeal did not agree, and the defendant's appeal failed. They then went on to say in the form of additional comments that judges should ordinarily allow an uplift of 5 per cent on the claimant's lawyers' costs, *including* the costs of any costs only proceedings awarded to them unless persuaded that a higher uplift was appropriate in the particular circumstances of the case.

They justified this apparent shift from by saying that at the time of the Court of Appeal's decision in *Callery* there was uncertainty about a number of matters concerning the recoverability of costs in a case like this. Because of the prevailing uncertainties when the CFA was made in this case, the costs judge was not wrong to hold that an uplift of 20 per cent was reasonable, given her wide discretion. However they then went on to say that following *Callery* it was time to reappraise the appropriate level of success fees that should be recoverable on these simple claims when they were settled without the need for court proceedings. They stated that in relation to all CFAs, however, they were structured, entered into on and after August 1, 2001 when both Court of Appeal *Callery* judgments had been published and the main uncertainties about costs recovery had been removed Judges should ordinarily allow an uplift of 5 per cent on the claimant's lawyers' costs unless persuaded that a higher uplift was appropriate in the particular circumstances of the case.

There are a number of strange things about these comments, not least the fact that there cannot be said to have been certainty in reality until after the decision in *Callery v Gray* in the House of Lords [2002] 3 All E.R. 417 (HL) in June 2002 rather than following the Court of Appeal's decision [2001] 3 All E.R. 833 (CA) in July 2001. The suggestion that this approach should be applied retrospectively is also difficult to understand or justify, as indeed it would have been if it had been an increase rather than a decrease which would have been totally unfair to defendant liability insurers.

We do not however believe that this decision should affect the procedure for risk assessment and setting the level of uplift set out above. It needs to be remembered that this was a very modest and straightforward road traffic accident involving a passenger and it should not relate directly to other types of claims. These comments were just that, comments, and the decision in *Callery* remains good law.

A claim that settles pre-issue need not necessarily be simple. For example it will be important for a claimant to be able to demonstrate if there was a compromise through use of their risk assessment even in a relatively modest or simple cases, if settled pre-issue, to ensure that a proper uplift is recovered.

This decision does not remove the importance of the protocol as set out above in *Callery*. It reinforces it. Even if a defendant fails to reply within the protocol and then settles just before issue of proceedings they should expect to face the *Callery* argument that they should pay a higher risk based success fee until settlement for failing to comply with or deliberately ignoring the protocol.

We do not believe there is any need to adopt a split success fee approach if a properly assessed uplift is included in the conditional fee agreement. The negotiation process should be all that is required.

8.014 The majority of claims are not for passengers in minor motor accidents. They are obviously not as "modest and straightforward" as *Callery* or *Halloran*. Even a single true risk factor should be sufficient to warrant a greater uplift even where there is a settlement without proceedings. Our method produces uplifts properly based on individual case risk assessment. The key to recovery of higher uplifts are proper risk assessments set of levels that envisage the real risks of cases in the event of litigation. There is no second chance to increase the proposed uplift if the case does not settle. There is however every opportunity to accept a reduced uplift if appropriate.

The Conditional Fee Agreements Regulations 2000 clearly

envisage this in the section dealing with the position if success fees are not assessed by the court:

Regulation 3(2) states: If the agreement relates to court proceedings, it must provide that where the percentage increase becomes payable as a result of those proceedings, then:

> "(c) (ii) if the legal representative agrees with any person liable as a result of the proceedings to pay fees subject to the percentage increase that a lower amount than the amount payable in accordance with the conditional fee agreement is to be paid instead, the amount payable under the conditional fee agreement in respect of those fees shall be reduced accordingly, unless the court is satisfied that the full amount should continue to be payable under it."

It is well accepted that "proceedings" includes "contemplated proceedings". In terms of recoverability of an after the event insurance premium this was considered in *Callery v Gray (No.1)* [2001] EWCA CIV 1117 and the Court of Appeal held that in the regulations "proceedings" included "contemplated proceedings". It must be the same for an uplift.

Why have this provision in the regulations if it was not envisaged that there would be the need to accept reduced uplifts in some cases? Note that it does not give the power to negotiate an increased uplift and override the agreement only to lower it. The success fee must therefore be calculated at it's justifiable maximum to allow for the potential to negotiate to take effect properly should it be appropriate to do so.

Finally, the *Callery* argument that success fees reflect the business risk is not altered by the comments in *Halloran*. If a firm demonstrates a business case with evidence for a higher than 5 per cent residual success fee where there is no risk assessment ot justify any case specific risks than the court can award that higher figure instead.

9

Control and Management of Risk

The explosion at Flixborough which we looked at in Chapter 8 **9.001**
on risk assessment showed the need for systems to control
risk generally. It also showed the need to control the extra
risks modifications including temporary ones can produce.
For modifications read alteration in the state of play. For
example a Part 36 payment or offer is a change in the state of
play in a case. No decision to continue with the case beyond
this point should be made until someone suitably qualified
and experienced has examined it systematically, looking for
unforeseen consequences and checking that it is not a figure
which must be accepted. This is just one simple example of
risk control and management in action.

All successful law firms have set up formal procedures for
the control of risk. Even so risk failures still occur because
there is no procedure, or it is not followed or it is followed in a
mechanical and unthinking way. Every fresh intake of
employees has to be trained in the control procedures and
why they are there, and old hands need to be reminded about
them from time to time. Instructions alone are not enough.
Checks and controls are essential.

An equally important lesson for us all from Flixborough is
the need for companies to employ people with the right
expertise. There have been two major recessions since 1974
and we have had the impact of the Woolf reforms. One result
is that staffing levels in a lot of law firms have been reduced
and, in addition, fewer real specialist lawyers are employed in
many firms. At a time when the risks of litigation are being
transferred to the lawyers themselves this could be a recipe

for disaster. In all too many firms experienced people are now looked upon as expenses to be eliminated rather than assets in which money has been invested. Even when the right people are available they may not be consulted. Making the best use of staff who should be a firms most important assets is a core element of risk control.

Flixborough started a debate on the extent to which governments should control hazardous industry. The United Kingdom approach is summed up in an article by D.V. Offord, a member of the Health and Safety Executive, entitled *"Can HSE prevent another Flixborough?"* He wrote, "On his own, the inspector is unlikely ever to be able to provide adequate safeguards or deterrents. He must and should rely heavily on industry, where the experience in a particular field is surely to be found. He must however learn the know-how necessary to identify and follow up weakness both in management and systems".

Transfer this to the management of your conditional fee based business. Ask yourself "Can we prevent a major disaster to the firm?" Remember that on his own, the fee earner is unlikely ever to be able to provide adequate safeguards or deterrents. He must and is entitled to rely on the firm as a whole, if a problem arises which poses a risk that needs to be addressed. He should know where the experience in any required field can be found. The fee earner should be taught the know-how necessary to identify problems and know what to do to follow them up by working with management and using their systems.

COMMON SENSE RULES FOR RUNNING A SUCCESSFUL CFA BUSINESS

9.002 Mix your funding base as far as you can. If a client has legal expenses insurance use it if possible. It's better to be paid less than not at all. Consider all the funding options in all cases. Not just to ensure success fee recovery but because you have a duty to the client and it makes good business sense. If a CFA is the right funding option and your client is happy with it use it, perhaps with other funding for the investigation stages.

Have a clear system in place for taking on CFA funded cases. Make sure that everyone understands and follows it. Allow no exceptions. From senior partner and junior paralegal, everyone should follow it. Unfortunately in some firms the more senior the fee earner the less willing they are to conform to standard practices. The need to set a good example is vital otherwise the system will not work as the less experienced will follow the lead of the more experienced. Ensure that you don't just have a paper system, have one that is used.

A risk assessment committee, in one form or another, is a vital element in the armoury of a successful firm. In smaller personal injury department, the risk assessment committee could include all the fee earners. Risk assessment meetings could then form part of regular departmental meetings. In bigger departments, ideally it should consist of two or three senior fee earners. If possible they should all have substantial experience in personal injury work. Some will inevitably have greater expertise than others and that asset should be made the most of. Sometimes it will be useful to bring in a fee earner to look at a particular case with the committee because of knowledge in a specialist area. An even number can produce problems. It is advisable to have a rule to reject rather than to accept cases unless there is a clear majority in favour. Odd numbers are best for obvious reasons. In most instances a committee of three will be large enough. Too many people can make the process more time consuming and that means it will not be cost effective. As long as a number of minds are applied to the case there should be a good chance that a clear and accurate assessment of the risk will be produced.

Multi-office firms can pose particular difficulties. There is no reason why there cannot be a system for sending the cases to a central committee. If counsel was being used they would be "sent out" and really this is no different. Some firms allow a fee earner to buddy up with another practitioner of their choice. That is a system that can lead to problems. There is no general standard being applied and it can be very difficult to monitor that sort of system and we do not recommend it.

However as an absolute minimum requirement no practitioner however experienced, should be allowed to take on a case without it being sanctioned following an appraisal by at least one other individual.

If you are a sole practitioner you should still try to have your assessments reviewed by someone else. Try linking up with another local practitioner in the same position as you. Work together for your mutual benefit. If you are the only personal injury practitioner in your firm and want to keep your assessments in house use an individual in another department with the closest experience you can find. As an alternative you could develop a relationship with a set of barristers' chambers or with one or more individual barristers. Many chambers now offer a risk assessment service, sometimes at no cost if a case is not recommended. Whatever option you choose will always be better than doing it yourself without the benefit of a second objective view of the case.

Difficult though it may be to accept, recognising that sometimes it is better to turn away cases rather that take them on is an essential element of managing your risks. Turn away cases that you are not experienced in dealing with. Complex areas require specialist lawyers. Don't dabble it's bad for you, the firm, the after the event insures and most of all your clients.

Risk assessment is ongoing. It is therefore essential to build in regular reviews of cases at set stages to ensure the risks of the case are still at an acceptable level. If not, you need to take action. Settle, abandon or (in a controlled way) get further information or evidence and review again. Always have a follow up organised and in the diary when a review has triggered obtaining further information or evidence. It is very easy at this stage to let a failing case struggle on. Biting the bullet to abandon or discontinue at the right time is essential. This can be a real problem area. All too often hope is allowed to stand in the place of reality for far too long.

Remember your duty to the insurer as well as your client. The insurer will expect you to occasionally loose or abandon some cases. However they will be very unhappy if they discover that your system is slack and allowed you to miss the right opportunity to terminate a case much earlier on when the adverse costs liabilities could have been contained. Slack systems mean bigger claims on the insurance policies and too many of those may risk your firm's insurability in the long term.

MAKING THE MOST OF YOUR ASSETS

A firm's best assets are its people. They need to be used wisely. You should try to fit the cases to the fee earners. Make sure the right cases go to the people with the appropriate experience. Ensure fee earners are up to the case. Keep their caseloads at a reasonable level so that you have a speedy turnover particularly of the smaller cases. This will help your cash-flow. Monitor the work to see that cases keep moving. If they are not moving fast enough make changes. You may need to reduce caseloads or re-allocate staff. You may need to re-allocate cases to others better equipped in terms of experience or with more capacity in terms of time. **9.003**

It should go without saying that you need to ensure that you keep up to date with the law and the rules. They develop and change all of the time. Don't take on a case on last year's law only to discover the change too late. Many risk assessments founder because of the simple failure to use knowledge that you have available but fail to get to the right people. Because of this, knowledge management to maximise the assets you have is vital.

KNOWLEDGE MANAGEMENT

Knowledge Management is the systematic process of finding, selecting, organising, distilling and presenting information in a way that improves people's understanding within a company in a specific area of interest. In industry knowledge management helps a firm to gain insight and understanding from its own experience and resources. Specific knowledge management activities should help focus the practice on acquiring, storing and utilising knowledge for such things as **9.003** problem solving, education, risk control, strategic planning and decision making. It also protects intellectual assets from being lost or under used. It provides increased flexibility. It makes you better at what you do.

Knowledge management is not really about managing knowledge in the true sense. We prefer terms such as knowledge-sharing, information systems, organised learning, intellectual asset management, all leading to better performance.

This is a good definition: "knowledge management is the practice of harnessing and exploiting intellectual capital to gain competitive advantage and client commitment through efficiency, innovation and faster and more effective decision-making."

How Does a Knowledge Management System Work?

9.005   Many firms do not "know what they know." This can often lead to duplication of effort throughout a practice. So to avoid this firms must ask themselves two important questions:

(1) What are our knowledge assets?

(2) How should we manage those assets to ensure a maximum return on them?

There are no right or wrong answers to these questions. Solutions will depend upon several factors such as the size of the firm, its culture and its needs. Nevertheless, effective management of knowledge focuses on solutions that encompass the entire practice: organisation, people and technology. Computers and communications systems are good at capturing, transforming and distributing highly structured knowledge that changes rapidly. Some companies in other areas are using analysis, planning and computer supported work systems to radically improve decision making, allocation of resources, management systems, access to information, to promulgate and process know-how and overall performance as a way to develop core strategic competencies.

Knowledge Management: Humbug!

Some people are put off by what they see as nothing more **9.006** than today's latest fad. Knowledge management is humbug they say. They are really missing a wonderful opportunity to increase profitability and give their clients an enhanced service. Knowledge as a concept, and knowledge management, are about being able to use data, information, knowledge, and your "wisdom". Knowledge Management is a means, not an end. Knowledge management is important, but it should simply be one of many co-operating means to an end, not the end in itself. The end is to simply enable you to work better. To enable you to control risks more effectively.

As much as 90 per cent, on some estimates, of the real value of intellectual capital is in the heads of you, your partners and staff. Their skills, experience, hard-won insight and intuition, and the trust they have invested and earned in relationships inside and outside of the practice. The right culture is needed to get the best out of everyone. If only the month's top fee earner gets a bonus, nobody is going to share their expertise and knowledge, no one is going to share what they learn.

To understand knowledge management you have to understand knowledge. Knowledge is not the same thing as information and information is not the same thing as data. Knowledge management involves the manipulation of all three. You often see a hierarchy that looks like this: data becomes information when it's organised; information becomes knowledge when it's placed in a usable or actionable context.

When you consider knowledge, it's important to distinguish between explicit and tacit knowledge. In the broadest terms, that is the difference between knowledge that can be written down and knowledge that cannot. Explicit knowledge can be processed by information systems; codified or recorded, archived and protected by the firm. Tacit knowledge exists in people's heads. Tacit knowledge is extremely difficult to transfer; explicit knowledge is much easier.

What's really important is to put it all into it's proper context. What are we trying to accomplish? CFA work means we have to have a strategy for the firm that recognises the basic risks inherent in this sort of funding. In other words "What's the objective?". The answer is to control the risks.

However managing knowledge well gives us much more than risk control. What about the competition? How do we gain a competitive edge? There is no point in offering to accept instructions unless you can answer the basic question, why us? There are very many firms who will offer to run the prospective client's case on a no win no fee basis. Even being the best is not enough, you need to get that message across. Being less than the best invites the prospective client to go elsewhere.

What about your performance? How do we deliver the results? If you manage your CFA based practice well there will be statistics that can prove it. However the best performance comes from the best management of your knowledge.

What about change? How do we cope with change? The world of personal injury law seems to be in almost continual change. Legal aid was a feather bed enabling complacency and second rate service to sometimes thrive and prosper. If you are good at what you do change is not your enemy it is your opportunity.

Of course as such, knowledge management, and everything else for that matter, is important only to the extent that it enhances your firm's ability and capacity to deal with, and develop in, the four dimensions, objective, competition, performance and change.

The Value of Knowledge Management

9.007 Knowledge is power! If you have it and use it gives you an edge and you win. If you have it and don't use it you may as well not have it al all. That is why you need to manage it and enable people to use it. In the first instance coping with information is knowledge management. Sometimes we feel totally swamped by information. The value of Knowledge Management relates directly to the effectiveness with which the managed knowledge enables the members of the organisation to deal with today's situations and effectively move things forward. Without on-demand access to managed knowledge, every situation is addressed based on what the individual or group brings to the situation with them. With on-demand access to managed knowledge, every situation is addressed with the sum total of everything anyone in the organisation has ever learned about a situation of a similar nature. Managing risk is about making the most of your "knowledge" as much as anything else.

Some Things You Can Do

Buy books & CD-ROMs and have a library with access to all **9.008** fee earners. Subscribe to legal journals and law reports and circulate them to all fee earners. See that they do circulate and don't simply pile up on the corner of someone's desk unread. See that the journals and law reports go back to the library and are kept there in a fashion that means your fee earners can find them when they need them when they need them.

Consider having your own intranet with your in firm with a data base of useful materials with full access to all fee earners. Provide shared data storage capacity giving the means to all fee earners to contribute to your intranet. Why ask someone to produce something that a colleague has already produced? It makes no sense at all.

Provide internet access with on everyone's desk or as a minimum with a library terminal open to all. If your fee earners cannot access the world wide web you have them working without the benefit of the best research tool that you could give to them.

Subscribe to at least one on line legal resource. Have daily updates delivered to the desk of every fee earner. Of course people don't read their emails. So create a digest and reduce the updates to the essentials and deliver a weekly bulletin to all of your fee earners desks. You will already be subscribing to journals law reports and you could include extracts of essentials materials from those in your digest.

Remember it is essential to provide training for all fee earners so that they can use the resources you put into place. It is almost as important as providing training in legal matters to keep people up to date. There is no point in running cases on the basis of the wrong legal assumptions old and outdated case law. Training should be seen as an essential, not a waste of fee earning time. Often the most difficult people to convince of this are the most senior and frequently they are the most in need of the training.

USING THE CPR

9.009 It is essential to cut down your risks at the earliest time you can. You need to ensure that you use the pre-action protocols to the full. They are designed for speed and efficiency. Use pre-action applications for disclosure or inspection to control the risk of litigating the wrong cases. Once proceedings are underway go for single issue trials. Split liability from quantum. Welcome trials on limitation don't avoid them. If the case is going to fail the message is stop the loss as soon as you can. If a case is going to fail the last place to be is in court at a full trial with all of the issues in dispute and all of the cost implications that go with it.

Delay rarely benefited claimants. Memories fade and risks increase. Parties should use the speed of the CPR to their advantage. Whichever party you act for you should use CPR Part 36 offers to protect your client and yourself and to produce early and realistic settlements. The earlier you do it the better and pro-actively not re-actively. Don't wait for your opponent to do it, do it first. CPR Part 36 focuses minds and leads to settlements yet claimants in particular still seem reluctant to use it perhaps fearing that to make an offer which is accepted will somehow mean that there was more that could have been recovered. If you know the offer is at the right level then there is nothing to fear by making it and everything to gain. It is an essential part of managing your risks.

DISCLOSURE AND THE INDEMNITY PRINCIPLE

There is much confusion about what has to be disclosed to **9.010**
your opponent when you are trying to recover your costs. In
particular people are confused about what entitlement if any
their opponent has to see their conditional fee agreement. This
has largely come about because of one particular case, *Dickinson v Rushmer*.[3] When it is considered it is also important to
look at the case of *South Coast Shipping v Havant BC*.[4] These
cases both concerned the extent to which a paying party is
entitled to see documents relied upon by the receiving party
as evidence that there is no breach of the indemnity principle.
They demonstrate a shift away from the "trust me, I'm a
solicitor" approach to the certificate on a bill of costs suggested by *Bailey v IBC Vehicles*[5] and instead seem to favour
considerations of natural justice. Even so both cases were in
fact decided on the basis of a restatement of pre-CPR and pre-
Human Rights Act decisions.

The first important point made by the *South Coast Shipping*
decision is that each decision will be based very much on the
facts of the case in question. It does not endorse a demand in
points of dispute for disclosure of all documents.

In *Dickinson* the defendant's appealed from a decision of
Deputy Costs Judge Jefferson on a preliminary issue that arose
in the course of a detailed assessment of the claimant's bills of
costs. The indemnity principle challenge to the claimant's bill
of over £88,000 was based on his inability to pay and the
possibility that the action was being maintained by a third
party. There was some evidence from the substantive proceedings to support both suggestions.

The point was taken at the detailed assessment and the
receiving party produced solicitor/client bills, a client care

---

[3] *John Dickinson (T/A John Dickinson Equipment Finance) v Duncan Rushmer
(T/A Fj Associates)*, Ch.D (Rimer J) 21/12/2001 IIR11/3/2002.
[4] *South Coast Shipping Co Ltd v Havant Borough Council*, Ch.D 21/12/2001
Pumfrey, J with Master O'Hare and Michael Seymour as Assessors.
[5] *Bailey v IBC Vehicles* [1998] 3 All E.R. 570.

letter and a calculation showing that the receiving party had paid about 40 per cent of the costs due under the bills to the costs judge but refused to produce them to the paying party on the ground of privilege.

The judge, having considered this evidence refused to order disclosure to the paying party holding that there was no breach of the indemnity principle. In reaching this decision he placed reliance on the solicitor's certificate on the bill in accordance with Bailey. The paying party appealed to Mr Justice Rimer, sitting with assessors.

In *South Coast Shipping*, there was an indemnity principle dispute in which the costs judge had given directions for the exchange of evidence, as a result of which he had before him a number of witness statements which were, of course, available to both parties. The judge was also shown material for which privilege was claimed and which he declined to order to be disclosed to the paying party.

In reliance upon the witness statements, the signature on the bills and the privileged documents the costs judge held that there was no indemnity principle issue which required further investigation. Again the paying party appealed.

In the *Dickinson* case, Mr Justice Rimer ruled on the classes of documents which were, in principle, privileged. He upheld a claim to privilege for solicitor and client bills, but rejected claims in relation to a client care letter and a calculation of the sums paid by the client on account of solicitor/client bills. However he said that a client care letter might, on the facts, be privileged but whether it was depended on the contents of the letter.

Rimer J. also held that in Dickinson there had been a breach of natural justice as the correct process had not been followed. The procedure adopted by the costs judge was unfair. An issue of fact had arisen on which the costs judge had to decide and he should have considered whether receiving evidence that the claimant was not willing to disclose to the defendant was consistent with one of the most basic rules of natural justice, namely the right of each party to know the other party's case and to comment on the other party's evidence in support of that case. Therefore, the unfair procedure necessarily resulted in an unfair disposal of the preliminary issue.

He ordered that the matter would have to be redetermined. Mr Justice Rimer allowed the appeal.

There was a waiver of privilege in South Coast Shipping, before Mr Justice Pumfrey, which had been declined by the receiving party below. He held that, once the costs judge decided to take account of the privileged material, the receiving party ought to have been put to its election, but that, ignoring the privileged material and considering only that available to both sides, no issue of breach of the indemnity principle arose. He held that the court had no power to override the privilege and only where it was necessary and proportionate should the receiving party be put to his election. Pumfrey J. rejected the appeal.

The analysis of the two judges on appeal was very similar. They can be summed up in three points. If a disputed issue of fact arises in the course of an assessment, the costs judge may direct production to him of a relevant document, or the receiving party may seek to rely upon a privileged document. It is not open to the costs judge to override the receiving party's privilege. However, he can allow that party to elect whether to rely upon the document or to seek to prove the fact by other means, such as the oral evidence of the solicitor in question. The decision whether to put the receiving party to its election is one for the costs judge, having regard to relevance and proportionality. However, where a document is of sufficient importance to be taken into account in determining the recoverability of costs, the receiving party must be put to this election. In other words they must be given the choice of waiving privilege if they wish to. If the receiving party seeks to prove the fact by other means, the paying party is not automatically entitled to see relevant documents in the possession of the receiving party if that party does not intend to rely upon them.

Giambrone v JMC Holidays Ltd[6] is a further case which considered the issues relevant to privilege. This was the claimants' appeal from a decision of Costs Judge Campbell on

---

[6] *Anita Giambrone & Ors v JMC Holidays Ltd* (Formerly T/A *Sunworld Holidays Ltd*) Q.B.D. (Nelson J) 22/3/2002 [2002] EWHC 495 (QB).

October 26, 2001 giving judgment on issues of principles regarding the detailed assessment of the claimant's costs. The litigation arose out of an incidence of food poisoning that afflicted 652 people staying at a hotel in Majorca on a holiday provided by the defendant tour operator. Four parts of the cost judge's decision were under appeal including an order that a partner of the claimants' firm of solicitors serve a witness statement on the defendant, exhibiting relevant documents showing whether the indemnity principle had been complied with.

Nelson J. held that Costs Judge Campbell was wrong in failing to follow Practice Direction 40.14. He should have directed the claimants to produce the witness statement together with relevant documents to him alone, after which he could decide whether to allow the claimants to elect to disclose the documents and rely on their contents or to decline disclosures and rely on witness statements alone.

The message seems finally to be getting through. In the Taunton County Court on September 11, 2001 in *Pratt v Bull* HH Judge Cotterill held that in challenging the validity of a conditional fee agreement, the defendant had to do more than merely assert points in dispute as to compliance. The claimant's solicitor's refusal to disclose the CFA did not raise a valid concern as it was a privileged document which was not required to be provided to the defendant under the Civil Procedure Rules 1998 (SI 1998/3132). The claimant's solicitor, by refusing disclosure of the CFA was showing good risk management. As we hope this book shows risk management has many elements. All need to be utilised not just one or two.

ESSENTIAL MATERIALS AND USEFUL PRECEDENTS

Funding Arrangements – Guide to Provisions*

The Law Society have produced a very useful and easy-to-follow **A1.001** guide to the provisions on funding arrangements. The provisions included in the guide were selected in order to provide an introduction to the most important aspects of the new legislative framework. The guide is not complete as there are other more minor provisions within the CPR that may also need to be considered. It should also be borne in mind that the general provisions with regards to costs within the CPR are of relevance to the operation of funding arrangements. For instance, the actual amount of money secured by the percentage increase within a CFA will be reduced if the base costs are assessed down by the Court whatever happens to the success fee.

The Law Society is keen to ensure that it is remembered that each of the provisions in relation to funding arrangements set out in the guide should not be seen in isolation. For instance, some provisions seem to indicate that a "no hindsight" rule applies, but others allow for hindsight to enter the arena. It might be dangerous to look solely at what needs to be written into a CFA and explained to the client at the time it was entered into, without also considering what evidence might need to be adduced at the costs assessment stage, for instance a memorandum setting out the circumstances that existed at that time

---

* Reproduced with the permission of the Law Society.

upon which the percentage increase was set or why a particular form of funding was preferred over another.

The Law Society recommends a thorough read of the provisions referred to in the guide and we echo that advice. They can all be found on the Lord Chancellor's website at http://www.open.gov.uk if you do not have a printed version readily available.

Conditional Fees–Funding Arrangements: Guide to Provisions

A1.002

	Conditional Fee Agreements	After the event LEI	Membership Organisations
Access to Justice Act 1999	S27	S29	S30
Conditional Fee Agreement Regulations 2000:-	Reg 1—Definitions Reg 2—Contents (and Reg 3—if success fee) Reg 4—Information to client.	N/A	N/A
Civil Procedure Rules:			
a) **Definitions**—"funding arrangements"; "additional liability"	CPR 43.2 PD S2. Also definition of "percentage increase"	CPR 43.2 PD S2. Also definition of "insurance premium"	CPR 43.2 PD S2. Also definition of "membership organisation"
b) **Limits on Recovery**—failure to provide information required by CPR, PD or Court order	CPR 44.3B PD S10. Also delay in payment element of success fee.	CPR 44.3B PD S10.	CPR 44.3B PD S10. Also notional cost of policy to cover other parties costs.
c) **Factors for deciding amount of costs**–Link	CPR 44.5 PD S11. Reasonableness of percentage increase	CPR 44.5 PD S11. Reasonableness of cost of premium	CPR 44.5 PD S11. Limited to the likely cost of a policy to cover

	Conditional Fee Agreements	After the event LEI	Membership Organisations
between "pro-portionality" and "additional liabilities"; the no-hind-sight rule. (The PD contains most of the information on funding arrangements, the CPR being relevant more to costs generally).	(11.8);	(11.10)	liability to other parties (11.11) (therefore PD 11.10 relevant as well)
d) **Costs-only proceedings**– where case set-tles before issue, parties agree who pays and application is not opposed. **Query**: are additional liabil-ities recoverable if proceedings not issued; no hindsight rule eroded. (see PD 17.8 (2)). **NB** other than this procedure, assessment usually done at detailed rather than summary assessment.	CPR 44.12A PD 17	CPR 44.12A PD 17	CPR 44.12A PD 17
e) **Providing information about funding arrangements**– notice of arrangement (but not amount or how calcu-	CPR 44.15 PD S19, especially, 19.4 (1) and (2)	CPR 44.15 PD 19, especially, 19.4 (1) and (3)	CPR 44.15 PD 19, especially, 19.4 (1) and (4)

	Conditional Fee Agreements	After the event LEI	Membership Organisations
lated) and any amendments to Court and parties **only** if an additional liability is claimed. Sets out time-limits, form, content etc			
f) **Adjournment to challenge disallowance of percentage increase**–procedure where percentage increase reduced to allow for client (and counsel) to attend if solicitor wishes to apply for balance against client. **NB. Reg 3 (2) (b) CFA Regs prevents this without an order.**	CPR 44.16 PD 20	N/A	N/A
g) **Solicitor and own client assessment in CFA cases**– allows for assessment of **pre-**April 2000 CFAs.	CPR 48.9 PD 55	N/A	N/A

Draft Letter Re: Legal Expenses Insurance

Thank you for instructing me in relation to your potential claim for **A1.003** damages for personal injury following your recent accident.

At this important stage, I need to advise you on methods that may be open to you that could be used to pay any bills for the legal work that could be involved in your case. This is what we call funding.

There are potentially a number of different funding methods that might be satisfactory. I want to make sure that however we fund your case we choose the best possible option for you. Initially I shall be grateful if you will please either bring or send to me at the office any of the following:

- Household Contents insurance documents

- Household Buildings insurance documents

- Motor insurance documents

- Any other insurance policy documents which you or other members of your household have which may include any legal expenses insurance cover. (This may include credit cards.)

If you think you may be entitled to cover under someone else's insurance on any policy please ask them for a copy of their policy document and for their permission for you to use any legal expenses insurance option which covers you.

[As you were injured as a passenger in a car you will need to ask the driver of the car that you were in at the time of the accident for a copy of their motor insurance policy and for their permission to use any legal expenses insurance option which may cover you.]

I need to examine the legal expenses aspects of any insurance policy to find out whether it will cover you in relation to your potential claim. I also want to make sure that if it does, it will provide you with adequate financial protection in respect of any potential legal bills that could arise in your case.

I propose to work for you on a "no win no fee" basis if that is the best choice for you. However, we need to look at legal expenses insurance options first before we can discuss that alternative.

If there are any queries at all please do not hesitate to contact me.

Law Society Conditional Fees–Checklist for use with Model Conditional Fee Agreement *

A1.004 If you think that a Conditional Fee Agreement is clearly the correct way forward in any particular case you may wish to consider using the Law Society Conditional Fees Checklist for use with Model Conditional Fee Agreement. It contains a non-exhaustive list of issues which should be considered *before* signing the conditional fee agreement. It may be a very useful document to use as a starting point for preparation of your own checklist.

THE LAW SOCIETY CONDITIONAL FEES–CHECKLIST FOR USE WITH MODEL CONDITIONAL FEE AGREEMENT

A1.005 The following is a non-exhaustive list of issues which should be considered *before* signing the conditional fee agreement.

HAVE YOU.........

1. TAKEN into account the overriding objective and proportionality in considering the potential net benefit of the case to your client?

2. CONSIDERED whether the case could be allocated to the Small Claims Track and the costs implications if that occurred.

3. CHECKED that you have the correct model agreement for this type of case?

4. UNDERTAKEN a thorough risk assessment.

5. APPLIED your risk assessment to your success fee, taking account of:

   - the prospects of success/failure
   - payments on account/financial subsidy
   - the risk that losing cases often have higher costs than winning ones and when setting your success fee,

* Reproduced with the permission of the Law Society.

- considered the element of the success fee relating to financial subsidy separately.
- recorded your reasons in writing and provided a copy to your client.

6. CONSIDERED the possibility of achieving success on liability but failure on enforceability?

7. DISCUSSED with your client whether a barrister will be used? If so, have you discussed:

- whether the barrister will be instructed on a conditional fee agreement?
- whether the conditional fee agreement with the barrister will be on the same terms as the conditional fee agreement with the client e.g. success fee.

8. EXPLAINED to your client the information required by the Conditional Fee Regulations:

- the circumstances which will make them liable to pay your costs or disbursements and discussed how the client will fund these amounts;
- when they can seek assessment of your costs and the procedure for doing so;
- the circumstances which will make them liable to pay the costs of any other party;
- whether their risk of becoming liable for costs is insured under an existing contract of insurance;
- other methods of financing costs;
- whether you believe a particular contract of insurance is appropriate (this should be confirmed in writing);
- the requirement of their consent to disclose to the court or opponent at the end of the case the reasons for setting the success fee.

9. CHECKED whether your client's proposed insurance will meet the other side's costs, if a Part 36 offer or payment is not beaten?

10. THOUGHT through the different clauses which can be used regarding Part 36 offers and payments? (There are two possible options if ALP insurance is used. Other insurers may have different approaches. Check the requirements of your AEI—they may specify the approach you must take.)

11. EXPLAINED to your client the information on costs required

by the Solicitors' Costs Information and Client Care Code 1999?

Remember the Code imposes a duty on you to:-

- give to your client the best costs information possible—paragraphs 4 (a) and (c);
- keep your client updated about costs as the matter progresses–paragraph 6.

12. EXPLAINED to your client that the agreement prevents the client from instructing you to accept an offer to settle which does not provide for your full success fee.

13. MADE SURE the agreement:

- specifies the proceedings to which it relates;
- will be signed by you and your client;
- specifies the reasons for setting the success fee, and specifies how much of the success fee, if any, relates to the cost of financial subsidy;

deals with appropriate funding methods and the insurance position.

Funding Options Checklist

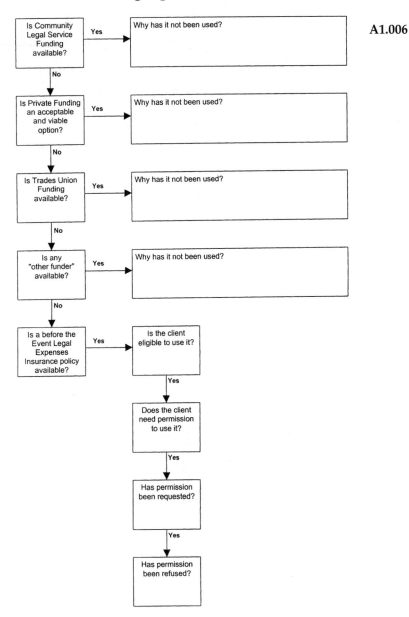

A1.006

Before The Event Legal Expenses Insurance Checklist

A1.007

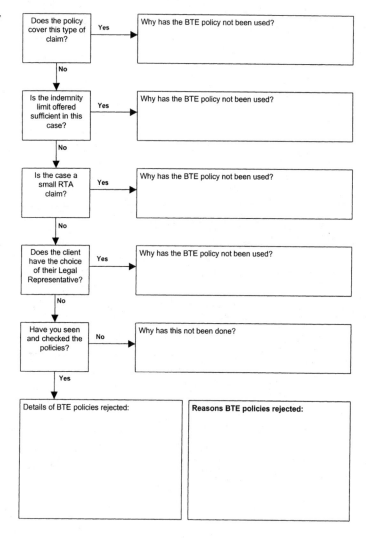

Model Collective Conditional Fee Agreement

This Agreement is made on [   ] between the [   ] **A1.008**
the United Kingdom of [   ] (the) and [solicitors of] ("the
solicitors")

Definitions

1. In this agreement the following terms have the following   **A1.009**
    meaning:

    (a) "Member": means a member of the
    (b) "Claim": means a claim made by a Member covered by
         this agreement whether or not proceedings are issued.
    (c) "Counterclaim": means a claim made by a Member's
         opponent against the member within the same proceed-
         ings.
    (d) "Appeal": means an appeal against the determination of
         a claim or counterclaim which has been conducted by the
         solicitors under the terms of this agreement, whether
         such appeal be made by the Member or his/her oppo-
         nent; this definition does not apply in the definitions of
         "interim dispute" or "finally entitled".
    (e) "Interim dispute": means a dispute or matter arising in
         the course of a claim other than the claim itself; examples
         are an application, an amendment, a directions hearing,
         an interim appeal or an enforcement procedure (this is
         not an exhaustive list).
    (f) "Win": a Member wins:

         (i)   a claim if s/he becomes finally entitled (whether by
               agreement, judgement or otherwise) to be paid by or
               on behalf of his/her opponent:

               (1) any damages (including provisional damages),
                    and/or
               (2) all or part of the costs of the claim:

         (ii) an interim dispute if s/he becomes finally entitled to
               be paid by his/her opponent all or part of the costs of
               the interim dispute.

         For the avoidance of doubt a Member is treated as enti-
         tled to be paid damages even if all such damages are paid
         to the Secretary of State under the Social Security

185

(Recovery of Benefits) Act 1997 or any statutory modification or replacement thereof.

(g) "Finally entitled": means that the Member's opponent is
not allowed to appeal against the entitlement, has not
appealed it in time or has lost an appeal; in the event that
any such appeal is allowed to proceed out of time and is
successful, then the entitlement of the solicitors will be
that which would have been obtained if the decision
appealed against had been the decision as varied by the
appeal court, and the solicitors shall immediately repay
any money which they have received to which they are
not entitled.

(h) "Lose": a Member loses if s/he does not win.

(i) "the Costs provision": means the additional amount in
respect of provision within the meaning of section 30 of
the Access to Justice Act 1999 made by or on behalf of the
[   ] to meet liabilities which a Member may
incur to pay the costs of other parties to proceedings.

(j) "Legal assistance": means the indemnity against legal
costs granted by the [   ] to a Member.

2. The solicitors charges payable under this agreement include:

(a) "basic charges", i.e. charges for work done by the solicitors, calculated on the basis of the higher of:

(i) the hourly rates allowable for the work in the court in
which the claim in question is conducted or would be
conducted if proceedings were to be issued and

(ii) the hourly rates allowable for equivalent work in the
solicitors local court;

(b) "success fee", i.e. the percentage increase applicable to
the basic charges in each case;

(c) "disbursements", i.e. expenses which the solicitors incur
on the Member's behalf in the course of a claim, such as
court fees, fees for experts, barristers' fees (including
success fees for barristers where appropriate), copying
charges made by others, travelling and hotel expenses
(this is not an exhaustive list);

(d) "VAT", Value Added Tax which is charged where
applicable at the applicable rate;

and, except where otherwise stated, references in this agreement to "the solicitors' charges" are references to the total of basic charges, success fee, disbursements and VAT.

Parties covered by the agreement

3. This agreement is made by the [   ] on its own behalf **A1.010** and on behalf of the Members for the time being with the intent that all Members whose claims are covered by the agreement are bound by the terms hereof.

4. All references to liability of the [   ] are to be taken as including the liability of the Member to the solicitors in respect of legal costs and the liability of the to identify the Member against such costs.

Coverage of the agreement

5. The agreement applies to: **A1.011**

    (a) all claims of Members referred by the [   ] to the solicitors for or including damages for personal injuries arising from or in the course of the Member's employ-ment or from an event or events occurring while the Member is travelling between home and work provided that such claim is or was brought at first instance by proceedings in a county court or in a civil division of the high court or would be so brought were proceedings to be issued unless:

        (i) it is agreed between the solicitors and the [   ] that this agreement should not apply to any such claim; or

        (ii) the solicitors decide that the correct venue for a Members claim is the Employment Tribunal in which case the solicitors should notify the [   ] thereof and the [   ] shall decide whether to provide further legal assistance to the member in his/her claim through its in-house lawyers or to make a separate agreement with the solicitors in relation to such claim;

    (b) appeals against the determination of any clause 5(a) claim, subject to the provisions of clause 27 of this agreement;

    (c) such further claims and/or counterclaims as may be agreed by the solicitors and the [   ] to be included: where such agreement is reached in relation to a counterclaim the subsequent provisions of this agreement shall apply reading "claim" as "counterclaim" and references to prosecuting the claim as defending the counterclaim;

(e) for the avoidance of doubt:

(i) a claim or appeal is treated as falling within this clause notwithstanding that it is resolved by mediation or some other form of alternative dispute resolution;

(ii) clause 5(a) does not include counterclaims and nothing in this agreement requires the solicitors to act for a Member in defending a counterclaim or the [   ] to indemnify a Member against any liability for the costs of a counterclaim unless the solicitors and the [   ] specifically so agree;

(iii) a claim includes proceedings to enforce any judgement or order.

6. The agreement applies to work done within clause 5:

(a) in all cases where the solicitors receive instructions after [date of arrangement], and

(i) after [date of arrangement] in such cases which are on-going at that date as shall be notified by the solicitors to the

Success

A1.012
7. If the Member wins a claim or interim dispute the [   ] is liable to pay the solicitors' charges for that claim or interim dispute. However in the case of an interim dispute the RCN's liability to pay is postponed until the conclusion of the proceedings unless the court orders that the party costs should be summarily assessed or subject to detailed assessment before the conclusion of the case.

8. If, in relation to a claim or interim dispute the Member is only entitled to be paid by his/her opponent:

(a) a stated proportion or element of his/her costs, or

(b) costs for a particular period, or

(c) costs relating to particular steps taken in the proceedings, or

(d) costs relating only to a distinct part of the proceedings, or

(e) costs relating to a particular issue, or

(f) costs excluding any costs described in clauses 8(a) to (e), or

(g) costs on the standard basis, or

(h) fixed costs

then the [   ] liability to pay the solicitors' charges is correspondingly reduced.

9. The solicitors are entitled to keep any interest on any of the solicitors' charges recovered from a Member's opponent.

10. If the Member wins a claim or interim dispute the solicitors will use their best endeavours to recover the costs provision from the Member's opponent and, if they are successful in doing so, will immediately pay the [   ] the amount so recovered together with any interest thereon recovered from the Member's opponent.

Success fees

11. The success fee will be 100% or such lesser percentage as is determined in accordance with this part of this agreement. **A1.013**

12. When accepting instructions[1] in relation to any specific proceedings the solicitors must prepare and retain a written statement containing:

(a) their assessment of the probability of the circumstances arising in which the success fee will become payable in relation to those proceedings ("the risk assessment");

(b) their assessment of the amount of the success fee in relation to those proceedings, having regard to the risk assessment; and

---

[1] "This requires a risk assessment on acceptance of instructions which will often, as discussed in con, be before a considered risk assessment can be carried out. I believe the decision in con was that this was all right because it tended to point to a higher success fee and the only downside was not recovering the full success fee on the risk assessment. It may be necessary to review this provision as it operates in practice. I can see a defendant's argument that so cavalier an assessment should result in a very low success fee— there is no logic in it but it might appeal to some insurance-minded DJs or judges. If that happens much then it will be necessary to introduce a review period not initially covered by the CCFA but retrospectively covered as soon as a sensible risk assessment has been carried out; alternatively a pre-CCFA CCFA with a separate risk assessment. The complications of that process speak for themselves.

(c) the reasons, by reference to the risk assessment, for setting the success fee at that level.

13. The [   ] and the Member agree that if any of the solicitors' charges which include a success fee are assessed by the court the solicitors may comply with any requirement of the court for disclosure of the written note of the success fees by the solicitors or the Member to the court or any other person

14. If any of the solicitors' charges which include a success fee are assessed by the court and any amount of the success fee is disallowed on the assessment on the ground that the level at which the increase was set was unreasonable in view of the facts which were or should have been known to the solicitors at the time it was set, that amount ceases to be payable under the agreement unless the court is satisfied that it should continue to be so payable.

15. If, in any situation other than that covered by clause 14, the solicitors agree with any person liable as a result of proceedings to pay fees subject to a success fee that a lower amount than the amount payable in accordance with this agreement to be paid, the amount payable under this agreement shall be reduced accordingly, unless the court is satisfied that the full amount should continue to be payable.

16. If a barrister is instructed on a case under a conditional fee agreement between the barrister and the solicitors, the barrister's fee may include a success fee which may not be the same as the success fee applicable to the work done by or on behalf or the solicitors.

Losing

A1.014

17. If the Member loses a claim or interim dispute the [   ] is not liable to pay any of the solicitors' charges for work done on that claim or interim dispute.

18. As examples for the avoidance of doubt:

(a) if the Member loses a claim but wins an interim dispute, the [   ] is liable to pay any of the solicitors' charges for the interim dispute;

(b) if the Member wins a claim but loses an interim dispute, the [   ] is not liable to pay the solicitors' charge for the interim dispute.

Action to be taken upon referral of claim

19. Upon receipt of instructions in relation to any specific claim **A1.015**
the solicitors shall consider the information with which they
have been provided and determine whether to accept
instructions under this agreement.

20. The solicitors may refuse to accept instruction under clause
5(a) of this agreement in relation to any specific claim if in
their professional judgment they consider that:

    (a) the chances of success in the claim are less than 50%
    (b) in view of the damages likely to be recovered any pro-
        ceedings would be likely to be allocated to the small
        claims track;
    (c) the risk in terms of costs does not justify the benefit likely
        to be achieved;
    (d) the claim will require unusually high investigative costs;
    (e) the claim is likely to be one of a number of similar claims
        for which special group litigation arrangements will need
        to be made, or
    (f) the claim falls outside the scope of clause 5(a) of this
        agreement

21. If the solicitors refuse to accept instructions under clause 5(a)
of this agreement they shall notify the [   ] in writing
as soon as possible:

    (a) of their decision, giving brief reasons, and
    (b) whether they would be prepared to accept instructions
        under clause 5(c) of this agreement or under a separate
        agreement.

22. If the [   ] decides to proceed with the specific claim
under clause 5(c) of this agreement, it shall notify the solicitors
in writing of that decision and in such a case the solicitors
shall be deemed to have accepted instructions under this
agreement from receipt of such notification from the
[   ].

Duties of the solicitor to advise

23. When accepting instructions in relation to any specific pro- **A1.016**
ceedings the solicitors must inform the Member as to the
circumstances in which the Member may be liable to pay the
solicitors' charges and, if the Member requires any further

explanation, advice or other information about that matter, the solicitors must provide such further explanation, advice or other information as the Member may reasonably require.

24. After accepting instructions in relation to any specific proceedings the solicitors must confirm their acceptance of instructions by writing a letter to the Member including all the information in the client care letter annexed to this agreement.

25. The solicitors shall:

   (a) send the [   ] a copy of the risk assessment as soon as it has been completed; and

   (b) report to the [   ] in writing as soon as is reasonably practicable:

      (i) any development (including but not limited to the discovery of any evidence, the expression of views by Counsel or an expert witness, a change of view by the solicitors, non co-operation, lying, misleading or failure to attend an appointment of any sort by the Member or an important witness) which substantially affects the risk assessment;

      (ii) their decision whether or not to continue the claim upon receipt of a reply from the Members opponent to the pre-action protocol letter or letter of claim;

      (iii) on receipt of an offer or payment, whether under CPR Part 36 or otherwise, affecting the [   ] potential liability for the opponent's costs;

      (iv) annually thereafter, on the anniversary of the receipt by the solicitors of instructions in the matter, with details of the state and progress of the proceedings;

      (v) the outcome of the claim by way of a short summary of the issues decided at trial or affecting the terms of settlement, the general and special damages claimed and/or recovered and the costs (including success fees) incurred and/or recovered.

      (vi) with notes of any judgement following trial.

   (c) At the same time as any of (b)(i) to (iv) above, advise the [   ] in writing of their view as to whether it is reasonable to continue to prosecute the claim or prosecute or defend the appeal, giving brief reasons taking into account not only the prospect of success but also whether the risk in terms of costs justifies the benefit likely to be achieved.

Appeals

26. This agreement applies to appeal with the following modifications: **A1.017**

    (a) In clauses 1(f), 7, 8, 10, 17 and 18 substitute "appeal" for "claim".

    (b) Clauses 19 to 22 shall not apply.

    (c) Upon receipt of instructions from a Member to make an appeal and on receipt of an appellant's notice from a Member's opponent the solicitors shall decide whether to accept instructions under this agreement in relation to such appeal.

    (d) The solicitors may refuse to accept instructions in relation o such appeal under this agreement if in their professional judgement they consider that:

        (i) the chances of success in the appeal are less than 50% or

        (ii) the risk in terms of costs does not justify the benefit likely to be achieved

    (e) If the solicitors refuse to accept instructions in relation to such appeal under this agreement they shall notify the [   ] in writing as soon as possible:

        (i) of their decision, giving brief reasons, and

        (ii) whether they would be prepared to accept instructions under a separate agreement.

    (f) In accepting instructions for an appeal under this agreement the solicitors must carry out a fresh risk assessment and paragraphs 12 to 16 shall apply in relation to the fresh risk assessment.

    (g) An appeal constitutes fresh "proceedings" for the purposes of clauses 23 and 24[2]

    (h) Clause 25 applies with the exclusion of sub-clause (b)(ii)

---

[2] This may be over-cautious, but in my view over-caution has to be the order of the day when the penalty for non-compliance with the Act is that the Agreement is unlawful, and no costs will be recoverable in any case under the agreement.

Early termination of retainers

A1.018
27. Each separate case taken on by the solicitors under this agreement constitutes a separate retainer subject to the terms of this agreement.

28. The [   ] is entitled in its absolute discretion to withdraw legal assistance from a Member or to transfer legal assistance in any particular case to another firm of solicitors.

29. The solicitors are entitled to terminate a retainer if:

   (a) the [   ] withdraws legal assistance from the Member or transfers legal assistance to another firm of solicitors;
   (b) the Member fails to give the solicitors instructions that allow them to do their work properly;
   (c) the Member requires the solicitor to work in an improper or unreasonable way
   (d) the Member deliberately misleads any of the solicitor's staff or any barrister or expert witness instructed by them;
   (e) the Member fails to co-operate with the solicitor's reasonable requirements;
   (f) the member fails to attend any appointment for a medical or expert examination conference with a barrister or court hearing;
   (g) the Member rejects the solicitors' reasonable recommendation to make or accept an offer or payment;
   (h) the Member rejects the solicitors' reasonable advice;
   (i) there has been a fundamental breakdown in the relationship between the solicitors and the Member.

30. A Member is entitled to terminate a retainer at any time.

31. A retainer terminates on the death of a Member; however, subject to sanction by the Council, the personal representatives of the deceased Member are entitled to instruct the solicitors to continue to act under the terms of this agreement and, if they do so, the retainer is treated as having continued despite the death of the Member and for these purposes the personal representatives shall have all the rights and obligations of a Member under this agreement.

32. Subject to clause 33, 34 and 35, if a retainer is terminated under clause 28, 29 or 30 the question of the [   ]

liability for payment of the solicitors' charges is deferred until the conclusion of the proceedings and then determined in accordance with clauses 7 to 18 of this agreement.

33. The [   ] is not liable to pay the solicitors' charges where:

   (a) The [   ] withdraws legal assistance from a Member following advice from the solicitors that the claim no longer has a reasonable chance of success or that it would be unreasonable to pursue the claim, or
   (b) The solicitors terminates the retainer because the Member has rejected their advice to withdraw or discontinue the claim.[3]

34. Any of the solicitors' charges which have become payable do not cease to be payable as a result of clause 32.

35. If, within 3 months of termination of a retainer the Member takes no steps to prosecute the claim, the [   ] shall, subject to clause 33, be liable to pay the solicitors charges (excluding any success fee).[4]

Variations

36. The terms of this agreement may be varied by agreement in writing signed by the [   ] and the solicitors and for the avoidance of any doubt any such variation may be retrospective to the date of this agreement.

A1.019

---

[3] This is not entirely satisfactory from the [   ] point of view. The aim is that the solicitors should not be paid in "lost" cases. There is no problem if the solicitors simply advise the client to drop the claim. However, that is relatively rare. More often one would go to the other side and try to get a "commercial" settlement. If that approach is successful then the [   ] remains liable in full for the costs, even if the settlement is far less than envisaged. The only way in my view to overcome this is to make the agreement even more complicated by trying to fix a lower limit of damages in each case and providing that if a client refused to accept a settlement at or below that lower limit the case should count as a failure. This would complicate risk assessment considerably and probably be unworkable in practice. However, I think the [   ] should be aware of the position.

[4] The problem here is proving it. However, normally the other side would be willing to say whether they had heard from the Member or new solicitors and in issued cases a Notice of Change would be served.

Termination

A1.020   37. Either the [   ] or the solicitors may terminate this agreement on six months' notice in writing to the other.

38. On such termination, subject to clause 28, all retainers in cases for Members which are still current will continue but no new retainers will be created under this agreement.

Severance

A1.021   39. If any provision of this agreement is held by a competent court to be invalid, illegal or unenforceable in whole or in part for whatever reason, then for the purpose of this proceedings in which such finding was made it shall be deemed to be severed from this agreement to the extent only of such invalidity, illegality or unenforceability and the remaining provisions of this agreement and the remainder of the provision in question shall continue in full force and effect unimpaired by such severance.

Signed: _____ (for the client)

Print Name:_____

Signed: _____ (for the solicitors)

Print Name:_____

Law Society Model Conditional Fee Agreement *

CONDITIONAL FEES—CONDITIONAL FEES AGREEMENT FOR USE
IN PERSONAL INJURY CASES

(Non-Clinical Negligence) June 2000   **A1.022**

Conditional fee agreement

For use in personal injury cases, but not clinical negligence.   **A1.023**
This agreement is a binding legal contract between you and your
solicitor/s. Before you sign, please read everything carefully.
Words like "our disbursements", "basic charges", "win" and
"lose" are explained in condition 3 of the Law Society Conditions
which you should also read carefully.

Agreement date
[....]

I/We, the solicitor/s
[....]

You, the client
[....]

What is covered by this agreement

- Your claim against [..........] for damages for personal injury
  suffered on [......................................].

- Any appeal by your opponent.

- Any appeal you make against an interim order during the
  proceedings.

- Any proceedings you take to enforce a judgment, order or
  agreement.

---

* Reproduced with the permission of the Law Society.

What is not covered by this agreement

- Any counterclaim against you.

- Any appeal you make against the final judgment order.

Paying us

If you win your claim, you pay our basic charges, our disbursements and a success fee. The amount of these is not based on or limited by the damages. You are entitled to seek recovery from your opponent of part or all of our basic charges, our disbursements, a success fee and insurance premium. Please also see conditions 4 and 6.

It may be that your opponent makes a Part 36 offer or payment which you reject and, on our advice, your claim for damages goes ahead to trial where you recover damages that are less than that offer or payment. We will not add our success fee to the basic charges for the work done after we received notice of the offer or payment.

If you receive interim damages, we may require you to pay our disbursements at that point and a reasonable amount for our future disbursements.

If you receive provisional damages, we are entitled to payment of our basic charges our disbursements and success fee at that point.

If you win but on the way lose an interim hearing, you may be required to pay your opponent's charges of that hearing. Please see conditions 3(h) and 5.

If on the way to winning or losing you win an interim hearing, then we are entitled to payment of our basic charges and disbursements related to that hearing together with a success fee on those charges if you win overall.

If you lose, you pay your opponent's charges and disbursements. You may be able to take out an insurance policy against this risk. Please also see conditions 3(j) and 5. If you lose, you do not pay our charges but we may require you to pay our disbursements.

If you end this agreement before you win or lose, you pay our basic charges. If you go on to win, you pay a success fee. Please also see condition 7(a).

We may end this agreement before you win or lose. Please also see condition 7(b) for details.

Basic charges

These are for work done from now until this agreement ends.

How we calculate our basic charges

These are calculated for each hour engaged on your matter [from now until the review date on [...]...]. Routine letters and telephone calls will be charged as units of one tenth of an hour. Other letters and telephone calls will be charged on a time basis. The hourly rates are:

- Solicitors with over four years' experience after qualification
  £ [...]

- Other solicitors and legal executives and other staff of equivalent experience
  £ [...]

- Trainee solicitors and other staff of equivalent experience
  £ [...]

[We will review the hourly rate on the review date and on each anniversary of the review date. We will not increase the rate by more than the rise in the Retail Prices Index and will notify you of the increased rate in writing.]

Success fee

This is [...]% of our basic charges
The reasons for calculating the success fee at this level are set out in Schedule 1 to this agreement.
You cannot recover from your opponent the part of the success fee that relates to the cost to us of postponing receipt of our charges and disbursements (as set out at paragraphs (a) and (b) at Schedule 1). This part of the success fee remains payable by you.

Value added tax (VAT)

We add VAT, at the rate (now [...]%) that applies when the work is done, to the total of the basic charges and success fee.

Law society conditions

The Law Society Conditions are attached because they are part of this agreement. Any amendments or additions to them will apply to you. You should read the conditions carefully and ask us about anything you find unclear.

Other points

Immediately before you signed this agreement, we verbally explained to you the effect of this agreement and in particular the following:

(a) the circumstances in which you may be liable to pay our disbursements and charges;

(b) the circumstances in which you may seek assessment of our charges and disbursements and the procedure for doing so;

(c) whether we consider that your risk of becoming liable for any costs in these proceedings is insured under an existing contract of insurance;

(d) other methods of financing those costs, including private funding, Community Legal Service funding, legal expenses insurance, trade union funding;

(e) (i) In all the circumstances, on the information currently available to us, we believe that a contract of insurance with [...] is appropriate. Detailed reasons for this are set out in Schedule 2.

(e) (ii) In any event, we believe it is desirable for you to insure your opponent's charges and disbursements in case you lose.

(e) (iii) We confirm that we do not have an interest in recommending this particular insurance agreement.

Signatures

Signed for the solicitor/s

Signed by the client

I confirm that my solicitor has verbally explained to me the matters in paragraphs (a) to (e) under "Other points" above.

Signed...(Client)

I specifically confirm that I verbally explained to the client the matters in paragraphs (a) to (e) under "Other points" and confirm the matters at (e) in writing in Schedule 2.

Signed..(Solicitors)

This agreement complies with the Conditional Fee Agreements Regulations 2000 (SI 2000/692).

SCHEDULE 1

The success fee

The success fee is set at [...]% of basic charges and cannot be more   **A1.024**
than 100% of the basic charges.
    The percentage reflects the following:

- (a) the fact that if you win we will not be paid our basic charges until the end of the claim;

- (b) our arrangements with you about paying disbursements;

- (c) the fact that if you lose, we will not earn anything;

- (d) our assessment of the risks of your case. These include the following:

- (e) any other appropriate matters.

The matters set out at paragraphs (a) and (b) above together make up [...]% of the increase on basic charges. The matters at paragraphs (c), (d) [and (e)] make up [...]% of the increase on basic charges. So the total success fee is [...]% as stated above.

SCHEDULE 2

The insurance policy

In all the circumstances and on the information currently available to   **A1.025**
us, we believe, that a contract of insurance with [...] is appropriate to
cover your opponent's charges and disbursements in case you lose.
    This is because

We are not, however, insurance brokers and cannot give advice on all products which may be available.

Law Society Conditions

1. Our responsibilities

A1.026   We must:

- always act in your best interests, subject to our duty to the court;
- explain to you the risks and benefits of taking legal action;
- give you our best advice about whether to accept any offer of settlement;
- give you the best information possible about the likely costs of your claim for damages.

2. Your responsibilities

You must:

- give us instructions that allow us to do our work properly;
- not ask us to work in an improper or unreasonable way;
- not deliberately mislead us;
- co-operate with us;
- go to any medical or expert examination or court hearing.

3. Explanation of words used

(a) Advocacy

Appearing for you at court hearings.

(b) Basic charges

Our charges for the legal work we do on your claim for damages.

(c) Claim

Your demand for damages for personal injury whether or not court proceedings are issued.

(d) Counterclaim

A claim that your opponent makes against you in response to your claim.

(e) Damages

Money that you win whether by a court decision or settlement.

(f) Our disbursements

Payment we make on your behalf such as:

- court fees;
- experts' fees;
- accident report fees;
- travelling expenses.

(g) Interim damages

Money that a court says your opponent must pay or your opponent agrees to pay while waiting for a settlement or the court's final decision.

(h) Interim hearing

A court hearing that is not final.

(i) Lien

Our right to keep all papers, documents, money or other property held on your behalf until all money due to us is paid. A lien may be applied after this agreement ends.

(j) Lose

The court has dismissed your claim or you have stopped it on our advice.

(k) Part 36 offers or payments

An offer to settle your claim made in accordance with Part 36 of the Civil Procedure Rules.

(l) Provisional damages

Money that a court says your opponent must pay or your opponent agrees to pay, on the basis that you will be able to go back to court at a future date for further damages if:

- you develop a serious disease; or

- your condition deteriorates;

in a way that has been proved or admitted to be linked to your personal injury claim.

(m) Success fee

The percentage of basic charges that we add to your bill if you win your claim for damages and that we will seek to recover from your opponent.

(n) Win

Your claim for damages is finally decided in your favour, whether by a court decision or an agreement to pay you damages. "Finally" means that your opponent:

- is not allowed to appeal against the court decision; or

- has not appealed in time; or

- has lost any appeal.

4. What happens if you win?

If you win:

- You are then liable to pay all our basic charges, our disbursements and success fee—please see condition 3(n).

- Normally, you will be entitled to recover part or all of our basic charges, our disbursements and success fee from your opponent.

- If you and your opponent cannot agree the amount, the court will decide how much you can recover. If the amount agreed or allowed by the court does not cover all our basic charges and our disbursements, then you pay the difference.

- You will not be entitled to recover from your opponent the part of the success fee that relates to the cost to us of postponing receipt of our charges and our disbursements. This remains payable by you.

- You agree that after winning, the reasons for setting the success fee at the amount stated may be disclosed:

  (i) to the court and any other person required by the court;
  (ii) to your opponent in order to gain his or her agreement to pay the success fee.

- If the court carries out an assessment and disallows any of the success fee percentage because it is unreasonable in view of what we knew or should have known when it was agreed, then that amount ceases to be payable unless the court is satisfied that it should continue to be payable.

- If we agree with your opponent that the success fee is to be paid at a lower percentage than is set out in this agreement, then the success fee percentage will be reduced accordingly unless the court is satisfied that the full amount is payable.

- It may happen that your opponent makes an offer that includes payment of our basic charges and a success fee. If so, unless we consent, you agree not to tell us to accept the offer if it includes payment of the success fee at a lower rate than is set out in this agreement.

- If your opponent is receiving Community Legal Service funding, we are unlikely to get any money from him or her. So if this happens, you have to pay us our basic charges, disbursements and success fee.

You remain ultimately responsible for paying our success fee.

You agree to pay into a designated account any cheque received by you or by us from your opponent and made payable to you. Out of the money, you agree to let us take the balance of the basic charges; success fee; insurance premium; our remaining disbursements; and VAT. You take the rest.

We are allowed to keep any interest your opponent pays on the charges.

Payment for advocacy is explained in condition 6.

If your opponent fails to pay

If your opponent does not pay any damages or charges owed to you, we have the right to take recovery action in your name to enforce a judgment, order or agreement. The charges of this action become part of the basic charges.

5. What happens if you lose?

If you lose, you do not have to pay any of our basic charges or success fee. You do have to pay:

- us for our disbursements;
- your opponent's legal charges and disbursements.

If you are insured against payment of these amounts by your insurance policy, we will make a claim on your behalf and receive any resulting payment in your name. We will give you a statement of account for all money received and paid out.

If your opponent pays the charges of any hearing, they belong to us.

Payment for advocacy is dealt with in condition 6.

6. Payment for advocacy

The cost of advocacy and any other work by us, or by any solicitor agent on our behalf, forms part of our basic charges. We shall discuss with you the identity of any barrister instructed, and the arrangements made for payment.

Barristers who have a conditional fee agreement with us

If you win, you are normally entitled to recover their fee and success fee from your opponent. The barrister's success fee is shown in the separate conditional fee agreement we make with the barrister. We will discuss the barrister's success fee with you before we instruct him or her. If you lose, you pay the barrister nothing.

Barristers who do not have a conditional fee agreement with us

If you win, then you will normally be entitled to recover all or part of their fee from your opponent. If you lose, then you must pay their fee.

7. What happens when this agreement ends before your claim for damages ends?

(a) Paying us if you end this agreement

You can end the agreement at any time. We then have the right to decide whether you must:

- pay our basic charges and our disbursements including barristers' fees when we ask for them; or

- pay our basic charges, and our disbursements including barristers' fees and success fees if you go on to win your claim for damages.

(b) Paying us if we end this agreement

(i) We can end this agreement if you do not keep to your responsibilities in condition 2. We then have the right to decide whether you must:

- pay our basic charges and our disbursements including barristers' fees when we ask for them; or
- pay our basic charges and our disbursements including barristers' fees and success fees if you go on to win your claim for damages.

(ii) We can end this agreement if we believe you are unlikely to win. If this happens, you will only have to pay our disbursements. These will include barristers' fees if the barrister does not have a conditional fee agreement with us.

(iii) We can end this agreement if you reject our opinion about making a settlement with your opponent. You must then:

- pay the basic charges and our disbursements, including barristers' fees;
- pay the success fee if you go on to win your claim for damages.

If you ask us to get a second opinion from a specialist solicitor outside our firm, we will do so. You pay the cost of a second opinion.

(iv) We can end this agreement if you do not pay your insurance premium when asked to do so.

(c) Death

This agreement automatically ends if you die before your claim for damages is concluded. We will be entitled to recover our basic charges up to the date of your death from your estate.

If your personal representatives wish to continue your claim for damages, we may offer them a new conditional fee agreement, as long as they agree to pay the success fee on our basic charges from the beginning of the agreement with you.

8. What happens after this agreement ends

After this agreement ends, we will apply to have our name removed from the record of any court proceedings in which we are acting unless you have another form of funding and ask us to work for you.

We have the right to preserve our lien unless another solicitor working for you undertakes to pay us what we are owed including a success fee if you win.

The Legal Costs Protection Model Conditional Fee Agreement

[This agreement is prepared to operate in conjunction
with Legal Costs Protection ATE Insurance.]

For use in personal injury cases (non-clinical negligence)

This agreement is a binding legal contract between you and your **A1.027**
solicitor/s. Before you sign, please read everything carefully.

Words like "our disbursements", "basic charges", "win" and
"lose" are explained in condition 3 of the Law Society Conditions.
which you should also read carefully.

Agreement date (dd/mm/yy)☐☐ ☐☐ ☐☐

I/We, the solicitor/s _____
You, the client _____

What is covered by this agreement

- Your claim against

  _____

  for damages for personal injury suffered on (dd/mm/yy)
  ☐☐ ☐☐ ☐☐

- Any appeal by your opponent.

- Any appeal you make against an interim order during the
  proceedings.

- Any proceedings you take to enforce a judgment, order or
  agreement.

What is not covered by this agreement

- Any counterclaim against you.

- Any appeal you make against the final judgment order.

Paying us

If you win your claim, you pay our basic charge, disbursements and a
success fee. The amount of these is not based on or limited by

reference to the damages. You are entitled to seek recovery of part or all of our disbursements, basic charges, success fee and the Legal Costs Protection insurance premium from your opponent. Please see conditions 4 and 6.

If your opponent makes a Part 36 offer or payment which you reject and, on our advice, your claim for damages goes ahead to trial where you recover damages that are less than that offer or payment, then you do not have to pay any of the basic charges or success fee for the work done after we received notice of the offer or payment.

If you receive provisional damages, we are entitled to payment of our basic charges, our disbursements and success fee at that point.

If you win but on the way lose an interim hearing, you may be required to pay your opponent's charges of that hearing. Please see conditions 3(h) and 5.

If on the way to winning or losing you win an interim hearing, then we are entitled to payment of our basic charges and disbursements related to that hearing together with a success fee on those charges if you win overall.

If you lose, you pay your opponent's charges and disbursements. You may be able to take out an insurance policy against this risk. Please also see conditions 3(j) and 5. If you lose, you do not pay our charges but we may require you to pay our disbursements.

If you end this agreement before you win or lose, you pay our basic charges. If you go on to win, you pay a success fee. Please see condition 7(a).

If we end this agreement before you win or lose, you pay our basic charges. If you go on to win, you pay a success fee. Please also see condition 7(a).

Basic charges

These are for work done from now until this agreement ends.

How we calculate our basic charges

These are calculated for each hour engaged on your matter (from now until the review date on [   ]). Routine letters and telephone calls will be charged as units of one tenth of an hour. Other letters and telephone calls will be charged on a time basis. The hourly rates are:

- Solicitors with over four years' experience after qualification
  £ _____

- Other solicitors and legal executives and other staff of equivalent experience
  £ _____

- Trainee solicitors and other staff of equivalent experience
  £ _____

We will review the hourly rate on the review date and on each anniversary of the review date. We will not increase the rate by more than the rise in the Retail Prices Index and will notify you of the increased rate in writing.

Success fee

This is [   ]% of the basic charge.

The reasons for calculating the success fee at this level are set out in Schedule 1 to this agreement.

You cannot recover from your opponent the part of the success fee that relates to the cost of us postponing receipt of our charges and disbursements (as set out at Paragraphs (a) and (b) at Schedule 1). This part of the success fee remains payable by you.

Value added tax (VAT)

We add VAT, at the rate (now [   ]%) that applies when the work is done, to the total of the basic charges and success fee.

Law society conditions

The Law Society Conditions are attached because they are part of this agreement. Any amendments or additions to them will apply to you. You should read the conditions carefully and ask us about anything you find unclear.

Legal Costs Protection

Legal Costs Protect is an insurance policy only made available to you by solicitors who are specifically approved to use it.

You agree to pay a premium of £ ____ for Legal Costs Protection Insurance when you sign this agreement. We undertake to make arrangements to send this to the Underwriters' on your behalf. If you lose or your case is abandoned Legal Costs Protection will cover our disbursements, your opponent's Legal Charges and the cost of the insurance premium. It will not cover fees to your barristers or advocates. The maximum cover is £100,000. The premium has been calculated to reflect the risk associated with your case which is being transferred to the underwriter.

If this agreement ends before your claim for damages ends, Legal Cost Protection ends automatically at the same time.

Other points

Immediately before you sign this agreement, we verbally explained to you the effect of this agreement and in particular the following:

(a) the circumstances in which you may be liable to pay our disbursements and charges

(b) the circumstances in which you may seek assessment of fees and expenses and the procedure for so doing

(c) whether we consider that your risk of incurring liability for costs in these proceedings is insured under an existing contract of insurance

(d) other methods of financing those costs, including private funding, Community Legal Service funding, legal expenses insurance, trade union funding.

(e) (i) in all circumstances we presently believe, on the information currently available to us, that a contract of insurance with Legal Costs Protection is appropriate. Detailed reasons for this are set out in Schedule 2.

Signatures

Signed for the solicitor/s.
Signed by the client.

I confirm that my solicitor has verbally explained to me the matters in paragraphs (a) to (e) under "Other Points" above.

Signed _____
(Client)

I specifically confirm that I verbally explained to the client the matter in paragraphs (a) to (e) under "Other Points" and confirm the matters at (e) in writing in Schedule 2.

Signed _____
(Solicitor)

This agreement complies with the Conditional Fee Agreement Regulations 2000 (SI 2000/692)

LAW SOCIETY CONDITIONS

1. Our responsibilities   A1.028

We must:

- always act in your best interests, subject to our duty to the court

- explain to you the risks and benefits of taking legal action

- give you our best advice about whether to accept any offer of settlement

- give you the best information possible about the likely costs of your claim for damages

2. Your responsibilities

You must

- give us instructions that allow us to do our work properly

- not ask us to work in an improper or unreasonable way

- not deliberately mislead us

- co-operate with us

- go to any medical or expert examination or court hearing

3. Explanation of words used

(a) Advocacy

Appearing for you at court hearings

(b) Basic charges

Our charges for the legal work we do on your claim for damages

(c) Claim

Your demand for damages for personal injury whether or not court proceedings are issued.

(d) Counterclaim

A claim that your opponent makes against you in response to your claim.

(e) Damages

Money that you win whether by a court decision or settlement.

(f) Our disbursements

Payment we make on your behalf such as:

- court fees
- experts' fees
- accident report fees
- travelling expenses

(g) Interim damages

Money that a court says your opponent must pay or your opponent agrees to pay while waiting for a settlement or the court's final decision.

(h) Interim hearing

A court hearing that is not final.

(i) Lien

Our right to keep all papers, documents, money or other property held on your behalf until all money due to us is paid. A lien may be applied after this agreement ends.

(j) Lose

The court has dismissed your claim or you have stopped it on our advice.

(k) Part 36 offers or payments

An offer to settle your claim made in accordance with Part 36 of the Civil Procedure Rules.

(l) Provisional damages

Money that a court says your opponent must pay or your opponent agrees to pay, on the basis that you will be able to go back to court at a future date for further damages if:

- you develop a serious disease; or

- your condition deteriorates;

in a way that has been proved or admitted to be linked to your personal injury claim.

(m) Success fee

The percentage of basic charges that we add to your bill if you win your claim for damages and that we will seek to recover from your opponent.

(n) Win

Your claim for damages is finally decided in your favour, whether by a court decision or an agreement to pay you damages. "Finally" means that your opponent:

- is not allowed to appeal against the court decision; or

- has not appealed in time; or

- has lost any appeal.

4. What happens if you win?

If you win:

- you are then liable to pay all our basic charges, disbursements and success fee—please see condition 3(n);

- normally, you will be able to recover part or all of our basic charges, success fee, disbursements and the Legal Costs Protection insurance premium from your opponent;

- if you and your opponent cannot agree the amount, the court will decide how much you can recover. If the amount agreed or allowed by the court does not cover all our basic charges and disbursements, you pay the difference;

- you will not be entitled to recover from your opponent the part of the success fee that relates to the cost of us postponing receipt of our charges and our disbursements. This remains payable by you;

- you agree that after winning, the reasons for setting the success fee at the amount stated may be disclosed;

  - to the court and any other person required by the court
  - to your opponent in order to gain his or her agreement to pay the success fee

- if the court carries out an assessment and the court disallows any of the success fee percentage because it is unreasonable in view of what we knew or should have known when it was agreed, then that amount ceases to be payable unless the court is satisfied that it should continue to be payable;

- if we agree with your opponent that the success fee is to be paid at a lower percentage than is set out in this agreement, the success fee percentage will be reduced accordingly unless the court is satisfied that the full amount is payable

- it may happen that your opponent makes an offer that includes payment of our basic charges and a success fee. If so, unless we consent, you agree not to tell us to accept the offer if it includes payment of the success fee at a lower rate than is set out in this agreement;

- if your opponent is receiving Community Legal Service Funding, we are unlikely to get any money from him or her.

So if this happens, you have to pay us our basic charges, disbursements and success fee.

You remain ultimately responsible for payment of our success fee.

You agree to pay into a designated account any cheque received by you or by us from your opponent and made payable to you. Out of the money, you agree to let us take the balance of the basic charges; success fee; Legal Costs Protection insurance premium (where applicable); remaining disbursements; and VAT. You take the rest.

We are allowed to keep any interest your opponent pays on the charges.

Payment for advocacy is explained in condition 6.

If your opponent fails to pay

If your opponent does not pay any damages or charges owed to you, we have the right to take recovery action in your name to enforce a judgment, order or agreement. The charges of this action become part of the basic charges.

5. What happens if you lose?

If you lose, you do not have to pay any of the basic charges or success fee. You do have to pay:

- us for our disbursements

- your opponent's legal charges and disbursements.

If you are insured against payment of these amounts by your Legal Costs Protection insurance policy, we will make a claim on your behalf and receive any resulting payment in your name. We will give you a statement of account for all money received and paid out.

If your opponent pays the charges of any hearing, they belong to us.

Payment for advocacy is dealt with in condition 6.

6. Payment for advocacy

The cost of advocacy and any other work by us, or by any solicitor agent on our behalf, forms part of our basic charges.

We shall discuss with you the identity of any barrister instructed, and the arrangements made for payment.

Barristers who have a conditional fee agreement with us

If you win, you are normally entitled to recover their fee and success fee from your opponent. The barrister's success fee is shown in the separate conditional fee agreement we make with the barrister. We will discuss the barrister's success fee with you before we instruct him or her. If you lose, you pay the barrister nothing.

Barristers who do not have a conditional fee agreement with us

If you win, then you will normally be entitled to recover all or part of their fee from your opponent. If you lose, then you must pay their fee.

7. What happens when this agreement ends before your claim for damages ends?

(a) Paying us if you end this agreement

You can end the agreement at any time. We then have the right to decide whether you must:

- pay our basic charges and our disbursements including barristers' fees when we ask for them; or

- pay our basic charges, and our disbursements including barristers' fees and success fees if you go on to win your claim for damages

(b) Paying us if we end this agreement

(i) We can end this agreement if you do not keep to your responsibilities in condition 2. We then have the right to decide whether you must:

- pay our basic charges and our disbursements including barristers' fees when we ask for them; or
- pay our basic charges and our disbursements including barristers' fees fees and success fee if you go on to win your claim for damages.

(ii) We can end this agreement if we believe you are unlikely to win. If this happens, you will only have to pay our disbursements. These will include barrister's fees if the barrister does not have a conditional fee agreement with us.

(iii) We can end this agreement if you reject our opinion about making a settlement with your opponent. You must then:

- pay the basic charges and our disbursements, including barristers' fees
- pay the success fee if you go on to win your claim for damages

If you ask us to get a second opinion from a specialist solicitor outside our firm, we will do so. You pay the cost of the second opinion.

(iv) We can end this agreement if you do not pay your insurance premium when asked to do so.

(c) Death

This agreement automatically ends if you die before your claim for damages is concluded. We will be entitled to recover our basic charge up to the date of your death from your estate.

If your personal representatives wish to continue your claim for damages, we may offer them a new conditional fee agreement, as long as they agree to pay the success fee on our basic charges from the beginning of the agreement with you. If a contract of insurance with Legal Costs Protection is in place then we will apply for authority to continue this insurance only if we agree to entering a new Conditional Fee Agreement. We must have written agreement for Legal Costs Protection to continue.

8. What happens after this agreement ends?

After this agreement ends, we will apply to have our name removed from the record of any court proceedings in which we are acting unless you have another form of funding and ask us to work for you.

We have the right to preserve our lien unless another solicitor working for you undertakes to pay us what we are owed including a success fee if you win.

Schedule 1

A1.029   The success fee

The success fee is set at [   ]% of basic charges and cannot be more than 100% of the basic charges.

The percentage reflects the following:

(a)   the fact that if you win we will not be paid our basic charges until the end of the claim;

(b)   our arrangements with you about paying disbursements;

(c)   the fact that if you lose, we will not earn anything;

(d)   our assessment of the risks of your case. These include the following:

(e)   any other appropriate matters.

The matters set out a paragraphs (a) and (b) above together make up [   ]% of the increase on basic charges. The matters at paragraphs (c), (d) [and (e)] make up [   ]% of the increase on basic charges. So the total success fee is [   ]% as stated above.

Schedule 2

A1.030   The insurance policy

In all the circumstances and on the information currently available to us, we believe that a contract of insurance with Legal Costs Protection is appropriate to cover your opponent's charges and disbursements in case you lose.

This is because:

●   the cover is comprehensive, fully underwritten and designed to meet the financial exposures you are likely to meet if you lose

●   we receive no commission from this insurance

●   the premium has been designed to be reasonable, comply with the Civil Procedure Rules and to be recoverable from your opponent if you win

- it enables us to obtain insurance on your behalf specifically relating to your case

- it is a reputable, quality Conditional Fee Agreement insurance policy.

We are not, however, insurance brokers and cannot give advice on all products which may be available.

Model Conditional Fee Agreement for Solicitor and Barrister

A1.031   APIL/PIBA 5 *

CONDITIONAL FEE AGREEMENT

Index of paragraphs

The nature of the agreement:

Obligations:

Of counsel

Termination:

Counsel's fees:

* Reproduced with the permission of APIL.

17 Counsel's success fee
18 Counsel's expenses
19 Success
20 Part 36 offers and payments
21 Failure
22 Errors and Indemnity for fees

Counsel's entitlement to fees on termination of the agreement:

23 Fees on termination
24 Challenge to fees
25 Return of work

Assessment and payment of fees:

26 Costs Assessment
27 Payment of fees
28 Interest
29 Challenge to Success Fee

Disclosing the reasons for success fee:

30 Disclosure of reasons

Counsels fees in the event of assessment or agreement:

31 Reduction of success fee
32 Reduction by agreement

NOTES: These paragraphs need to be completed by counsel or counsel's **A1.032**
clerk: 1; 2; 3; 10(10); 16; 17(1), (2) & (3); 25(1).

CONDITIONAL FEE AGREEMENT
BETWEEN
SOLICITORS AND COUNSEL

The nature of the agreement

1. In this agreement: **A1.033**

    "Counsel" means: _____
    and any other counsel either from Chambers or recommended

by counsel in accordance with clause 25 who signs this agreement at any time at the solicitors request;

"the solicitor" means the firm:
Messrs: _____

"the client" means: _____

[acting by his Litigation Friend. _____]

"Chambers" means members of chambers at _____

2.   This agreement forms the basis on which instructions are accepted by counsel from the solicitor to act on a conditional fee basis for the client in his/her claim against:

_____

("the Opponent(s)")

for damages for personal injuries suffered on:

_____

until

1)   the claim is won, lost or otherwise concluded or

2)   this agreement is terminated.

3.   This agreement relates to

1)   issues of jurisdiction;

2)   issues of breach of duty;

3)   issues of causation;

4)   issues of limitation

5)   issues of damages;

6)   any appeal by the client's opponent(s);

7)   any appeal by the client against an interim order;

8) any appeal by the client advised by counsel;

9) any proceedings to enforce a judgment or order.

It does not cover:

10) any other appeal by the client;

11) any counterclaim or defence by way of set-off;

12) any part 20 claim

13) part only of the proceedings unless specifically incorporated in this agreement.

[NOTE: delete those parts of the proceedings to which the agreement does NOT relate]

4. This agreement is not a contract enforceable at law. The relationship of counsel and solicitor shall be governed by the Terms of Work under which barristers offer their services to solicitors and the Withdrawal of Credit Scheme as authorised by the General Council of the Bar as from time to time amended and set out in the Code of Conduct of the Bar of England and Wales, save that where such terms of work are inconsistent with the terms of this agreement the latter shall prevail.

5. Counsel has been provided with:

1) A copy of the conditional fee agreement between the solicitor and the client and the Law Society's Conditions as they apply to the claim;

2) written confirmation that "after the event" or other similar insurance is in place, or a written explanation why it is not; and

3) where more than one defendant is sued, copies of correspondence between the solicitor and the "after the event" insurers clarifying whether and when defendants costs are to be covered if the claimant does not succeed or win against all of the defendants; and

4) all relevant papers and risk assessment material, including all advice from experts and other solicitors or barristers to the client or any Litigation Friend in respect of the claim, which is currently available to the solicitor.

> 5) Any offers of settlement already made by the client or the defendant.

6. The solicitor confirms that:

> 1) he/she has complied with Regulation 4 of the Conditional Fee Agreements Regulations 2000 No. 692 and the client has confirmed by signing the solicitor/client agreement that Regulation 4 has been complied with; and
>
> 2) the client or any Litigation Friend has consented to the terms and conditions set out in this agreement insofar as they relate to the client.
>
> 3) Either:
>
> > (a) there are no other methods of financing costs available to the client, or
> > (b) Notwithstanding there are other methods of financing costs available to the client, namely [], the client has reasonably decided to fund this claim with conditional fees.

7. Counsel is not bound to act on a conditional fee basis until he/she has signed this agreement.

Obligations of counsel

A1.034 8. Counsel agrees to act diligently on all proper instructions from the solicitor subject to paragraph 9 hereof.

9. Counsel is not bound to accept instructions:

> 1) to appear at an interlocutory hearing where it would be reasonable
>
> > (a) to assume that counsel's fees would not be allowed on assessment or
> > (b) to instruct a barrister of less experience and seniority, provided that counsel has first used his/her best endeavours to ensure that an appropriate barrister will act for the client on the same terms as this agreement;
>
> 2) to draft documents or advise if a barrister of similar seniority would not ordinarily be instructed so to do if not instructed on a conditional fee basis;
>
> 3) outside the scope of this agreement.

Obligations of the solicitor

10. The solicitor agrees: **A1.035**

1) promptly to supply a copy of this agreement to the client or any Litigation Friend;

2) to comply with all the requirements of the CPR, the practice direction about costs supplementing parts 43 to 48 of the CPR (PD Costs), the relevant pre-action protocol and any court order relating to conditional fee agreements and in particular promptly to notify the Court and the opponent of the existence and any subsequent variation of the CFA with the client and this CFA and whether he/she has taken out an insurance policy or made an arrangement with a membership organisation and of the fact that additional liabilities are being claimed from the opponent.

3) promptly to apply for relief from sanction pursuant to CPR part 3.8 if any default under part 44.3B(1)(c) or (d) occurs and to notify counsel of any such default.

4) to act diligently in all dealings with counsel and the prosecution of the claim;

5) to consult counsel on the need for advice and action following:

    (a) the service of statements of case and if possible before the allocation decision; and
    (b) the exchange of factual and expert evidence;

6) to deliver within a reasonable time papers reasonably requested by counsel for consideration;

7) promptly to bring to counsel's attention:

    (a) any priority or equivalent report to insurers;
    (b) any Part 36 or other offer to settle;
    (c) any Part 36 payment into Court;
    (d) any evidence information or communication which may materially affect the merits of any issue in the case;
    (e) any other factor coming to the solicitor's attention which may affect counsel's entitlement to success fees whether before or after the termination of this agreement.

8) promptly to communicate to the client any advice by counsel:

    (a) to make, accept or reject any Part 36 or other offer;

(b) to accept or reject any Part 36 payment in;

(c) to incur, or not incur, expenditure in obtaining evidence or preparing the case;

(d) to instruct Leading counsel or a more senior or specialised barrister;

(e) that the case is likely to be lost;

(f) that damages and costs recoverable on success make it unreasonable or uneconomic for the action to proceed;

9) promptly to inform counsel's clerk of any listing for trial;

10) to deliver the brief for trial not less than [   ] weeks/ days before the trial;

11) if any summary assessment of costs takes place in the absence of counsel, to submit to the court a copy of counsel's risk assessment and make representations on counsel's behalf in relation to his/her fees;

12) to inform counsel in writing within 2 days of any reduction of counsel's fees on summary assessment in the absence of counsel and of any directions given under PD Costs 20.3(1) or alternatively to make application for such directions on counsel's behalf;

13) where points of dispute are served pursuant to CPR part 47.9 seeking a reduction in any percentage increase charged by counsel on his fees, to give the client the written explanation required by PD Costs 20.5 on counsel's behalf;

14) where more than one defendant is sued, the solicitor will write to the "after the event" insurers clarifying whether and when defendants costs are to be covered if the claimant does not succeed or win against all of the defendants, and send that correspondence to counsel.

15) When drawing up a costs bill at any stage of the case to include in it a claim for interest on counsel's fees.

Termination of the agreement by counsel

A1.036 11. Counsel may terminate the agreement if:

1) Counsel discovers that the solicitor is in breach of any obligation in paragraph 10 hereof;

2) the solicitor, client or any Litigation Friend rejects counsel's advice in any respect set out in paragraph 10(8) hereof;

3) Counsel is informed or discovers the existence of any set-off or counter-claim which materially affects the likelihood of success and/or the amount of financial recovery in the event of success;

4) Counsel is informed or discovers the existence of information which has been falsified or knowingly withheld by the solicitor, client or any Litigation Friend, of which counsel was not aware and which counsel could not reasonably have anticipated, which materially affects the merits of any substantial issue in the case;

5) Counsel is required to cease to act by the Code of Conduct of the Bar of England and Wales or counsel's professional conduct is being impugned; provided that counsel may not terminate the agreement if so to do would be a breach of that Code, and notice of any termination must be communicated promptly in writing to the solicitor.

Termination of the agreement by the solicitor

12. The solicitor may terminate the agreement at any time on the instructions of the client or any Litigation Friend. **A1.037**

Automatic termination of the agreement

13. This agreement shall automatically terminate if: **A1.038**

1) Counsel accepts a full-time judicial appointment;

2) Counsel retires from practice;

3) the solicitor's agreement with the client is terminated before the conclusion of the case;

4) Legal Services Commission funding is granted to the client;

5) the client dies;

6) The court makes a Group Litigation Order covering this claim.

Client becoming under a disability

14. If the client at any time becomes under a disability then the solicitor will: **A1.039**

1) consent to a novation of his Conditional Fee Agreement with the client to the Litigation Friend; and

2) where appropriate, apply to the Court to obtain its consent to acting under a conditional fee agreement with the Litigation Friend.

Thereafter, the Litigation Friend shall, for the purposes of this agreement, be treated as if he/she was and has always been the client.

Counsel taking silk

A1.040 15. If counsel becomes Queen's Counsel during the course of the agreement then either party may terminate it provided he/she does so promptly in writing.

Counsel's normal fees

A1.041 16. 1) Counsel's fees upon which a success fee will be calculated (the normal fees) will be as follows:-

(a) Advisory work and drafting
In accordance with counsel's hourly rate obtaining for such work in this field currently £[   ] per hour.

(b) Court appearances

(i) **Brief fee**

(a) **Trial**

For a trial whose estimated duration is up to 2 days (including—hours of preparation) £[   ], 3 to 5 days (including—hours of preparation) £[[   ], 5 to 8 days (including—hours of preparation) £[   ], 8 to 12 days (including—hours of preparation), £[   ], and 13 to 20 days (including—hours of preparation) £[   ].

(b) **Interlocutory hearings**

For an interlocutory hearing whose estimated duration is up to 1 hour (including—hours of preparation), £[   ], 1 hour to 1/2 day (including—hours of preparation) £[   ], 1/2 day to 1 day (including hours of preparation) £[   ], over 1 day (including—hours of preparation) will be charged as if it was a trial.

(ii) **Refreshers**

In accordance with counsel's daily rate obtaining for such work in this field, currently £[   ], per day.

(iii) **Renegotiating counsel's fees**

(a) To the extent that the hours of preparation set out above are reasonably exceeded then counsel's hourly rate will apply to each additional hour of preparation.

(b) If the case is settled or goes short counsel will consider the solicitor's reasonable requests to reduce his/her brief fees set out above.

2) The normal fees will be subject to review with effect from each successive anniversary of the date of this agreement but counsel will not increase the normal fees by more than any increase in the rate of inflation measured by the Retail Prices Index.

Counsel's success fee

17.(1) The rate of counsel's success fee will be [   ]% of **A1.042** counsel's normal fees;

(2) The reasons, briefly stated, for counsel's success fee are that at the time of entry into this agreement:

(i) the prospects of success are estimated by counsel as [   ](X)% as more fully set out in counsel's risk assessment, and a percentage increase of [   ](Y)% reflects those prospects

(ii) the length of postponement of the payment of counsel's fees and expenses is estimated at [   ] year, and a further increase of [   ](Z)% relates to that postponement

[Note: the success fee at paragraph 17(1) must be the sum of Y% and Z%]

(3) The reasons for counsel's success fee are more fully set out in counsel's risk assessment which is* / is not* (*please delete as appropriate) attached to this agreement.

Counsel's expenses

A1.043 18. If a hearing, conference or view takes place more than 25 miles from counsel's chambers the solicitor shall pay counsel's reasonable travel and accommodation expenses which shall:

1) appear separately on counsel's fee note;

2) attract no success fee and

3) subject to paragraph 21 be payable on the conclusion of the claim or earlier termination of this agreement.

Counsel's entitlement to fees—winning and losing [if the agreement is not terminated]

A1.044 19. 1) "Success" means the same as "win" in the Conditional Fee Agreement between the solicitor and the client.

2) Subject to paragraphs 20, 23 & 26 hereof, in the **event of success** the solicitor will pay counsel his/her normal and success fees.

3) If the client is successful at an interim hearing counsel may apply for summary assessment of solicitors basics costs and counsels normal fees.

20. If the amount of damages and interest awarded by a court is **less than a Part 36 payment into Court or effective Part 36 offer** then:

1) if counsel advised its rejection he/she is entitled to normal and success fees for work up to receipt of the notice of Part 36 payment into Court or offer but only normal fees for subsequent work;

2) if counsel advised its acceptance he/she is entitled to normal and success fees for all work done.

21. Subject to paragraph 22(1) hereof, if the case is lost or on counsel's advice ends without success then counsel is not entitled to any fees or expenses.

Errors and indemnity for fees

A1.045 22. 1) If, because of a breach by the solicitor but not counsel of his/

her duty to the client, the client's claim is dismissed or struck out:

a) for non compliance with an interlocutory order; or
b) for want of prosecution, or
c) by rule of court or the Civil Procedure Rules; or becomes unenforceable against the MIB for breach of the terms of the Uninsured Drivers Agreement:

the solicitor shall (subject to sub paragraphs (3)–(6) hereof) pay counsel such normal fees as would have been recoverable under this agreement.

(2) If, because of a breach by counsel but not the solicitor of his/her duty to the client, the client's claim is dismissed or struck out:

a) for non compliance with an interlocutory order; or
b) for want of prosecution, or
c) by rule of court or the Civil Procedure Rules

counsel shall (subject to sub paragraphs (3)–(6) hereof) pay the solicitor such basic costs as would have been recoverable from the client under the solicitor's agreement with the client.

(3) If, because of non-compliance by the solicitor but not by counsel of the obligations under sub-paragraphs (2), (3), (11), (12) or (13) of paragraph 10 above, counsel's success fee is not payable by the Opponent or the client then the solicitor shall (subject to sub-paragraphs (5) to (7) hereof) pay counsel such success fees as would have been recoverable under this agreement.

(4) No payment shall be made under sub paragraph (1), (2) or (3) hereof in respect of any breach by the solicitor or counsel which would not give rise to a claim for damages if an action were brought by the client;

Adjudication on disagreement

(5) In the event of any disagreement as to whether there has been an actionable breach by either the solicitor or counsel, or as to the amount payable under sub paragraph (1), (2) or (3) hereof, that disagreement shall be referred to adjudication by a panel consisting of a Barrister nominated by PIBA and a solicitor nominated by APIL who shall be requested to resolve the issue on written representations and on the basis of a proce-

dure laid down by agreement between PIBA and APIL. The costs of such adjudication shall, unless otherwise ordered by the panel, be met by the unsuccessful party.

(6) In the event of a panel being appointed pursuant to sub paragraph (5) hereof:

    a)   if that panel considers, after initial consideration of the disagreement, that there is a real risk that they may not be able to reach a unanimous decision, then the panel shall request APIL (where it is alleged there has been an actionable breach by the solicitor) or PIBA (where it is alleged that the has been an actionable breach by counsel) to nominate a third member of the panel;

    b)   that panel shall be entitled if it considers it reasonably necessary, to appoint a qualified costs draftsman, to be nominated by the President for the time being of the Law Society, to assist the panel;

    c)   the solicitor or counsel alleged to be in breach of duty shall be entitled to argue that, on the basis of information reasonably available to both solicitor and barrister, the claim would not have succeeded in any event. The panel shall resolve such issue on the balance of probabilities, and if satisfied that the claim would have been lost in any event shall not make any order for payment of fees or costs.

Cap

(7) the amount payable in respect of any claim under sub paragraph (1) or (2) or (3) shall be limited to a maximum of £25,000.

Counsel's entitlement to fees on termination of the agreement

A1.046   23.(1) **Termination by counsel** If counsel terminates the agreement under paragraph 11 then, subject to sub-paragraphs (b) and (c) hereof, counsel may elect either:

    (a)   to receive payment of normal fees without a success fee which the solicitor shall pay not later than three months after termination: ("Option A"), or

(b) to await the outcome of the case and receive payment of normal and success fees if it ends in success: ("Option B").

(2) If counsel terminates the agreement because the solicitor, client or Litigation Friend rejects advice under paragraph 10(8)(e) hereof counsel is not entitled to any fee.

(3) If counsel terminates the agreement because the solicitor, client or Litigation Friend rejects advice under paragraph 10(8)(f) counsel is entitled only to "Option B".

(4) **Termination by the solicitor** If the solicitor terminates the agreement under paragraph 12, counsel is entitled to elect between "Option A" and "Option B".

(5) **Automatic Termination and counsel taking silk**

(a) If the agreement terminates under paragraph 13(1) (judicial appointment) or 13(2) (retirement) or 15 (counsel taking silk) counsel is entitled only to "Option B".

(b) If the agreement terminates under paragraph 13(3) (termination of the solicitor/client agreement) then counsel is entitled to elect between "Option A" and "Option B" save that:

   (i) if the solicitor has ended the solicitor/client agreement because he considers that the client is likely to lose and at the time of that termination counsel considers that the client is likely to win, and the client goes on to win, the solicitor will pay counsel's normal and success fees;

   (ii) if the solicitor has ended the solicitor/client agreement because the client has rejected the advice of the solicitor or counsel about making a settlement the solicitor will pay counsel's normal fee in any event and, if the client goes on to win the case, will also pay counsel's success fee.

(c) If the agreement terminates under paragraph 13(4) (Legal Services Commission) or paragraph 13(5) (death of client) or paragraph 13(6) (group litigation order) counsel is entitled only to "Option B".

24. If the client or any Litigation Friend wishes to challenge:

(a) the entitlement to fees of counsel or the level of such fees following termination of the agreement [   ] or

(b) any refusal by counsel after signing this agreement to accept instructions the solicitor must make such challenge in accordance with the provisions of paragraphs 14 and 15 of the Terms of Work upon which barristers offer their services to solicitors (Annexe G to the Code of Conduct of the Bar of England and Wales).

Return of work

A1.047 25. If counsel in accordance with the Bar's Code of Conduct is obliged to return any brief or instructions in this case to another barrister, then:

1) Counsel will use his/her best endeavours to ensure that an appropriate barrister agrees to act for the client on the same terms as this agreement; if counsel is unable to secure an appropriate replacement barrister to act for the client on the same terms as this agreement counsel will

*(a) be responsible for any additional barristers' fees reasonably incurred by the solicitor or client and shall pay the additional fees to the solicitor promptly upon request and in any event within 3 months of such a request by the solicitor

*(b) not be responsible for any additional fee incurred by the solicitor or client.

2) Subject to paragraph 25(3) hereof, if the case ends in success counsel's fees for work done shall be due and paid on the conditional fee basis contained in this agreement whether or not the replacement barrister acts on a conditional fee basis; but

3) if the solicitor or client rejects any advice by the replacement barrister of the type described in paragraph 10(8) hereof, the solicitor shall immediately notify counsel whose fees shall be paid as set out in paragraph 23(1) hereof.

[NOTE: delete 25(1)(a) or 25(1)(b)]

Assessment and payment of costs/fees

A1.048 26. 1) If:

(a) a costs order is anticipated or made in favour of the client at an interlocutory hearing and the costs are summarily assessed at the hearing; or

(b) the costs of an interlocutory hearing are agreed between the parties in favour of the client; or

(c) an interlocutory order or agreement for costs to be assessed in detail and paid forthwith is made in favour of the client:

then

(i) the solicitor will include in the statement of costs a full claim for counsel's normal fees; and

(ii) the solicitor will promptly conclude by agreement or assessment the question of such costs; and

(iii) within one month of receipt of such costs the solicitor will pay to counsel the amount recovered in respect of his/her fees, such sum to be set off against counsel's entitlement to normal fees by virtue of this agreement.

27. 1) The amounts of fees and expenses payable to counsel under this agreement

(a) are not limited by reference to the damages which may be recovered on behalf of the client and

(b) are payable whether or not the solicitor is or will be paid by the client or opponent.

2) Upon success the solicitor will promptly conclude by agreement or assessment the question of costs and within one month after receipt of such costs the solicitor will pay to counsel the full sum due under this agreement.

28. The solicitor will use his best endeavours to recover interest on costs from any party ordered to pay costs to the client and shall pay counsel the share of such interest that has accrued on counsel's outstanding fees.

29. 1) The solicitor will inform counsel's clerk in good time of any challenge made to his success fee and of the date, place and time of any detailed costs assessment the client or opponent has taken out pursuant to the Civil Procedure Rules and unless counsel is present or represented at the assessment hearing will place counsel's risk assessment, relevant details and any written representations before the assessing judge and argue counsel's case for his/her success fee.

2)   If counsel's fees are reduced on any assessment then:

    (a)   the solicitor will inform counsel's clerk within seven days and confer with counsel whether to apply under Regulation 3(2)(b) of the CFA Regulations 2000 for an order that the client should pay the success fee and make such application on counsel's behalf;

    (b)   subject to any appeal, counsel will accept such fees as are allowed on that assessment and will repay forthwith to the solicitor any excess previously paid.

30. Disclosing the reasons for the success fee

1)   If

    (a)   a success fee becomes payable as a result of the client's claim and

    (b)   any fees subject to the increase provided for by paragraph 17(1) hereof are assessed and

    (c)   Counsel, the solicitor or the client is required by the court to disclose to the court or any other person the reasons for setting such increase as the level stated in this agreement, he / she may do so.

31. Counsel's fees in the event of assessment or agreement

If any fees subject to the said percentage increase are assessed and any amount of that increase is disallowed on assessment on the ground that the level at which the increase was set was unreasonable in view of the facts which were or should have been known to counsel at the time it was set, such amount ceases to be payable under this agreement unless the court is satisfied that it should continue to be so payable.

32.   If the Opponent offers to pay the client's legal fees at a lower sum than is due under this agreement then the solicitor:

    (a)   will calculate the proposed pro-rata reductions of the normal and success fees of both solicitor and counsel, and

    (b)   inform counsel of the offer and the calculations supporting the proposed pro-rata reductions referred to in paragraph (a) above, and

    (c)   will not accept the offer without counsel's express consent.

If such an agreement is reached on fees, then counsel's fees shall be limited to the agreed sum unless the court orders otherwise.

Dated:_____

Signed by counsel _____

or by his/her clerk [with counsel's authority]_____

*[Additional interlocutory counsel_____]

*[Additional interlocutory counsel_____]
*see paragraph 1

Signed by: _____

Solicitor/employee in Messrs:_____
The solicitors firm acting for the client:

APIL Conditional Fee Checklist to be Signed by Client Prior to Entering into Conditional Fee Agreement *

A1.049   Client's name
Matter No.
Fee earner
Date
Time signed (ensure that this is signed prior to the Conditional Fee Agreement).

CONFIRMATION

1.   It has been explained to me when I may be liable to pay the costs of legal representation.
2.   I have been informed of my right to a detailed assessment of my solicitor's fees and expenses.
3.   My solicitor has discussed with me how disbursements are to be paid and it has been agreed that I will/will not pay for these as the case progresses.
4.   I have checked to see if I or anyone in my household (and the driver of the car in which I was a passenger) has any pre-purchased legal expenses insurance.
5.   My solicitor has discussed with me and I and been advised of other methods of financing the case.
6.   My solicitor has discussed after the event insurance and it has been agreed that a contract of insurance is/is not appropriate. My solicitor has informed me why the insurance we have chosen is appropriate and the interest s/he has in recommending this policy of insurance that is [   ].
7.   My solicitor has explained the effect of the conditional fee agreement to me.
8.   I confirm that the Conditional Fee Agreement has been explained to me and that my solicitor has answered the questions I have in relation to the agreement.
9.   I have received written confirmation about my solicitor's interest in the insurance policy and a written explanation of the effect of the conditional fee agreement.

Signed..

Dated...

* Reproduced with the permission of APIL.

Pre-action Protocol for Personal Injury Claims

ANNEX A—TEMPLATE FOR LETTER OF CLAIM (DRAFT FOR ACCIDENT CASE)

LETTER OF CLAIM   A1.050

To

Defendant

Dear Sirs

Re: Claimant's full name
       Claimant's full address
       Claimant's National Insurance Number
       Claimant's Date of Birth
       Claimant's Clock or Works Number
       Claimant's (*name and address*)

We are instructed by the above named to claim damages in connection with an accident at work/ road traffic accident / tripping accident on day of year at (place of accident which must be sufficiently detailed to establish location)

Please confirm the identity of your insurers. Please note that the insurers will need to see this letter as soon as possible and it may affect your insurance cover and/or the conduct of any subsequent legal proceedings if you do not send this letter to them.

The circumstances of the accident are:- (brief outline)

The reason why we are alleging fault is:- (simple explanation e.g. defective machine, broken ground)

A description of our clients' injuries is as follows:- (brief outline)

(In cases of road traffic accidents)

Our client (state hospital reference number) received treatment for the injuries at name and address of hospital).

He is employed as (occupation) and has had the following time off work (dates of absence). His approximate weekly income is (insert if known).

If you are our client's employers, please provide us with the usual earnings details which will enable us to calculate his financial loss.

We are obtaining a police report and will let you have a copy of the same upon your undertaking to meet half the fee.

We have also sent a letter of claim to (name and address) and a copy of that letter is attached. We understand their insurers are (name, address and claims number if known).

At this stage of our enquiries we would expect the documents contained in parts (insert appropriate parts of standard disclosure list) to be relevant to this action.

Please note that we have entered into a conditional fee agreement with our client dated in relation to this claim which provides for a success fee within the meaning of section 58(2) of the Courts and Legal Services Act 1990. Our client has taken out an insurance policy dated with (name of insurance company) to which section 29 of the Access to Justice Act 1999 applies in respect of this claim.

A copy of this letter is attached for you to send to your insurers. Finally we expect an acknowledgement of this letter within 21 days by yourselves or your insurers.

Yours faithfully

Pre-action Protocol for Disease and Illness Claims

To:- Defendant **A1.051**

Dear Sirs

Re: Claimant's full name
        Claimant's full address
        Claimant's National Insurance Number
        Claimant's Date of Birth
        Claimant's Clock or Works Number
        Claimant's (*name and address*)

We are instructed by the above named to claim damages in connection with a claim for:-

Specify occupational disease

We are writing this letter in accordance with the pre-action protocol for disease and illness claims.

Please confirm the identity of your insurers. Please note that your insurers will need to see this letter as soon as possible and it may affect your insurance cover if you do not send this to them.

The Claimant was employed by you (*if the claim arises out of public or occupiers' liability give appropriate details*) as *job description* from *date* to *date.* During the relevant period of his employment he worked:-

description of precisely where the Claimant worked and what he did to include a description of any machines used and details of any exposure to noise or substances

The circumstances leading to the development of this condition are as follows:-

Give chronology of events

243

The reason why we are alleging fault is:-
Details should be given of contemporary and comparable employees who have suffered from similar problems if known; any protective equipment provided; complaints; the supervisors concerned, if known.

Our client's employment history is attached.

We have also made a claim against:-
Insert details
Their insurers' details are:-
Insert if known
e.g. Occupational health notes; GP notes

We have obtained a medical report from (name) and will disclose this when we receive your acknowledgement of this letter.
(This is optional at this stage)

(i)   the Claimant first became aware of symptoms on *(insert approximate date)*
(ii)   the Claimant first received medical advice about those symptoms on *(insert date) (give details of advice given if appropriate)*
(iii)   the Claimant first believed that those symptoms might be due to exposure leading to this claim on *(insert approximate date)*

This should be sufficiently detailed to allow the Defendant to put a broad value on the claim. (Where the client has any rehabilitation needs you may wish to advise the defendant at this stage).

He has the following time off work:
Insert dates

He is presently employed as a *job description* and his average net weekly income is £[   ]

If you are our client's employers, please provide us with the usual earnings details, which will enable us to calculate his financial loss.

Please note that we have entered into a conditional fee agreement with our client dated in relation to this claim which provides for a success fee within the meaning of section 58(2) of the Courts and Legal Services Act 1990. Our client has taken out an insurance

policy dated with (name of insurance company) to which section 29 of the Access to Justice Act 1999 applies in respect of this claim.

A copy of this letter is attached for you to send to your insurers. Finally we expect an acknowledgement of this letter within 21 days by yourselves or your insurers.

Yours faithfully

Pro Forma for Risk Assessment and Ranking of Risk

A1.052

If a risk applies in the case enter it and then calculate the level of risk							
	Likelihood			Severity			Risk Rate
Areas of Risk to Consider:	Low <u>1</u>	Med <u>2</u>	High <u>3</u>	Low <u>1</u>	Med <u>2</u>	High <u>3</u>	Lx S = RR
Facts • • • •							
Liability • • • •							
Limitation • • • •							
Defendant • • • •							
Causation • • • •							
Quantum • • • •							
Any Other Matters • • • •							

Risk View:	
1. Does the case involve significant risk factors?	Yes/No
2. Can the case be run at reasonable cost relative to value?	Yes/No
3. Is the case acceptable to take on within the firm's guidelines?	Yes/No

Overall Assessment of Risk:
High/Medium/Low

Suggested uplift based on the risks from this assessment is: %

These actions, in order of priority, should be taken to mitigate the risks
identified:-

RISK ASSESSMENT RECORD

CLIENT NAME AND TITLE:	
ADDRESS:	
DATE OF BIRTH:	
ACCIDENT DATE:	
DATE FIRST INSTRUCTED:	
REASON FOR DELAY IN APPLYING FOR CFA IF ACCIDENT MORE THAN 6 MONTHS AGO:	
ACCIDENT TYPE:	
INJURIES SUFFERED:	
BRIEF CIRCUMSTANCES OF THE ACCIDENT:	
NAME OF POTENTIAL DEFENDANT:	
INSURERS:	
SOLICITORS:	

BASIS OF CASE IN LAW	
PRIMARY ALLEGATIONS OF NEGLIGENCE:	
BREACHES OF STATUTES TO BE ALLEGED:	
BREACHES OF REGULATIONS TO BE ALLEGED:	
POTENTIAL ALLEGATIONS OF CONTRIBUTORY NEGLIGENCE:	
TRACK:	**MULTI/FAST**
ESTIMATE OF GENERAL DAMAGES:	
BEST ESTIMATE OF TOTAL DAMAGES:	
ANTICIPATED HEADS OF DAMAGE:	

LIABILITY RISK FACTORS

HIGH RISK FACTORS:	REASONS:
MEDIUM RISK FACTORS:	REASONS:
LOW RISK FACTORS:	REASONS:

QUANTUM RISK FACTORS

HIGH RISK FACTORS:	REASONS:
MEDIUM RISK FACTORS:	REASONS:
LOW RISK FACTORS:	REASONS:

OVERALL RISK ASSESSMENT

CASE RISK CATEGORY	LOW/ MEDIUM / HIGH
SUCCESS FEE :	50% / 75% / 100%
RISK CONTROL FACTORS TO BE APPLIED TO CASE	

Reference............... Signed................................... Dated........................

The Conditional Fee Agreements Regulations 2000

(SI 2000/692)

The Lord Chancellor, in exercise of the powers conferred on him by **A1.053** sections 58(3)(c), 58A(3) and 119 of the Courts and Legal Services Act 1990 and all other powers enabling him hereby makes the following Regulations:

Citation, commencement and interpretation

1.—(1) These Regulations may be cited as the Conditional Fee **A1.054** Agreements Regulations 2000.

(2) These Regulations come into force on 1st April 2000.

(3) In these Regulations—

"client" includes, except where the context otherwise requires, a person who—

(a) has instructed the legal representative to provide the advocacy or litigation services to which the conditional fee agreement relates, or

(b) is liable to pay the legal representative's fees in respect of those services; and

"legal representative" means the person providing the advocacy or litigation services to which the conditional fee agreement relates.

Requirements for contents of conditional fee agreements: general

2.—(1) A conditional fee agreement must specify— **A1.055**

(a) the particular proceedings or parts of them to which it relates (including whether it relates to any appeal, counterclaim or proceedings to enforce a judgement or order),

(b) the circumstances in which the legal representative's fees and expenses, or part of them, are payable,

(c) what payment, if any, is due—

(i)   if those circumstances only partly occur,

(ii) irrespective of whether those circumstances occur, and

(iii) on the termination of the agreement for any reason, and

(d) the amounts which are payable in all the circumstances and cases specified or the method to be used to calculate them and, in particular, whether the amounts are limited by reference to the damages which may be recovered on behalf of the client.

(2) A conditional fee agreement to which regulation 4 applies must contain a statement that the requirements of that regulation which apply in the case of that agreement have been complied with.

Requirements for contents of conditional fee agreements providing for success fees

A1.056   3.—(1) A conditional fee agreement which provides for a success fee—

(a) must briefly specify the reasons for setting the percentage increase at the level stated in the agreement, and

(b) must specify how much of the percentage increase, if any, relates to the cost to the legal representative of the post-ponement of the payment of his fees and expenses.

(2) If the agreement relates to court proceedings, it must provide that where the percentage increase becomes payable as a result of those proceedings, then—

(a) if—

(i)   any fees subject to the increase are assessed, and

(ii) the legal representative or the client is required by the court to disclose to the court or any other person the reasons for setting the percentage increase at the level stated in the agreement,

he may do so,

(b) if—

(i)   any such fees are assessed, and

(ii) any amount in respect of the percentage increase is dis-allowed on the assessment on the ground that the level at which the increase was set was unreasonable in view of facts which were or should have been known to the legal representative at the time it was set,

that amount ceases to be payable under the agreement, unless the court is satisfied that it should continue to be so payable, and

(c) if—

    (i) sub-paragraph (b) does not apply, and

    (ii) the legal representative agrees with any person liable as a result of the proceedings to pay fees subject to the percentage increase that a lower amount than the amount payable in accordance with the conditional fee agreement is to be paid instead,

the amount payable under the conditional fee agreement in respect of those fees shall be reduced accordingly, unless the court is satisfied that the full amount should continue to be payable under it.

(3) In this regulation "percentage increase" means the percentage by which the amount of the fees which would be payable if the agreement were not a conditional fee agreement is to be increased under the agreement.

Information to be given before conditional fee agreements made

4.—(1) Before a conditional fee agreement is made the legal representative must— **A1.057**

(a) inform the client about the following matters, and

(b) if the client requires any further explanation, advice or other information about any of those matters, provide such further explanation, advice or other information about them as the client may reasonably require.

(2) Those matters are—

(a) the circumstances in which the client may be liable to pay the costs of the legal representative in accordance with the agreement,

(b) the circumstances in which the client may seek assessment of the fees and expenses of the legal representative and the procedure for doing so,

(c) whether the legal representative considers that the client's risk of incurring liability for costs in respect of the proceedings to which agreement relates is insured against under an existing contract of insurance,

(d) whether other methods of financing those costs are available, and, if so, how they apply to the client and the proceedings in question,

(e) whether the legal representative considers that any particular method or methods of financing any or all of those costs is appropriate and, if he considers that a contract of insurance is appropriate or recommends a particular such contract—

(i) his reasons for doing so, and
(ii) whether he has an interest in doing so.

(3) Before a conditional fee agreement is made the legal representative must explain its effect to the client.

(4) In the case of an agreement where—

(a) the legal representative is a body to which section 30 of the Access to Justice Act 1999 (recovery where body undertakes to meet costs liabilities) applies, and

(b) there are no circumstances in which the client may be liable to pay any costs in respect of the proceedings,

paragraph (1) does not apply.

(5) Information required to be given under paragraph (1) about the matters in paragraph (2)(a) to (d) must be given orally (whether or not it is also given in writing), but information required to be so given about the matters in paragraph (2)(e) and the explanation required by paragraph (3) must be given both orally and in writing.

(6) This regulation does not apply in the case of an agreement between a legal representative and an additional legal representative.

Form of agreement

A1.058   5.—(1) A conditional fee agreement must be signed by the client and the legal representative.

(2) This regulation does not apply in the case of an agreement between a legal representative and an additional legal representative.

Amendment of agreement

6. Where an agreement is amended to cover further proceedings or parts of them— **A1.059**

    (a) regulations 2, 3 and 5 apply to the amended agreement as if it were a fresh agreement made at the time of the amendment, and

    (b) the obligations under regulation 4 apply in relation to the amendments in so far as they affect the matters mentioned in that regulation.

Revocation of 1995 regulations

7. The Conditional Fee Agreements Regulations 1995 are revoked. **A1.060**

The Collective Conditional Fee Agreements Regulations 2000

(SI 2000/2988)

A1.061 The Lord Chancellor, in exercise of the powers conferred upon him by sections 58(3)(c), 58A(3) and 119 of the Courts and Legal Services Act 1990 hereby makes the following Regulations:

Citation, commencement and interpretation

A1.062 1.—(1) These regulations may be cited as the Collective Conditional Fee Agreements Regulations 2000, and shall come into force on 30th November 2000.

(2) In these Regulations, except where the context requires otherwise—

"client" means a person who will receive advocacy or litigation services to which the agreement relates;

"collective conditional fee agreement" has the meaning given in regulation 3;

"conditional fee agreement" has the same meaning as in section 58 of the Courts and Legal Services Act 1990;

"funder" means the party to a collective conditional fee agreement who, under that agreement, is liable to pay the legal representative's fees;

"legal representative" means the person providing the advocacy or litigation services to which the agreement relates.

Transitional provisions

A1.063 2. These Regulations shall apply to agreements entered into on or after 30th November 2000, and agreements entered into before that date shall be treated as if these Regulations had not come into force.

Definition of "collective conditional fee agreement"

A1.064 3.—(1) Subject to paragraph (2) of this regulation, a collective conditional fee agreement is an agreement which—

(a) disregarding section 58(3)(c) of the Courts and Legal Services Act 1990, would be a conditional fee agreement; and

(b) does not refer to specific proceedings, but provides for fees to be payable on a common basis in relation to a class of proceedings, or, if it refers to more than one class of proceedings, on a common basis in relation to each class.

(2) An agreement may be a collective conditional fee agreement whether or not—

(a) the funder is a client; or

(b) any clients are named in the agreement.

Requirements for contents of collective conditional fee agreements: general

4.—(1) A collective conditional fee agreement must specify the circumstances in which the legal representative's fees and expenses, or part of them, are payable.
A1.065

(2) A collective conditional fee agreement must provide that, when accepting instructions in relation to any specific proceedings the legal representative must—

(a) inform the client as to the circumstances in which the client may be liable to pay the costs of the legal representative; and

(b) if the client requires any further explanation, advice or other information about the matter referred to in sub-paragraph (a), provide such further explanation, advice or other information about it as the client may reasonably require.

(3) Paragraph (2) does not apply in the case of an agreement between a legal representative and an additional legal representative.

(4) A collective conditional fee agreement must provide that, after accepting instructions in relation to any specific proceedings, the legal representative must confirm his acceptance of instructions in writing to the client.

Requirements for contents of collective conditional fee agreements providing for success fees

5.—(1) Where a collective conditional fee agreement provides for a success fee the agreement must provide that, when accepting
A1.066

instructions in relation to any specific proceedings the legal representative must prepare and retain a written statement containing—

(a) his assessment of the probability of the circumstances arising in which the percentage increase will become payable in relation to those proceedings ("the risk assessment");

(b) his assessment of the amount of the percentage increase in relation to those proceedings, having regard to the risk assessment; and

(c) the reasons, by reference to the risk assessment, for setting the percentage increase at that level.

(2) If the agreement relates to court proceedings it must provide that where the success fee becomes payable as a result of those proceedings, then—

(a) if—

(i) any fees subject to the increase are assessed, and

(ii) the legal representative or the client is required by the court to disclose to the court or any other person the reasons for setting the percentage increase at the level assessed by the legal representative,

he may do so,

(b) if—

(i) any such fees are assessed by the court, and

(ii) any amount in respect of the percentage increase is disallowed on the assessment on the ground that the level at which the increase was set was unreasonable in view of facts which were or should have been known to the legal representative at the time it was set

that amount ceases to be payable under the agreement, unless the court is satisfied that it should continue to be so payable, and

(c) if—

(i) sub-paragraph (b) does not apply, and

(ii) the legal representative agrees with any person liable as a result of the proceedings to pay fees subject to the percentage increase that a lower amount than the amount

payable in accordance with the conditional fee agreement
is to be paid instead,

the amount payable under the collective conditional fee
agreement in respect of those fees shall be reduced accordingly, unless the court is satisfied that the full amount should
continue to be payable under it.

(3) In this regulation "percentage increase" means the percentage
by which the amount of the fees which would have been payable if
the agreement were not a conditional fee agreement is to be increased
under the agreement.

Form and amendment of collective conditional fee agreement

6.—(1) Subject to paragraph (2), a collective conditional fee **A1.067**
agreement must be signed by the funder, and by the legal representative.

(2) Paragraph (1) does not apply in the case of an agreement
between a legal representative and an additional legal representative.

(3) Where a collective conditional fee agreement is amended, regulations 4 and 5 apply to the amended agreement as if it were a fresh
agreement made at the time of the amendment.

Amendment to the conditional fee agreements regulations 2000

7. After regulation 7 of the Conditional Fee Agreements Regula- **A1.068**
tions 2000 there shall be inserted the following new regulation:—

> **"Exclusion of collective conditional fee agreements**
> **8.** These Regulations shall not apply to collective condi-
> tional fee agreements within the meaning of regulation 3 of
> the Collective Conditional Fee Agreements Regulations
> 2000.".

The Access to Justice (Membership Organisations) Regulations 2000

(SI 2000/693)

The Lord Chancellor, in exercise of the powers conferred on him by section 30(1) and (3) to (5) of the Access to Justice Act 1999 and all other powers enabling him hereby makes the following Regulations:

Citation, commencement and interpretation

1.—(1) These Regulations may be cited as the Access to Justice (Membership Organisations) Regulations 2000.

(2) These Regulations come into force on 1st April 2000.

Bodies of a prescribed description

2. The bodies which are prescribed for the purpose of section 30 of the Access to Justice Act 1999 (recovery where body undertakes to meet costs liabilities) are those bodies which are for the time being approved by the Lord Chancellor for that purpose.

Requirements for arrangements to meet costs liabilities

3.—(1) Section 30(1) of the Access to Justice Act 1999 applies to arrangements which satisfy the following conditions.

(2) The arrangements must be in writing.

(3) The arrangements must contain a statement specifying—

(a) the circumstances in which the member or other party may be liable to pay costs of the proceedings,

(b) whether such a liability arises—

(i) if those circumstances only partly occur,
(ii) irrespective of whether those circumstances occur, and
(iii) on the termination of the arrangements for any reason,

(c) the basis on which the amount of the liability is calculated, and

(d) the procedure for seeking assessment of costs.

(4) A copy of the part of the arrangements containing the statement must be given to the member or other party to the proceedings whose liabilities the body is undertaking to meet as soon as possible after the undertaking is given.

Recovery of additional amount for insurance costs

4.—(1) Where an additional amount is included in costs by virtue of section 30(2) of the Access to Justice Act 1999 (costs payable to a member of a body or other person party to the proceedings to include an additional amount in respect of provision made by the body against the risk of having to meet the member's or other person's liabilities to pay other parties' costs), that additional amount must not exceed the following sum.

(2) That sum is the likely cost to the member of the body or, as the case may be, the other person who is a party to the proceedings in which the costs order is made of the premium of an insurance policy against the risk of incurring a liability to pay the costs of other parties to the proceedings.

Pre-action Protocol for Personal Injury Claims

A1.069   1 INTRODUCTION

A1.070   1.1   Lord Woolf in his final Access to Justice Report of July 1996 recommended the development of pre-action protocols:

"To build on and increase the benefits of early but well informed settlement which genuinely satisfy both parties to dispute."

1.2   The aims of pre-action protocols are:

- more pre-action contact between the parties
- better and earlier exchange of information
- better pre-action investigation by both sides
- to put the parties in a position where they may be able to settle cases fairly and early without litigation
- to enable proceedings to run to the court's timetable and efficiently, if litigation does become necessary.

1.3   The concept of protocols is relevant to a range of initiatives for good litigation and pre-litigation practice, especially:

- predictability in the time needed for steps pre-proceedings
- standardisation of relevant information, including documents to be disclosed.

1.4   The Courts will be able to treat the standards set in protocols as the normal reasonable approach to pre-action conduct. If proceedings are issued, it will be for the court to decide whether non-compliance with a protocol should merit adverse consequences. Guidance on the court's likely approach will be given from time to time in practice directions.

1.5   If the court has to consider the question of compliance after proceedings have begun, it will not be concerned with minor infringements, e.g. failure by a short period to provide relevant information. One minor breach will not exempt the "innocent" party from following the protocol. The court will look at the

effect of non-compliance on the other party when deciding
whether to impose sanctions.

2 NOTES OF GUIDANCE

2.1   The protocol has been kept deliberately simple to promote ease   **A1.071**
of use and general acceptability. The notes of guidance which
follow relate particularly to issues which arose during the
piloting of the protocol.

Scope of the protocol

2.2   This protocol is intended to apply to all claims which include a
claim for personal injury (except industrial disease claims) and
to the entirety of those claims: not only to the personal injury
element of a claim which also includes, for instance, property
damage.

2.3   This protocol is primarily designed for those road traffic, tripping and slipping and accident at work cases which include an
element of personal injury with a value of less than £15,000
which are likely to be allocated to the fast track. This is because
time will be of the essence, after proceedings are issued, especially for the defendant, if a case is to be ready for trial within 30
weeks of allocation. Also, proportionality of work and costs to
the value of what is in dispute is particularly important in lower
value claims. For some claims within the value "scope" of the
fast track some flexibility in the timescale of the protocol may be
necessary, see also paragraph 3.8.

2.4   However, the "cards on the table" approach advocated by the
protocol is equally appropriate to some higher value claims.
The spirit, if not the letter of the protocol, should still be followed for multi-track type claims. In accordance with the sense
of the civil justice reforms, the court will expect to see the spirit
of reasonable pre-action behaviour applied in all cases,
regardless of the existence of a specific protocol. In particular
with regard to personal injury cases worth more than £15,000,
with a view to avoiding the necessity of proceedings parties are
expected to comply with the protocol as far as possible e.g. in
respect of letters before action, exchanging information and
documents and agreeing experts.

2.5   The timetable and the arrangements for disclosing documents and obtaining expert evidence may need to be varied to suit the circumstances of the case. Where one or both parties consider the detail of the protocol is not appropriate to the case, and proceedings are subsequently issued, the court will expect an explanation as to why the protocol has not been followed, or has been varied.

Early notification

2.6 The claimant's legal representative may wish to notify the defendant and/or his insurer as soon as they know a claim is likely to be made, but before they are able to send a detailed letter of claim, particularly for instance, when the defendant has no or limited knowledge of the incident giving rise to the claim or where the claimant is incurring significant expenditure as a result of the accident which he hopes the defendant might pay for, in whole or in part. If the claimant's representative chooses to do this, it will not start the timetable for responding.

The letter of claim

2.7 The specimen letter of claim at Annex A will usually be sent to the individual defendant. In practice, he/she may have no personal financial interest in the financial outcome of the claim/ dispute because he/she is insured. Court imposed sanctions for non-compliance with the protocol may be ineffective against an insured. This is why the protocol emphasises the importance of passing the letter of claim to the insurer and the possibility that the insurance cover might be affected. If an insurer receives the letter of claim only after some delay by the insured, it would not be unreasonable for the insurer to ask the claimant for additional time to respond.

Reasons for early issue

2.8 The protocol recommends that a defendant be given three months to investigate and respond to a claim before proceedings are issued. This may not always be possible, particularly where a claimant only consults a solicitor close to the end of any relevant limitation period. In these circumstances, the claimant's solicitor should give as much notice of the intention to issue proceedings as is practicable and the parties should consider whether the court might be invited to extend time for service of the claimant's supporting documents and for service of any defence, or alternatively, to stay the proceedings while the recommended steps in the protocol are followed.

Status of letters of claim and response

2.9 Letters of claim and response are not intended to have the same status as a statement of case in proceedings. Matters may come to light as a result of investigation after the letter of claim has been sent, or after the defendant has responded, particularly if disclosure of documents takes place outside the recommended three-month period. These circumstances could mean that the "pleaded" case of one or both parties is presented slightly differently than in the letter of claim and response. It would not be consistent with the spirit of the protocol for a party to "take a point" on this in the proceedings, provided that there was no obvious intention by the party who changed their position to mislead the other party.

Disclosure of documents

2.10 The aim of the early disclosure of documents by the defendant is not to encourage "fishing expeditions" by the claimant, but to promote an early exchange of relevant information to help in clarifying or resolving issues in dispute. The claimant's solicitor can assist by identifying in the letter of claim or in a subsequent letter the particular categories of documents which they consider are relevant.

Experts

2.11 The protocol encourages joint selection of, and access to, experts. Most frequently this will apply to the medical expert, but on occasions also to liability experts, e.g. engineers. The protocol promotes the practice of the claimant obtaining a medical report, disclosing it to the defendant who then asks questions and/or agrees it and does not obtain his own report. The Protocol provides for nomination of the expert by the claimant in personal injury claims because of the early stage of the proceedings and the particular nature of such claims. If proceedings have to be issued, a medical report must be attached to these proceedings. However, if necessary after proceedings have commenced and with the permission of the court, the parties may obtain further expert reports. It would be for the court to decide whether the costs of more than one expert's report should be recoverable.

2.12 Some solicitors choose to obtain medical reports through medical agencies, rather than directly from a specific doctor or hospital. The defendant's prior consent to the action should be sought and, if the defendant so requests, the agency should be asked to provide in advance the names of the doctor(s) whom they are considering instructing.

Negotiations/settlement

2.13 Parties and their legal representatives are encouraged to enter into discussions and/or negotiations prior to starting proceedings. The protocol does not specify when or how this might be done but parties should bear in mind that the courts increasingly take the view that litigation should be a last resort, and that claims should not be issued prematurely when a settlement is in reasonable prospect.

Stocktake

2.14 Where a claim is not resolved when the protocol has been followed, the parties might wish to carry out a "stocktake" of the issues in dispute, and the evidence that the court is likely to need to decide those issues, before proceedings are started. Where the defendant is insured and the pre-action steps have been conducted by the insurer, the insurer would normally be expected to nominate solicitors to act in the proceedings and the claimant's solicitor is recommended to invite the insurer to nominate solicitors to act in the proceedings and do so 7–14 days before the intended issue date.

3 THE PROTOCOL

Letter of claim

A1.072   3.1   The claimant shall send to the proposed defendant two copies of a letter of claim, immediately sufficient information is available to substantiate a realistic claim and before issues of quantum are addressed in detail. One copy of the letter is for the defendants, the second for passing on to his insurers.

3.2   The letter shall contain a **clear summary of the facts** on which the claim is based together with an indication of the **nature of any injuries** suffered and of **any financial loss incurred**. In cases of road traffic accidents, the letter should provide the name and address of the hospital where treatment has been obtained and the claimant's hospital reference number.

3.3 Solicitors are recommended to use a **standard format** for such a letter—an example is at Annex A: this can be amended to suit the particular case.

3.4 The letter should ask for **details of the insurer** and that a copy should be sent by the proposed defendant to the insurer where appropriate. If the insurer is known, a copy shall be sent directly to the insurer. Details of the claimant's National Insurance number and date of birth should be supplied to the defendant's insurer once the Defendant has responded to the letter of claim and confirmed the identity of the insurer. This information should not be supplied in the letter of claim.

3.5 **Sufficient information** should be given in order to enable the defendant's insurer/solicitor to commence investigations and at least put a broad valuation on the "risk".

3.6 The **defendant should reply within 21 calendar days** of the date of posting of the letter identifying the insurer (if any). If there has been no reply by the defendant or insurer within 21 days, the claimant will be entitled to issue proceedings.

3.7 The **defendant**('s insurers) will have a **maximum of three months** from the date of acknowledgment of the claim **to investigate**.No later than the end of that period the defendant (insurer) shall reply, stating whether liability is denied and, if so, giving reasons for their denial of liability.

3.8 Where the accident occurred outside England and Wales and/ or where the defendant is outside the jurisdiction, the time periods of 21 days and three months should normally be extended up to 42 days and six months.

3.9 Where **liability is admitted**, the presumption is that the defendant will be bound by this admission for all claims with a total value of up to £15,000.

Documents

3.10 If the **defendant denies liability**, he should enclose with the letter of reply, **documents** in his possession which are **material to the issues** between the parties, and which would be likely to be ordered to be disclosed by the court, either on an application for pre-action disclosure, or on disclosure during proceedings.

3.11 Attached at Annex B are **specimen**, but non-exhaustive, **lists** of documents likely to be material in different types of claim. Where the claimant's investigation of the case is well advanced, the letter of claim could indicate which classes of documents are considered relevant for early disclosure. Alternatively these could be identified at a later stage.

3.12 Where the defendant admits primary liability, but alleges contributory negligence by the claimant, the defendant should give reasons supporting those allegations and disclose those documents from Annex B which are relevant to the issues in dispute. The claimant should respond to the allegations of contributory negligence before proceedings are issued.

Special damages

3.13 The claimant will send to the defendant as soon as practicable a Schedule of Special Damages with supporting documents, particularly where the defendant has admitted liability.

Experts

3.14 Before any party instructs an expert he should give the other party a list of the **name**(s) of **one or more experts** in the relevant speciality whom he considers are suitable to instruct.

3.15 Where a medical expert is to be instructed the claimant's solicitor will organise access to relevant medical records—see specimen letter of instruction at Annex C.

3.16 **Within 14 days** the other party may indicate **an objection** to one or more of the named experts. The first party should then instruct a mutually acceptable expert. It must be emphasised that if the Claimant nominates an expert in the original letter of claim, the Defendant has 14 days to object to one or more of the named experts after expiration of the period of 21 days within which he has to reply to the letter of claim, as set out in paragraph 3.6.

3.17 If the second party objects to all the listed experts, the parties may then instruct **experts of their own choice**. It would be for the court to decide subsequently, if proceedings are issued, whether either party had acted unreasonably.

3.18 If the **second party does not object to an expert nominated**, he shall not be entitled to rely on his own expert evidence within that particular speciality unless:

(a) the first party agrees,

(b) the court so directs, or

(c) the first party's expert report has been amended and the first party is not prepared to disclose the original report.

3.19 **Either party may send to an agreed expert written questions** on the report, relevant to the issues, via the first party's solicitors. The expert should send answers to the questions separately and directly to each party.

3.20 The cost of a report from an agreed expert will usually be paid by the instructing first party: the costs of the expert replying to questions will usually be borne by the party which asks the questions.

3.21 Where the defendant admits liability in whole or in part, before proceedings are issued, any medical report obtained by agreement under this protocol should be disclosed to the other party. The claimant should delay issuing proceedings for 21 days from disclosure of the report, to enable the parties to consider whether the claim is capable of settlement. The Civil Procedure Rules Part 36 permit claimants and defendants to make offers to settle pre-proceedings. Parties should always consider before issuing if it is appropriate to make Part 36 Offer. If such an offer is made, the party making the offer must always supply sufficient evidence and/or information to enable the offer to be properly considered.

ANNEX A
LETTER OF CLAIM

To   **A1.073**

Defendant

Dear Sirs

Re: Claimant's full name
Claimant's full address
Claimant's Clock or Works Number
Claimant's Employer (*name and address*)

We are instructed by the above named to claim damages in connection with *an accident at work/road traffic accident/tripping accident* on day of *(year)* at *(place of accident which must be sufficiently detailed to establish location)*

Please confirm the identity of your insurers. Please note that the insurers will need to see this letter as soon as possible and it may affect your insurance cover and/or the conduct of any subsequent legal proceedings if you do not send this letter to them.

The circumstances of the accident are:-
(brief outline)

The reason why we are alleging fault is:
(simple explanation e.g. defective machine, broken ground)

A description of our clients' injuries is as follows:-
(brief outline)

(In cases of road traffic accidents)

Our client (state hospital reference number) received treatment for the injuries at name and address of hospital).

He is employed as *(occupation)* and has had the following time off work *(dates of absence)*. His approximate weekly income is *(insert if known)*.

If you are our client's employers, please provide us with the usual earnings details which will enable us to calculate his financial loss.

We are obtaining a police report and will let you have a copy of the same upon your undertaking to meet half the fee.

We have also sent a letter of claim to *(name and address)* and a copy of that letter is attached. We understand their insurers are *(name, address and claims number if known)*

At this stage of our enquiries we would expect the documents contained in parts *(insert appropriate parts of standard disclosure list)* to be relevant to this action.

A copy of this letter is attached for you to send to your insurers.

Finally we expect an acknowledgment of this letter within 21 days by yourselves or your insurers.

Yours faithfully

ANNEX B
STANDARD DISCLOSURE LISTS

Pre-action personal injury protocol
Fast track disclosure
RTA cases

Section A

In all cases where liability is at issue—   **A1.074**

   (i) Documents identifying nature, extent and location of damage to defendant's vehicle where there is any dispute about point of impact.

   (ii) MOT certificate where relevant.

   (iii) Maintenance records where vehicle defect is alleged or it is alleged by defendant that there was an unforeseen defect which caused or contributed to the accident.

Section B

Accident involving commercial vehicle as potential defendant—

   (i) Tachograph charts or entry from individual control book.

   (ii) Maintenance and repair records required for operators' licence where vehicle defect is alleged or it is alleged by defendants that there was an unforeseen defect which caused or contributed to the accident.

Section C

Cases against local authorities where highway design defect is alleged.

   (i) Documents produced to comply with Section 39 of the Road

Traffic Act 1988 in respect of the duty designed to promote road safety to include studies into road accidents in the relevant area and documents relating to measures recommended to prevent accidents in the relevant area.

Highway tripping claims

Documents from Highway Authority for a period of 12 months prior to the accident—

(i)   Records of inspection for the relevant stretch of highway.

(ii) Maintenance records including records of independent contractors working in relevant area.

(iii) Records of the minutes of Highway Authority meetings where maintenance or repair policy has been discussed or decided.

(iv) Records of complaints about the state of highways.

(v)   Records of other accidents which have occurred on the relevant stretch of highway.

Workplace claims

(i)   Accident book entry.

(ii)   First aider report.

(iii) Surgery record.

(iv)   Foreman/supervisor accident report.

(v)   Safety representatives accident report.

(vi)   RIDDOR report to HSE.

(vii) Other communications between defendants and HSE.

(viii) Minutes of Health and Safety Committee meeting(s) where accident/matter considered.

(ix)   Report to DSS.

(x)   Documents listed above relative to any previous accident/matter identified by the claimant and relied upon as proof of negligence.

(xi)   Earnings information where defendant is employer.

Documents produced to comply with requirements of the Management of Health and Safety at Work Regulations 1992—

   (i) Pre-accident Risk Assessment required by Regulation 3.

  (ii) Post-accident Re-Assessment required by Regulation 3.

 (iii) Accident Investigation Report prepared in implementing the requirements of Regulations 4, 6 and 9.

 (iv) Health Surveillance Records in appropriate cases required by Regulation 5.

  (v) Information provided to employees under Regulation 8.

 (vi) Documents relating to the employees health and safety training required by Regulation 11.

Workplace claims—disclosure where specific regulations apply

Section A—workplace (health safety and welfare) regulations 1992

   (i) Repair and maintenance records required by Regulation 5.

  (ii) Housekeeping records to comply with the requirements of Regulation 9.

 (iii) Hazard warning signs or notices to comply with Regulation 17 (Traffic Routes).

Section B—provision and use of work equipment regulations 1992

   (i) Manufacturers' specifications and instructions in respect of relevant work equipment establishing its suitability to comply with Regulation 5.

  (ii) Maintenance log/maintenance records required to comply with Regulation 6.

 (iii) Documents providing information and instructions to employees to comply with Regulation 8.

 (iv) Documents provided to the employee in respect of training for use to comply with Regulation 9.

  (v) Any notice, sign or document relied upon as a defence to alleged breaches of Regulations 14 to 18 dealing with controls and control systems.

(vi) Instruction/training documents issued to comply with the requirements of Regulation 22 insofar as it deals with maintenance operations where the machinery is not shut down.

(vii) Copies of markings required to comply with Regulation 23.

(viii) Copies of warnings required to comply with Regulation 24.

Section C—personal protective equipment at work regulations 1992

(i) Documents relating to the assessment of the Personal Protective Equipment to comply with Regulation 6.

(ii) Documents relating to the maintenance and replacement of Personal Protective Equipment to comply with Regulation 7.

(iii) Record of maintenance procedures for Personal Protective Equipment to comply with Regulation 7.

(iv) Records of tests and examinations of Personal Protective Equipment to comply with Regulation 7.

(v) Documents providing information, instruction and training in relation to the Personal Protective Equipment to comply with Regulation 9.

(vi) Instructions for use of Personal Protective Equipment to include the manufacturers' instructions to comply with Regulation 10.

Section D—manual handling operations regulations 1992

(i) Manual Handling Risk Assessment carried out to comply with the requirements of Regulation 4(1)(b)(i).

(ii) Re-assessment carried out post-accident to comply with requirements of Regulation 4(1)(b)(i).

(iii) Documents showing the information provided to the employee to give general indications related to the load and precise indications on the weight of the load and the heaviest side of the load if the centre of gravity was not positioned centrally to comply with Regulation 4(1)(b)(iii).

(iv) Documents relating to training in respect of manual handling operations and training records.

Section E—health and safety (display screen equipment) regulations 1992

(i) Analysis of work stations to assess and reduce risks carried out to comply with the requirements of Regulation 2.

(ii) Re-assessment of analysis of work stations to assess and reduce risks following development of symptoms by the claimant.

(iii) Documents detailing the provision of training including training records to comply with the requirements of Regulation 6.

(iv) Documents providing information to employees to comply with the requirements of Regulation 7.

Section F—control of substances hazardous to health regulations 1988

(i) Risk assessment carried out to comply with the requirements of Regulation 6.

(ii) Reviewed risk assessment carried out to comply with the requirements of Regulation 6.

(iii) Copy labels from containers used for storage handling and disposal of carcinogenics to comply with the requirements of Regulation 7(2A)(h).

(iv) Warning signs identifying designation of areas and installations which may be contaminated by carcinogenics to comply with the requirements of Regulation 7(2A)(h).

(v) Documents relating to the assessment of the Personal Protective Equipment to comply with Regulation 7(3A).

(vi) Documents relating to the maintenance and replacement of Personal Protective Equipment to comply with Regulation 7(3A).

(vii) Record of maintenance procedures for Personal Protective Equipment to comply with Regulation 7(3A).

(viii) Records of tests and examinations of Personal Protective Equipment to comply with Regulation 7(3A).

(ix) Documents providing information, instruction and training in relation to the Personal Protective Equipment to comply with Regulation 7(3A).

(x) Instructions for use of Personal Protective Equipment to include the manufacturers' instructions to comply with Regulation 7(3A).

(xi) Air monitoring records for substances assigned a maximum exposure limit or occupational exposure standard to comply with the requirements of Regulation 7.

(xii) Maintenance examination and test of control measures records to comply with Regulation 9.

(xiii) Monitoring records to comply with the requirements of Regulation 10.

(xiv) Health surveillance records to comply with the requirements of Regulation 11.

(xv) Documents detailing information, instruction and training including training records for employees to comply with the requirements of Regulation 12.

(xvi) Labels and Health and Safety data sheets supplied to the employers to comply with the CHIP Regulations.

Section G—construction (design and management) regulations 1994

(i) Notification of a project form (HSE F10) to comply with the requirements of Regulation 7.

(ii) Health and Safety Plan to comply with requirements of Regulation 15.

(iii) Health and Safety file to comply with the requirements of Regulations 12 and 14.

(iv) Information and training records provided to comply with the requirements of Regulation 17.

(v) Records of advice from and views of persons at work to comply with the requirements of Regulation 18.

Section H—pressure systems and transportable gas containers regulations 1989

(i) Information and specimen markings provided to comply with the requirements of Regulation 5.

(ii) Written statements specifying the safe operating limits of a system to comply with the requirements of Regulation 7.

(iii) Copy of the written scheme of examination required to comply with the requirements of Regulation 8.

(iv) Examination records required to comply with the requirements of Regulation 9.

(v) Instructions provided for the use of operator to comply with Regulation 11.

(vi) Records kept to comply with the requirements of Regulation 13.

(vii) Records kept to comply with the requirements of Regulation 22.

Section I—lifting plant and equipment (records of test and examination etc.) regulations 1992

(i) Record kept to comply with the requirements of Regulation 6.

Section J—the noise at work regulations 1989

(i) Any risk assessment records required to comply with the requirements of Regulations 4 and 5.

(ii) Manufacturers' literature in respect of all ear protection made available to claimant to comply with the requirements of Regulation 8.

(iii) All documents provided to the employee for the provision of information to comply with Regulation 11.

Section K—construction (head protection) regulations 1989

(i) Pre-accident assessment of head protection required to comply with Regulation 3(4).

(ii) Post-accident re-assessment required to comply with Regulation 3(5).

Section L—the construction (general provisions) regulations 1961

  (i) Report prepared following inspections and examinations of excavations etc. to comply with the requirements of Regulation 9.

  (ii) Report prepared following inspections and examinations of work in cofferdams and caissons to comply with the requirements of Regulations 17 and 18.

N.B. Further Standard Discovery lists will be required prior to full implementation.

Annex C

Letter of Instruction

To medical expert

A1.075 Dear Sir,

Re: *(Name and Address)*

D.O.B.—

Telephone No.—

Date of Accident—

We are acting for the above named in connection with injuries received in an accident which occurred on the above date. The main injuries appear to have been **(main injuries)**.

We should be obliged if you would examine our Client and let us have a full and detailed report dealing with any relevant pre-accident medical history, the injuries sustained, treatment received and present condition, dealing in particular with the capacity for work and giving a prognosis.

It is central to our assessment of the extent of our Client's injuries to establish the extent and duration of any continuing disability. Accordingly, in the prognosis section we would ask you to specifically comment on any areas of continuing complaint or disability or impact on daily living. If there is such continuing disability you should comment upon the level of suffering or inconvenience caused and, if you are able, give your view as to when or if the complaint or disability is likely to resolve.

Please send our Client an appointment direct for this purpose. Should you be able to offer a cancellation appointment please contact our Client direct. We confirm we will be responsible for your reasonable fees.

We are obtaining the notes and records from our Client's GP and Hospitals attended and will forward them to you when they are to hand/or please request the GP and Hospital records direct and advise that any invoice for the provision of these records should be forwarded to us.

In order to comply with Court Rules we would be grateful if you would insert above your signature a statement that the contents are true to the best of your knowledge and belief.

In order to avoid further correspondence we can confirm that on the evidence we have there is no reason to suspect we may be pursuing a claim against the hospital or its staff.

We look forward to receiving your report within _____ weeks. If you will not be able to prepare your report within this period please telephone us upon receipt of these instructions.

When acknowledging these instructions it would assist if you could give an estimate as to the likely time scale for the provision of your report and also an indication as to your fee.

Yours faithfully

Insurance Policy Wording

A1.076

WHAT IS COVERED BY THIS SOLICITORS SERVICES — LEGAL COSTS PROTECTION POLICY

SUBJECT ALWAYS to acceptance of cover by Us and payment of The Premium:

1. You are insured on an annual basis up to the maximum limit We will pay under this Policy provided Your CFA shown in the Schedule remains in effect. This Policy relates only to Your Personal Injury Claim.

2. You are insured for liability You may incur to pay:

Your Opponent s Legal Charges:
- When You are ordered to pay them by a Court following a judgment against You.
- When You are ordered to pay them by a Court after an award of damages is made to You which are less than Your Opponent has paid into Court in accordance with Part 36.
- When You are ordered to pay them when You, Your Solicitor and We agree to discontinue against Your Opponent.

Your Disbursements and The Premium:
- When the Court has dismissed Your case and makes an order by consent or otherwise that You must pay Your Opponents Costs.
- When a Court makes no order as to costs when You, Your Solicitor and We agree to discontinue.
- When Your Personal Injury Claim is abandoned before Court proceedings are commenced strictly provided that a Letter of Claim has been sent by Your Solicitor and a response received from Your Opponent.

Your Opponent s Legal Charges which We may be liable to pay will always be subject to agreement by Us before any claim on this indemnity is paid.

3. It may be that during Your Personal Injury Claim You receive an award of damages in which case We will pay:

- Your Opponent s Legal Charges if ordered by a Court where there is a failure to beat a payment made into Court in respect of Part 36, Your Disbursements incurred after the date of the payment into Court under Part 36.

In all other circumstances where damages or other monies are agreed or awarded to You the liability under this Policy to pay your Opponent s Legal Charges and Your Disbursements will only be payable to the extent that they exceed the award.

Where any of Your Opponent s Legal Charges or Your Disbursements have already been paid by Us and You receive a payment of damages or other monies for Your Personal Injury Claim We will be entitled to claim reimbursement out of those damages or other monies.

4. You are insured under this Policy for any proceedings other than small claims within the jurisdiction and the Law of the Courts of England and Wales for Personal Injury that You suffer anywhere in the world.

5. You are insured for The Premium, Your Disbursements and Your Opponent s Legal Charges which We are liable to pay from Your Personal Injury Claim to a maximum indemnity limit of £100,000 inclusive of VAT. We shall not under any circumstances be liable to pay more than this maximum limit in respect of You and Your Personal Injury under any or all Policies.

6. The Insurance starts when We have agreed to accept cover under this Policy, You have signed a Conditional Fee Agreement, You have paid The Premium or made arrangements to have The Premium paid to Us by Your Solicitor, who has undertaken to do this on Your behalf, and You have been issued the Policy. The Policy is subject to review at the annual anniversary.

7. The Insurance ends at the annual anniversary of the Policy start date. Your Personal Injury Claim will be reviewed and if We agree the Policy will continue as a renewal. Your Solicitor will explain this to You.

The Policy ends when the Conditional Fee Agreement ends or if earlier, on termination of Your CFA or termination of your Personal Injury Claim by settlement or otherwise subject to the cancellation provisions of the Policy.

8. **Making a claim under this Policy**
It may be that Your Personal Injury Claim is unsuccessful in total or in part. Subject always to Our agreement:

We will pay:
- Opponent s Legal Charges when the Opponent s Legal Charges which You are ordered by the Court to pay have been agreed with Your Opponent by Us or when they have been assessed by the Court and agreed by Us.
- Your Disbursements and The Premium when a Court orders You to pay Your Opponent s Legal Charges or at the time of discontinuance if the Court makes no order as to costs if Your Personal Injury Claim is discontinued or, with Our agreement, at the time of abandonment before Court Proceedings are commenced provided that a Letter of Claim has been sent and a response received from Your Opponent.

In all circumstances, any payment is subject always to Our agreement.

9. You are not insured and will not be entitled to cover under the Policy for:
- Your Solicitor s legal charges or success fee
- anything which is not related to your Personal Injury Claim
- anything after the annual anniversary of the Policy unless Our written agreement to continue is given
- any claim for recovery by Your Solicitor of any shortfall in legal charges, success fees, The Premium or other monies
- anything if We have not accepted cover, if You have not signed a Conditional Fee Agreement, or if You have not paid The Premium or made arrangements to have The Premium paid to Us by Your Solicitor
- any appeal You make against any final judgement or order without Our agreement in writing
- any claim dealt with in the Small Claims Court
- any claim which relates to clinical negligence or to pharmaceutical or drug related claims (including but not limited to claims relating to tobacco or tobacco products)
- any claim for libel or slander and/or the mental or other effect of libel or slander
- any counterclaim made against You
- any action which You discontinue, abandon or from which You withdraw without agreement in writing from Us
- anything incurred before the Policy start date
- anything incurred after The Conditional Fee Agreement ends
- any enforcement proceedings
- any of Your Opponent s Legal Charges without Our agreement in writing
- Your advocate s or Your barrister s fees
- Your Disbursements and The Premium if Your Personal Injury Claim is abandoned before a Letter of Claim has been issued and a response received from Your Opponent.

SOLICITORS SERVICES — LEGAL COSTS PROTECTION POLICY CONDITIONS

You have a responsibility under this Insurance. You must:

- always give instructions that will allow Your Solicitor to work properly and You must not ask Your Solicitor to work in an improper or unreasonable way or deliberately mislead Your Solicitor
- co-operate fully with Your Solicitor when asked
- go to any medical or expert examination or Court hearing when asked
- authorise Us to receive from Your Solicitor any specific information, document or advice even if privileged and on Our request instruct Your Solicitor to release such information
- ensure the cost of any claim under this Insurance is minimised. This includes, but is not limited to allowing Us or Our representative to negotiate and approve the amount claimed from the indemnity of this Insurance which We are liable to pay either by agreement or representing You at the assessment of any Opponent s Legal Charges or disbursements
- comply with the conditions and the terms of this Insurance in respect of anything You should or should not do and understand that failure to comply may result in Our refusing to meet Your claim
- assign to Us or Our representative any rights or causes of action which may enable Us to recover an outlay under the terms of the Policy.

YOUR SOLICITOR AND US

Your Solicitor has a responsibility to Us.

Unless You are acting with Our prior written authorisation We will not be bound by any promise or undertaking You give to Your Solicitor.

You have entered into a Conditional Fee Agreement with Your Solicitor. Your Solicitor has also entered into an agreement with Us so that We can provide the Policy to You.

If You or Your Solicitor by breach of conduct, duty, authority under the Policy or by act of negligence or fraud should prejudice Our position We reserve Our rights to investigate the matter and where necessary, instruct Our legal representative to take remedy.

If Your Solicitor by breach of conduct, duty, authority under the Policy or by act of negligence or fraud should prejudice Your position in relation to Your Personal Injury Claim, You agree to assign to Us any rights or causes of action You may have so that We may investigate the matter and where necessary, instruct Our legal representative to take remedy.

Cancellation

The Policy may be cancelled by You without return of The Premium at any time.

The Policy may be cancelled by Us without return of The Premium if:

(a)   You fail to meet any of Your responsibilities
(b)   Your Solicitor believes You are unlikely to succeed in Your Personal Injury Claim but You wish to continue nonetheless
(c)   You reject Your Solicitor s opinion about making a settlement with Your Opponent
(d)   We believe You are unlikely to succeed in Your Personal Injury Claim but You and Your Solicitor disagree. If, following arbitration as provided for below, the arbitrator agrees with You, the cover will be reinstated from the date of cancellation
(e)   Your breach of any of the terms of Your Conditional Fee Agreement or any of the terms of the Policy. In these circumstances You will render the Policy invalid and You will not be able to make any claim from the Policy and The Premium will not be returned.

If the Policy is cancelled We will not pay any of Your Opponent s Legal Charges or any Disbursements (whether incurred before or after the date of cancellation).

The exception to this is that if We cancel as described in Cancellation clause (d) above, our liability for Your Opponent s Legal Charges and Your Disbursements and The Premium incurred prior to the date of such cancellation will not be affected.

If any fraudulent claim is made or if any fraudulent means or devices are used to obtain any benefit under the Policy, this Insurance shall be void and The Premium shall be forfeited. Any benefits claimed, received or paid must be repaid to Us by You.

General Exceptions

The Policy does not cover any expense, consequential loss, legal liability or loss, damage or Personal Injury directly or indirectly caused by or arising from or contributed to by:

- pressure waves caused by aircraft or other aerial devices
- ionising radiation or contamination by radioactivity from any nuclear fuel or from any nuclear waste from the combustion of nuclear fuel
- the radioactive, toxic, explosive or other hazardous properties of any explosive nuclear assembly or nuclear component
- war, invasion, act of foreign enemy, terrorism, hostilities (whether war be declared or not), civil war, rebellion, revolution, insurrection, military or usurped power, civil commotion, or riot
- the actual or potential inability of any computer, data processing equipment or media, microchip, integrated circuit or similar device or any computer software or stored programme to correctly recognise any date as its true calendar date or to continue to function correctly in respect of or beyond that date.

Arbitration

It may be that a dispute arises between You and Us. If this happens the dispute shall be subject to arbitration under the process in effect at the time.

Any dispute between You and Us shall be referred to a single arbitrator pursuant to the Arbitration Act 1996 as amended from time to time (or to a mutually agreed alternative) who shall be either a solicitor on whom We both agree or, if We cannot agree, one who is nominated by the Chairman of the British Insurance Law Association.

The Insurance and any dispute arising in respect of its interpretation, application, operation or otherwise shall   be governed by the Laws of England & Wales.

Nothing in the Insurance shall prevent the parties from engaging in voluntary mediation or some other mutually agreeable method of dispute resolution.

We will pay all costs of arbitration, whatever the outcome, in relation to any dispute brought to arbitration as a result of cancellation under Cancellation Clause (d) above.

In all other arbitration disputes the costs of arbitration shall be met in full by the party against whom the decision is made.

If the decision is not clearly made against either party, the arbitrator shall have the power to apportion costs.

Data Protection

It is understood by You that any information provided to Us regarding You will be processed by Us, in compliance with the provisions of the Data Protection Act 1998, or any subsequent revisions or amendments for the purpose of providing Insurance and handling claims, if any, which may necessitate providing such information to third parties.

Third Party Rights

A person who is not a party to this contract has no right under the Contracts (Rights of Third Parties) Act 1999 or any subsequent revisions or amendments to enforce any term of this contract but this does not affect any right or remedy of a third party which exists or is available apart from that Act.

Complaints

We aim to provide a first class service at all times. However, if You have any complaint regarding the standard of service You have received under Your Policy, the following procedure is available to You to resolve the situation.

1.   In the first instance please write to the Managing Director, Solicitors Services Limited, TMS House, Cray Avenue, Orpington, Kent BR5 3QB. We will endeavour to deal fully with your complaint within four weeks of receipt.

2.   Our decision is final and based on the evidence presented. If You feel that there is any new evidence or information that may change Our decision You have the right to make an appeal which should be addressed to the Quality Department, Europ Assistance Holdings Limited, Sussex House, Perrymount Road, Haywards Heath, West Sussex, RH16 1DN.

3.   Should You remain dissatisfied or fail to receive a final answer within eight weeks (this depends on You responding immediately to any correspondence We send You) of Us receiving Your complaint, You have the right to refer the matter to the Financial Ombudsman Service at: South Quay Plaza, 183 Marsh Wall, London, E14 9SR. Telephone : 0207 964 1000

This referral is in addition to your contractual rights under the insurance.

- N.B. The time scales given above are dependent on you responding immediately to any correspondence we send you.

Pre-action Protocol for Personal Injury Claims

THE SCHEDULE

INSURANCE POLICY NUMBER: _____

NAME OF INSURED: _____

ADDRESS OF INSURED: _____

_____ POST CODE: _____

PREMIUM £ _____
(INCLUSIVE OF INSURANCE PREMIUM TAX)

PREMIUM PAID THROUGH LEGAL COSTS FUNDING? ☐ Y ☐ N

POLICY START DATE: ☐☐ / ☐☐ / ☐☐

POLICY REVIEW DATE: ☐☐ / ☐☐ / ☐☐

CONDITIONAL FEE AGREEMENT DATE: ☐☐ / ☐☐ / ☐☐

ACCIDENT TYPE: [Accident type in words] _____

YOUR SOLICITOR: _____

YOUR SOLICITOR S ADDRESS: _____

_____ POST CODE: _____

This Insurance

The benefits under this Insurance Policy are underwritten by Europ Assistance Insurance Limited and apply during the period of Insurance subject always to the terms, conditions and exclusions contained in this Policy and following payment of The Premium. This Insurance is effected in and is subject to the Laws of England and Wales.

We will provide You with the security of Legal Costs Protection in return for payment of The Premium and conditional upon You entering into and maintaining a Conditional Fee Agreement with Your Solicitor.

This Schedule and Policy should be read carefully at the same time as Your Conditional Fee Agreement, and should be kept in a safe place. Your Solicitor will explain anything that is not clear to You.

Unless We specifically agree in writing, this Insurance is not transferable.

Signed for Europ Assistance Insurance Limited

Managing Director

MEANING OF WORDS
Wherever the following words and phrases shown here in bold appear in this Policy, they will always have these meanings:

We, Us, Our
Solicitors Services Limited, agents appointed by Europ Assistance Insurance Limited, the underwriters of this Policy, who manage the Policy.

You, Your
The person accepted for cover under this Policy of Insurance and shown in the Schedule as the Insured Person; or if unable to act for him/herself their legal personal representative.

Your Conditional Fee Agreement - CFA
The Agreement dated in the Schedule between You and Your Solicitor which relates to the payment of Your Solicitor s basic Legal Charges and Success Fee in a specific claim for damages after You have suffered Personal Injury. The Agreement must comply with the Conditional Fee Agreements Regulations 2000 and any subsequent revisions and amendments to them.

Your Personal Injury
A disease or impairment of Your physical or mental condition for which damages may be claimed and which is recognised in English Law.

Your Personal Injury Claim
Your claim for damages for Your Personal Injury to which Your Conditional Fee Agreement relates.

Your Solicitor
The Solicitor or firm of Solicitors with whom You have entered into Your Conditional Fee Agreement. Your chosen Solicitor must be authorised by Us to implement this policy.

Your Opponent
The party or parties from whom You are seeking to recover damages under Your Personal Injury Claim.

Opponent s Legal Charges
Your Opponent s Solicitor s reasonable Legal Charges including their disbursements.

Your Disbursements
Reasonable and necessary payments to third parties (not including advocate s or barrister s fees of any kind) made or incurred by Your Solicitor on Your behalf in connection with Your Personal Injury Claim which would be allowable as recoverable by a Court under the Civil Procedure Rules provided always that they are incurred after the Policy start date and during the period of this Insurance. Examples include Court fees, accident report fees and expert report fees, including any funding costs arising from the use of Legal Costs Funding.

Schedule
The Schedule, which forms part of the Policy shows Your name and address, Your Conditional Fee Agreement date, the Policy start date, The Premium and information relating to the Policy.

The Premium
The amount indicated in the Schedule which is agreed by and paid to Us and from which Your Solicitor receives no commission. Any payment arising from a claim agreed under this Policy will include any funding costs where applicable from the Use of Solicitors Services - Legal Costs Funding. In certain circumstances an amount of The Premium may be rebated. Your Solicitor will advise You of these circumstances and make application on Your behalf where necessary. The Policy is subject to renewal at the annual anniversary. Your Solicitor will advise when any Premium payments are due and what they will be.

The Civil Procedure Rules
All reference to legal procedure in the Policy shall be interpreted in accordance with the Civil Procedure Rules of England and Wales and any subsequent reviews or amendments to them.

Notice of Funding of Case or Claim

Notice of Funding of Case or Claim

Click here to clear all fields

A1.077

Notice of funding by means of a conditional fee agreement, insurance policy or undertaking given by a prescribed body should be given to the court and all other parties to the case:

- on commencement of proceedings
- on filing an acknowledgment of service, defence or other first document; and
- at any later time that such an arrangement is entered into, changed or terminated

In the	
Claim No.	
Claimant (include Ref.)	
Defendant (include Ref.)	

Take notice that in respect of [all claims herein][the following claims . . . .]
the case of . . . . *(specify name of party)*

[is now][was] being funded by:
(Please tick those boxes which apply)

☐ a conditional fee agreement dated . . . . which provides for a success fee;

☐ an insurance policy issued on *(date)* . . . . . . by *(name of insurers)* . . . . ;

☐ an undertaking given on *(date)* . . . . . by *(name of prescribed body)* . . . . in the following terms . . . .

The funding of the case has now changed:

☐ the above funding has now ceased

☐ the conditional fee agreement has been terminated

☐ a conditional agreement dated . . . . which provides for a success fee has been entered into

☐ the insurance policy dated . . . . has been cancelled

☐ an insurance policy has been issued by *(name of insurer)* . . . . on *(date)* . . . .

☐ the undertaking given on *(date)* . . . . has been terminated

☐ an undertaking has been given on *(date)* . . . . . by *(name of prescribed body)* . . . . in the following terms . . . .

Signed . . . . Date . . . .
Solicitor for the (claimant) (defendant) (Part 20 defendant) (respondent)(appellant)

The court office at

is open between 10 am and 4 pm Monday to Friday. When corresponding with the court, please address forms or letters to the Court Manager and quote the claim number.
N251 Notice of funding of case or claim (7.00) The Court Service Publications Unit

APPENDIX 2

CALLERY v GRAY

Report on the Facts and History of the Case

CALLERY v GRAY [2002] UKHL 28, HL
JUNE 27, 2002 (LORDS BINGHAM, NICHOLLS, HOFFMANN, HOPE
AND SCOTT)

On June 27, 2002 the long awaited decision of the House of Lords in **A2.001**
Callery v Gray [2002] UKHL 28 was delivered. The decision on the
appeal from the Court of Appeal in costs-only proceedings was of
course concerned with the arrangements for financing the cost of
personal injury litigation. The Court of Appeal had given it's decision
(EWCA Civ 1246) in two separate judgments reported in July 2001. It
is central to the whole question of recoverability both of insurance
premiums and uplifts. It is also the starting point for anyone setting a
success fee in a CFA funded case.

On April 2, 2000 Mr Callery was a passenger in a car which was
struck side-on by a vehicle driven by Mr Gray. Mr Callery sustained
minor injuries. He instructed solicitors, Messrs Amelans, to pursue a
claim for damages against Mr Gray. Amelans are a firm who deal
with a large number of road traffic accident claims. They are specialists in this field. Mr Callery's claim was commonplace. There are
thousands of such claims every year. They rarely reach the courts. Mr
Callery entered into a CFA with Amelans at the same time as
instructing them to pursue his damages claim. The CFA was dated
April 28, 2000. It said that if Mr Callery succeeded in his claim for
damages he would pay Amelans' basic charges and a success fee. It
said that, win or lose, Mr Callery would have to pay their dis-

bursements. It set the success fee at 60 per cent of Amelans' basic charges.

On May 4, 2000 Mr Callery took out an after the event insurance policy with Temple Legal Protection Ltd. This was the date on which Amelans' first letter to Mr Gray, informing him of the claim, was sent. The policy was taken out before Mr Callery or his legal advisers, Amelans, could have come to the conclusion that litigation to pursue the claim would be necessary or even likely. The premium for the policy was £350 plus £17.50 tax, a total of £367.50. The broad scope of the cover under the policy meant that Temple agreed to indemnify Mr Callery, up to a limit of £100,000, for any sum in respect of Mr Gray's costs that might be ordered by the court to be paid by Mr Callery; and for disbursements paid out by Amelans in the event that the litigation came to an end without the disbursements becoming payable by Mr Gray.

A feature of the policy was that the premium of £350 would not become payable until the conclusion of the legal proceedings in respect of which the policy had been taken out and, if the amount of the premium were challenged by Mr Gray in any cost assessment process, the recoverable amount of the premium would be reduced to the amount payable by Mr Gray under the assessment.

A2.002   On May 4, 2000, the day on which the policy was taken out, Amelans wrote to Mr Gray giving notice of their client's damages claim and enclosing a copy of the letter for his insurers. The letter asked for an acknowledgement within 21 days from Mr Gray or his insurers.

On May 19, 2000, Mr Gray's insurers, CGU Insurance, replied. Their reply said that they were able "to admit liability as to negligence but not to causation". Following an exchange of offer and counter-offer, the parties reached agreement on August 2, 2000 that Mr Callery should receive damages of £1500. Amelans wrote on August 7, 2000 to CGU confirming "acceptance of your offer in the sum of £1500 in respect of our client's damages" and that "acceptance of the offer is subject to payment of our client's reasonable costs and disbursements ...". However, the parties were unable to agree the amount of the "reasonable costs and disbursements".

There were two main issues. First, CGU took the view that a 60 per cent success fee for Amelans was unreasonably high. It was always certain, they thought, that Mr Callery would succeed in recovering damages. He had been a passenger in a vehicle struck side-on by Mr Gray's vehicle. He had been injured in the accident. He was bound to recover something. So this was not a case in which there was any risk that Amelans, in pursuing the claim on Mr Callery's behalf, would be working for nothing. It followed that any success fee should be very low.

Second, CGU contended that the £350 premium was an item of expenditure that had not been reasonably incurred. The likelihood of litigation being necessary was always very remote. At the least Mr Callery should have waited until a response to Amelans' letter of May 4, 2000 had been received before taking out a policy to protect himself against the costs consequences of litigation that was unlikely ever to materialise.

On September 12, 2000 Mr Callery commenced proceedings under **A2.003** CPR Part 8 asking the court to assess his reasonable costs of and occasioned by his damages claim against Mr Gray. The particulars of claim pleaded the agreement that had been reached that Mr Gray would pay £1500 damages and Mr Callery's reasonable costs. The assessment hearing took place before District Judge Wallace on November 7, 2000. The District Judge assessed Amelans' basic charges, reduced the success fee from 60 per cent to 40 per cent of the basic charges and allowed the after the event insurance premium of £350 plus tax as a disbursement. The assessment allowed a total of £1008, plus VAT, for fees and £617.50 for disbursements.

Mr Gray (prompted by CGU) appealed to the circuit judge. The appeal was heard by Judge Edwards in the Chester County Court on January 29, 2001. Two points were taken on the appeal, one relating to Amelans' success fee under the CFA, the other relating to the after insurance premium. The appeal was dismissed on both points.

CGU took the view that important points of principle were at stake, with implications for personal injury litigants and their insurers generally, and prompted Mr Gray to apply to the Court of Appeal for permission to bring a second appeal to that court. On March 16, 2001 Lady Justice Hale granted permission on condition that Mr Gray, if successful, would not seeks costs from Mr Callery unless his liability to pay were covered in full by the terms of the after the event policy.

Further evidence was, with the permission of the Court of Appeal, introduced at the hearing of the appeal and written and oral intervention by the Law Society, the ABI, the After Event Insurers Group Forum, APIL and FOIL was authorised. On appeal *Russell v Pal Pak Corrugated Ltd* was also considered as similar success fee issues arose.

The Court of Appeal heard the appeal on June 5, 6 and 7, 2001. On **A2.004** July 17, 2001 the court handed down the judgment of the court on the success fee issue, reducing Amelans' success fee from the 40 per cent fixed by the district judge to 20 per cent (and dismissing the appeal in *Russell v Pal Pak*) [2001] 1 W.L.R. 2112. In addition the court ruled that an after the event insurance premium could in principle be recovered as part of a claimant's costs in "costs only" proceedings. But the court formed the view that, on the evidence available, it was not possible to come to a conclusion as to the reasonableness in amount of the £350 premium. So the court postponed judgment on the issue relating to the amount of the after the event insurance premium pending an inquiry by a costs judge, Master O'Hare. A separate judgment on that issue awaited Master O'Hare's report.

In principle the premium was held to be recoverable notwithstanding that the policy had been taken out before the commencement of litigation for the purpose of recovering damages had become necessary, or even likely. As it was put at p. 2134, para 100 of the judgment: "we have concluded that where, at the outset, a reasonable uplift is agreed and after the event insurance at a reasonable premium is taken out, the costs of each are recoverable from the defendant in the event that the claim succeeds, or is settled on terms that the defendant pay the claimant's costs."

Master O'Hare's report was dated July 23, 2001. The purpose of his report was expressed to be "to enable the Court of Appeal to give guidance in its judgment as to the practice to be adopted in future in taking out [ATE] insurance." Master O'Hare had received written submissions from a number of interested parties but nonetheless concluded that: "For several reasons it is not possible to state standard or average premiums for different classes or categories of ATE insurance." He concluded that the industry was still immature and this was not the time to publish guideline figures for after the event premiums.

On July 31, 2001 Lord Phillips of Worth Matravers, sitting with Brooke LJ, handed down the judgment of the court dealing with the reasonableness of the amount of Mr Callery's ATE premium [2001] 1 W.L.R. 2142. The Court concluded that "the amount of the premium does not strike us as manifestly disproportionate to the risk". So the appeal on the insurance premium point was dismissed. The appeal on the success fee point had been allowed by the reduction of the percentage uplift from 40 per cent to 20 per cent.

A2.005   There were ten issues before the House of Lords:

(1) Was the insurance premium recoverable given the stage when the policy was taken out? (prematurity).

(2) Was the amount of the premium reasonable having regard to the characteristics of the instant case?

(3) Was the amount of the premium reasonable having regard to prematurity?

(4) Was the Court of Appeal wrong not to resolve doubt—if any—as to the amount of the recoverable premium in favour of the paying party?

(5) Should the defendant be liable for any part of the premium which covers adverse costs orders and all aspects of own costs, however incurred?

(6) The success fee ("uplift"): is the full uplift recoverable given the stage when the CFA was effected?

(7) Was the 20 per cent uplift a reasonable maximum for simple accident cases?

(8) Was the Court of Appeal's assessment of 20 per cent uplift for the instant case wrong?

(9) Should an uplift be assessed by reference to the risk in the particular case, or on a more general, and if so what, basis?

(10) Should uplift levels be conditioned, and if so how, by public interest considerations?"

The Lords held, with Lord Scott dissenting, that the responsibility for monitoring and controlling the developing practice in this field lay with the Court of Appeal and not the House of Lords. They said that the House of Lords should be very slow to interfere with the findings of the Court of Appeal on such issues.

They said that the present issues arose at a very early stage in the practical development of the new funding regime when reliable factual material was sparse, market experience was meagre and trends were hard to discern. They said that the Court of Appeal therefore rightly did not lay down rules applicable for all time but gave provisional guidance to be reviewed in the light of increased knowledge and developing experience.

The commented that the new funding system should be watched closely to ensure that it did not become unbalanced or unfairly prejudicial to liability insurers and to the general body of motorists whose insurance policy premiums provided the money with which liability insurers met personal injury claims and costs.

In his dissenting judgment Lord Scott held that the appeal should be allowed to the extent of disallowing Mr Callery to recover the insurance premium, which was not reasonable given the stage when the policy was taken out. The other four law lords did not agree. The Appeal was dismissed.

Index

Trade Associations
  funding options, and, 1.013
Trade unions
  funding options, and, 1.013
Training
  knowledge management, and,
    9.008
Trends
  risk assessment, and, 6.022

Uncertainty
  risk assessment in CFAs, and,
    6.020, 6.022

Unpredictability
  risk assessment in CFAs, and,
    6.019

Variation of agreements
  model collective CFAs, and,
    A1.019

Workplace claims
  disclosure under pre-action
    personal injury protocol,
    A1.074